Praise for

Cashing In on Pre-foreclosures and Short Sales

"I've traveled the globe with Chip Cummings and consider him a great friend. Chip's expertise, insight, and success in the real estate vertical market is unparalleled. If you're interested in cashing in on pre-foreclosure properties—Get this book!"

—Ralph Roberts, author of *Flipping Houses for Dummies, Foreclosure Investing for Dummies,* and *Foreclosure Self-Defense for Dummies*

"Another home run from Chip Cummings! If you want to learn how to buy smart when everyone else is running scared, read this book. Real estate is still the only investment you can buy with the bank's money and pay for with the tenant's income. Twenty years from now, you'll wish you owned more!"

—Robert Helms and Russell Gray, hosts of *The Real Estate Guys* radio and TV shows

"Foreclosures are an unfortunate consequence of our economic times. Fortunately, Chip shows anyone how they can position themselves to create long-term wealth while helping people along the way. *Cashing In* is a great read, with practical easy-to-follow steps!"

—Sig Anderman, CEO, Ellie Mae, Inc.

"We are entering into one of the greatest periods for real estate investment in our lifetimes. *Cashing In on Pre-foreclosures and Short Sales* will show you exactly how to take advantage of the investment opportunities available, and develop long-term profits in these challenging times."

—Mitch Freifeld, investor and Branch Marketing expert

"The real estate 'crash of 2008' may go down in history as one of the greatest opportunities to acquire properties at bargain basement prices. Don't miss out! Chip teaches you the why and how to get in on the action."

—Tim Kleyla, President, The Mortgage House; past President, MMBA

"*Cashing In on Pre-foreclosures and Short Sales* provides practical, actionable education to help the bold and savvy investor get in on the greatest buyers market we've seen in decades. I've already purchased six new properties this year!"

—Aaron Metaj, real estate investor

A Real Estate Investor's Guide to Making a
Fortune—Even in a Down Market!

CASHING IN on PRE-FORECLOSURES and SHORT SALES

CHIP CUMMINGS

WILEY

John Wiley & Sons, Inc.

Published by John Wiley & Sons, Inc., Hoboken, New Jersey.
Published simultaneously in Canada.

Limit of Liability/Disclaimer of Warranty: While the publisher and author have used their best efforts in preparing this book, they make no representations or warranties with respect to the accuracy or completeness of the contents of this book and specifically disclaim any implied warranties of merchantability or fitness for a particular purpose. No warranty may be created or extended by sales representatives or written sales materials. The advice and strategies contained herein may not be suitable for your situation. You should consult with a professional where appropriate. Neither the publisher nor author shall be liable for any loss of profit or any other commercial damages, including but not limited to special, incidental, consequential, or other damages.

For general information on our other products and services or for technical support, please contact our Customer Care Department within the United States at (800) 762-2974, outside the United States at (317) 572-3993 or fax (317) 572-4002.

Wiley also publishes its books in a variety of electronic formats. Some content that appears in print may not be available in electronic books. For more information about Wiley products, visit our web site at www.wiley.com.

Library of Congress Cataloging-in-Publication Data:

Cummings, Chip.
  Cashing in on pre-foreclosures and short sales : a real estate investor's guide to making a fortune - even in a down market / by Chip Cummings.
    p.   cm.
  Includes bibliographical references and index.
  ISBN 978-0-470-41981-6 (pbk.)
    1. Real estate investment—United States.   2. Foreclosure—United States.   3. Mortgage loans—United States.   4. House buying—United States.   5. Residential real estate—Purchasing—United States.   I. Title.
  HD255.C857   2009
  332.63'24—dc22
                                                                                      2008042921

Printed in the United States of America.
10 9 8 7 6 5 4 3 2 1

*To my wife Lisa—my number one fan, best friend,
and life partner*

TABLE OF CONTENTS

CONTENTS

CONTENTS

CONTENTS

Throughout the book, you will see many forms, letters, and worksheets that I and other investors have used in pursuing foreclosure deals. You are welcome to use them for your business, and to make it easier, you can access all of these forms electronically in Microsoft Word format at www.ChipCummings.com/CashingIn.

Once downloaded, you can modify, reword, or even add your logo and customize them a bit. Here is a list of materials that are available for electronic download. (Additional versions of these documents are available for download as well.)

10.1	Marketing Letter to Real Estate Agents
10.2	Marketing Letter to Attorneys
10.3	Marketing Letter to Mortgage Broker
11.4	Foreclosure Tracking Worksheet
13.1	Letter to Homeowner #1
13.2	Letter to Homeowner #2
13.3	Letter to Homeowner #3
13.4	Letter to Homeowner #4
13.5	Letter to Homeowner #5
13.6	Letter to Homeowner #6
13.7	Congratulations Letter to Homeowner
13.8	Initial Telephone Script
14.1	Homeowner Profile Worksheet
14.2	Property Loan Worksheet
14.3	Borrower Authorization Form
14.4	Lender Estoppel Letter
14.5	Borrower Release Form—Private Lender

Chip Cummings is a recognized expert in the areas of real estate lending and e-Marketing, and a Certified Mortgage Consultant (CMC) with over 26 years in the mortgage industry and over a billion dollars in real estate volume. Having purchased his first foreclosure property at the age of 19, Chip is an experienced real estate investor of both residential and commercial properties.

Chip has written hundreds of articles and appeared numerous times on radio and television with FOX News, NBC, ABC, and the *Neil Cavuto Show,* and in various magazines including *Entrepreneur, Mortgage Originator, Real Estate Banker/ Broker,* and *The Mortgage Press.* He is experienced in all areas of real estate financing and investing, including residential and commercial mortgages, government lending, regulatory and compliance issues, is the past president of the MMBA, and is a licensed broker and mortgage lender in Michigan.

As an international speaker, he has addressed groups and organizations of all types, and trains thousands of mortgage and real estate professionals each year. Chip is a certified trainer of continuing education in over 40 states and has served as an expert witness in state and federal courts. He is also the author of *Foreclosure Myths: 77 Secrets to Making Money on Distressed Properties* (Hoboken, NJ: John Wiley & Sons, 2008), *Mortgage Myths: 77 Secrets to Saving Thousands on Home Financing* (Hoboken, NJ: John Wiley & Sons, 2008) and *Financing Real Estate Investments for Dummies* (John Wiley & Sons, 2009) with Ralph Roberts, *ABC's of FHA Lending* (Northwind: 2008), and *Stop Selling and Start Listening! Marketing Strategies That Create Top Producers* (Northwind, 2005).

To learn more about Chip Cummings, his many success products, or how he can help your organization as a speaker or business consultant, visit www .ChipCummings.com.

To receive a complimentary subscription to his multimedia e-newsletter "The Marketing Minute," check out www.TheMarketingMinute.com, or www.eCoaching-Club.com. You can also reach Chip by emailing him at info@ChipCummings.com or by calling 616-977-7900.

Chip lives in Rockford, Michigan, with his wife Lisa and three children, Katelyn, CJ, and Joe.

I f you are thinking about buying property (and you should be), now is the time to act and this is the book you will want to read. Whether you want to begin (or add to) your property investments or whether you want to buy a home, it is unlikely that you will again witness the opportunities that are available today.

What opportunities? Bargain prices matched with low interest rates (rates that future inflation will certainly push higher). Why this book? Because *Cashing In on Pre-foreclosures and Short Sales* provides the most thorough coverage and most helpful discussion of foreclosures that I have seen. As a welcome bonus, Chip Cummings' writing style combines worldly experience with a flair for simple, easy-to-read, straight talk. You can't beat his tried and true path to build wealth: Timing + Practical Knowledge = Great Profits.

In the investment classic, *The Intelligent Investor* (even though originally published in 1948, the latest revised edition still sits near the top of bestselling business titles), the legendary stock market analyst, Ben Graham, created the true-to-life story of "Mr. Market." Mr. Market represents that chameleon mass character whose moods persistently shift from irrational exuberance to pessimistic confusion. Which market mood gives us the best time to buy? You know the answer. When Mr. Market holes up in a cave, when fear triumphs over greed, when journalists write never-ending stories of gloom and despair.

In fact, for my book, *The Beginner's Guide to Real Estate Investing, 2nd edition* (Wiley, 2008), I researched back 60 years and showed how each downturn of the property cycle has brought forth a journalistic chorus (often quoting supposedly expert economists) who declared the "end of real estate" as we know it. As far back as 1947 (with average homes selling for around $8,500), *Time Magazine* warned that housing prices were too high and buyers could no longer expect to profit from appreciation.

During the intermittent property recessions of the 1970s, the 1980s, and the 1990s, media stories time and again put forth the notion that "real estate is no longer a good investment." In fact, in 1996, on the brink of one of the biggest booms in property prices in U.S. history, a major California newspaper proclaimed, "A home is where the bad investment is." Aren't you seeing similar stories today?

Now think: Who today enjoys the highest net worth? Those buyers/investors who understand the psychological moods of Mr. Market? Those buyers/investors who jumped into the market during those earlier downturns? Or those who watched opportunity pass them by—or maybe those who waited and finally bought at or near the cyclical peak? You know the answer. After each previous property recession, property prices recovered their losses and continued upwards to set ever-higher price records. Experience leaves no doubts. Investors who buy when "blood is running in the streets," profit big.

Fortunately, with the know-how you'll achieve from *Cashing In on Pre-foreclosures and Short Sales,* you won't even have to wait for market recovery to start banking the gains that you'll earn when you buy now. In *Cashing In*, Chip Cummings—an outstanding real estate pro, I might add—guides you to below-market deals. When you invest below-market in a down cycle, you can rocket blast your profit potential.

However, unlike so many foreclosure books, seminars, and CDs, *Cashing In* does not feed you pie-in-the sky. Chip does not promise that you can buy for dimes on the dollar. He does not mislead you into believing that you can suit up for the game without preparation—or by merely following five easy steps. He does, though, illustrate how with preparation, with dedication, and most importantly, with action even beginners can outperform those investors who are more experienced.

In other words, Chip guides you through the real world of profiting from foreclosures—and he does it from an ethical, win-win perspective. Chip gives you a full set of checklists, questions, sample letters, and helpful forms that are sure to lead you to a rewarding—and risk-avoiding—property investment. I urge you to read through the chapter contents. You will find that *Cashing In* leaves nothing out.

My editor at Wiley knows that I do not recommend many books, but I am pleased to recommend *Cashing In on Pre-foreclosures and Short Sales*. In fact, this is a book I wish I had written. Indeed, I would make only one change. The super title says, "A Real Estate Investor's Guide to Making a Fortune—*Even* in a Down Market." I would say, ***Especially*** in a Down Market. You are now living quite possibly a once in a lifetime opportunity. Do not let this chance to earn big profits pass you by.

—Gary W. Eldred, PhD

ACKNOWLEDGMENTS

As with any project of this magnitude, it takes a great number of people to help pull it off, but I want to offer special thanks to my dedicated staff at Northwind Financial Corporation and Chip Cummings Unlimited!, especially my personal assistant Debbie Forth and production assistant Lindsay Pate.

Special thanks goes to my fearless acquisitions editor Shannon Vargo, and the rest of the John Wiley & Sons team who made things happen, kept the project on track, and ensured a great finished product. Jessica Langan-Peck, Kate Lindsay, Brian Neill, Beth Zipko, and Kim Dayman deserve a special round of applause for making it fun and making me look good. Thanks also go to my agents Cynthia Zigmund and John Willig for their hard work and enthusiasm. Separately, my chief editor Dennis Ross deserves a great deal of praise for spending a lot of extra hours and long nights poring over the text to make me look and sound good!

Over the years, I have been fortunate to work with some incredible associations and organizations, who graciously offered technical assistance and support for this book, including:

Fannie Mae

Freddie Mac

U.S. Department of Housing and Urban Development

Federal Housing Administration

U.S. Department of Veterans Affairs

Realty Trac

National Association of Mortgage Brokers

Mortgage Bankers Association

Rental Property Owners Association

National Association of Realtors

Michigan Association of Realtors

Michigan Association of Mortgage Brokers

WriteInvestment.com

In addition, there were some key individuals that I have had the pleasure of working with that donated their time, talent, and experiences with stories and practical tips to help readers understand key points. My sincere thanks go out to

Russell Gray and Robert Helms—"The Real Estate Guys," Terri Murphy with US Learning, Mark Baragar with ReMax of Grand Rapids, Tim Kearns of First Priority Financial, Giff Cummings with Creative Property Services, and Nate Martinez, who rules the Phoenix area with Re/Max Professionals.

And last, but not least, thanks to my family who puts up with some long days and even longer nights, and still seem to smile and laugh through it all. Their patience and willingness to allow me to do what I do on a daily basis gives me the ability and energy to make a difference in the lives of so many people out there— I love you all very much!

In just one month, 272,171 properties were touched by foreclosures—a 55 percent increase from just one year ago. This is a new record that means one out of every 464 U.S. households received a foreclosure notice. Worse yet, one out of every five homes with a mortgage is "upside-down."*

Many say it's a sign of the times caused by a tough economic climate, loss of manufacturing jobs to overseas, over extended homeowners, over zealous lending programs, or even investor speculation. It's probably a combination of at least a dozen such factors. But it happens, it's real, and for some—it's an opportunity.

Foreclosures happen every day and, at this pace, over 3.2 million homes will be affected in some way over the next 12 months. Will all of these homeowners end up losing their home? No, of course not, but many of them will need help. They will need help understanding what they're going through, help with their finances, help picking up the pieces—and help to keep the dream of homeownership from turning into a nightmare.

Investing in real estate is not a new concept, nor is investing in foreclosure properties. There has always been good money to be made for those who had the time and cash to jump on the deals. But the rules have changed, the players have changed, and the opportunities for investors have never been better.

My first foreclosure purchase actually happened by mistake. I was young and "green." I didn't have a clue about what I was doing. But there were some great real estate pros who believed in me, were willing to show me the ropes, and who taught me how to play the game without losing my ass along the way. I promised that when the time came, I'd share my strategies so others didn't have to learn the "secrets" to creating wealth the hard way—through the expensive school of hard knocks. I wrote this book for you, so that you could discover the opportunities that are out there and to provide a road map of how to navigate the sometimes turbulent and stressful waters of purchasing foreclosure properties.

---

*RealtyTrac.com, July 2008, November 2008.

Here's your opportunity to dive in and help others and the opportunity to help yourself. An opportunity to solve problems for distressed homeowners and lenders, and an opportunity to build a future for you and your family—your opportunity for *Cashing In on Pre-Foreclosures and Short Sales!*

—Chip Cummings

This publication is designed to provide accurate and authoritative information with regard to the subject matter covered. It is sold with the understanding that the publisher, author, and individual contributors are not engaged in rendering professional services. If professional advice or other expert assistance is required, the services of a competent professional should be sought.

As with any type of printed material, information is subject to change. All reference items, web sites, addresses, phone numbers, and program requirements were current as of date of publishing, but may change from time to time. For current updated information and releases, go to www.ChipCummings.com/CashingIn.

Bulk quantities of this publication are available at a reduced cost for educational, non profit, corporate, or association distribution.

For your convenience, I have highlighted certain topics and points that are not to be overlooked. Here are the icons used throughout this book:

Important Tip—This highlights an important item that you need to make a note of for future reference.

Warning—This illustrates a critical step that could cost you money if you skip or ignore!

Info Spot—Here I point out key "Chip Tips" designed to save you time and eliminate errors!

Download—This icon indicates that this particular form is available for electronic download at www.ChipCummings.com/CashingIn.

WHERE TO START

My philosophy has always been that the best place to start is right at the beginning.

Whether you are a true beginner in the world of foreclosure investing or an experienced professional, inside this book there are years and years of practical experiences, strategies, and street-smart insights designed to save you time and money and help you create your own personal fortune through investing in foreclosures. Also included are many expensive lessons learned from the "school of hard knocks" to illustrate what NOT to do!

To help make it easier for you to navigate, I have divided this book into three parts. Part I is designed for those just getting into the world of foreclosures for the first time. As I travel around the country, one of the biggest frustrations for most people I talk to is they simply don't know where to begin. So to get you ready to become a foreclosure investor, I will start out by teaching you about the process, common terminology, opportunities, risks, and information about the foreclosure market.

We'll also explore what you need to know about state laws and regulations, how to quickly evaluate a property, and where to find financing. Don't skip the last two chapters, as we set you up to do the foreclosure business the right way, and look at how to build a team of professionals to help you create wealth.

Thanks for investing your time and money with me, and I promise to share all the details of how to create a personal fortune with pre-foreclosures and short sales. So if you're ready, fasten your seatbelt and let's get started!

CHAPTER 1

A Crash Course in Pre-foreclosures and Short Sales

Congratulations! You have taken an important step in securing your financial future, and I'm honored that you've decided to take it with me. I bought my first foreclosure property at the age of 19—and it was actually by mistake! Although I had a few fellow real estate brokers showing me the ropes, I didn't know what I was doing, and had no formal training or education on foreclosure investing. At that time, there was no such thing.

Just like there are very few classes that teach our kids about credit and how to manage their finances, no one has set up a curriculum to teach you the ropes of evaluating, investing, and managing foreclosures. You learn by doing.

My goal is to shorten the learning curve for you. Right now, the entire foreclosure process may seem quite foreign, and even a bit secretive, but once you get into it, you'll find that it's actually quite simple!

People buy a home, then, for any number of reasons they stop making payments, and the lender has to take the home back. Pretty simple. Although there are a certainly a few more steps in between, that one sentence pretty much sums up the foreclosure process. The trick is learning how to make money between the steps. In this first chapter, I'll take you through a crash course on the foreclosure process to help you start to identify where the real opportunities lie.

What Are Foreclosures?

The first thing you need is a clear understanding of what a foreclosure is. When you mention the word *foreclosure,* most people think of unfortunate people who got in over their heads and lost their property to the bank.

This is only partially accurate. While there is certainly an element of truth in this statement, the concept of foreclosures is actually bigger than that. There are many reasons why properties go through foreclosure, and it involves an entire process whose pieces can be broken down into three basic phases—pre-foreclosure, public auction, and post-auction.

What Are Pre-foreclosures?

As you will soon see, this is where the "real" money is made. I have purchased properties in all different steps of the process, but this is where your efforts will yield the greatest reward.

Pre-foreclosures simply defined is the time period between when a homeowner misses his or her first mortgage payment, and the date when the property is sold at public auction or a trustee's sale.

What Are Short Sales?

During a foreclosure process, the lender will always lose money. Sometimes a great deal of it. With the advent of creative mortgages over the past several years, combined with a cycle of soft or declining real estate markets, some homeowners actually become "upside-down" in their property, that is to say, they can't afford to sell. By the time they pay a real estate commission, all the costs and fees, as well as the debts associated with the property, they actually end up owing the lender money to in order to sell their home. In fact, according to RealtyTrac.com, a national foreclosure tracking service, as of the end of 2008, one out of every five homes that had a mortgage were upside-down. That's 20 percent!

In these circumstances, many homeowners and lenders are faced with the difficult choice of the lesser of two evils. This effect is compounded when a property enters the foreclosure stage, as the payments and penalties start to add up quickly. Enter the *short sale.*

A short sale is where the lender agrees to accept full payment for the mortgage debt in an amount that is less than the homeowner actually owes. Most homeowners don't know that this is even possible, and they certainly don't know how to structure a short sale transaction. When the circumstances are right, you'll be in a position to help.

Steps in the Foreclosure Process

Most people believe that the foreclosure process starts with a notice published in their local newspaper or at the courthouse. In reality, it starts way before that. It starts as soon as the homeowner misses a payment.

I mentioned the three phases of foreclosure, but in a typical foreclosure process, there are actually 16 steps. So you understand all the differences, and how to determine where the homeowner is in the progression, let's take a quick look at each one:

1. *The missed payment:* For a variety of reasons, a payment is missed, and once a borrower gets behind, it is difficult to get caught up.

2. *The payment reminder:* Hoping that it's just an oversight, the lender will send a gentle reminder to the borrower within the first 10 to 25 days.

3. *No response:* If the payment still hasn't found its way to the lender, there will be a series of more strongly worded letters, followed by a few phone calls to the homeowner to find out what's wrong.

4. *Collection:* If the lender and homeowner have not reached a resolution to get the payments caught up, usually by the sixtieth day of delinquency, the lender will turn the matter over to its internal collection department, or what's known as the "loss mitigation" department.

5. *Outside collection:* Once the homeowner has missed three payments, the lender knows that the problem is serious, and the likelihood of them catching up is slim. Now 90 days past due, the matter is usually referred to outside attorneys to begin hounding the homeowner. They aren't typically as nice as the lender's own employees.

6. *Work out:* If the attorney can talk to the homeowner (the homeowner is probably getting really skilled at dodging phone calls), they will try and do a *work-out,* or loan modification to get the borrower back on track. This can include partial payments for a short period of time, payments added to the end of the loan, or any other of several scenarios based on the borrower's situation. This is a mandatory step for most loans and can work great if the borrower can demonstrate that his circumstances are only temporary.

7. *The Notice of Default:* If a work-out arrangement cannot be agreed on, or if the borrower does not follow through on the arrangements, a Notice of Default will be posted through the local newspaper or legal news, and the foreclosure process officially begins.

8. *Sheriff notification:* At this point, the county sheriff's office receives the paperwork, and the attorney or trustee for the lender will set the opening bid. This amount represents the balance due on the loan, plus late fees, penalties, and costs.

9. *Posting the property:* The sheriff or a representative may visit the house and post a notice of foreclosure action, and inspect the property. If the property appears to be abandoned, the court may decide to expedite the process. In all states, a notice must be posted on the property. At this point, the homeowner can still

redeem the property and reinstate the loan by paying the delinquent amount, plus any fees and costs incurred.

10. *Bid adjustment:* Just before the date of the public foreclosure auction, the lender will adjust the bid up or down slightly based on a final accounting of the loan and delinquency costs.

11. *Auction day:* If the homeowner has not somehow gotten his act together, the property is auctioned off to the highest bidder, or is liquidated to pay off the lender. This is usually an anticlimactic event, except for the homeowner. This is the day he or she really starts to lose the property.

12. *Hammer time:* When the hammer comes down (the motion of the auctioneer to indicate the final bid), the lender or an investor wins the bidding for the property. Sometimes the sale is handled by a trustee. The lender will simply make a bid for what it is owed, or an investor purchases the property. If there are no other bids, the property is turned over to the lender. Regardless of whether the lender or an investor wins the bid, the property may be subject to a redemption period.

13. *Redemption and possession:* Based on where the property is located, the lender or investor could take immediate possession, or in states with redemption periods, there is a mandatory waiting period. Sometimes called a "cooling off period," a redemption period gives the borrower one last chance to redeem the property by paying off the high bidder, plus certain reasonable costs. This redemption period could last just a few days—or it could last a year.

14. *Redemption period expires:* At the end of that redemption period, there may be another court hearing with the homeowners before the new owner (the lender or the investor) can take possession of the property. In certain circumstances, such as abandonment, the redemption period can be waived by the court.

15. *Eviction:* If the previous owner is not already out, the new owner will have the sheriff's department evict the previous owners. This eviction is done without any further notice, and without fanfare, and all of the previous owner's belongings are put out on the street. This step can get ugly.

16. *New owner moves in:* Once the property has been secured, the new owner or investor can fully take over. If the lender has ended up with the property, then it is brought back up to marketable condition and put up for sale as quickly as possible.

The Best Market Is Now

In the past two years, foreclosures have increased in every state in the country. We look at some of the many reasons for this in a moment, but it is a trend that is likely to continue for several years. As a result, the opportunities for investors have never been better.

But is this just another cycle? Will you be able to capitalize when the market changes back? In Chapter 3, we take a detailed look at how the markets work in your favor—no matter what the real estate conditions are.

Real estate in general works in cycles. There are good years, and some not-so-good years, but overall, values will eventually increase. This has been the case for well over 100 years. But foreclosure cycles operate differently. Although some cycles are driven by real estate values, there are other factors that drive them as well, such as a major factory closing down, or an increase in the cost of living. Interest rate spikes on subprime loans or major tax increases in a certain metropolitan area also affect foreclosure rates.

But for the investor, the best market and the best time to get started is now. Foreclosures happen every day, and regardless of your level of experience, or the present market conditions, I can teach you how to effectively evaluate each opportunity and pick the right ones for success. They exist in every city, in every state, in every market condition. But to fully appreciate how the markets play into your hands, let's look at the reasons why the numbers of foreclosures have been increasing.

Reasons Foreclosures Are Increasing

The biggest reason that foreclosures keep increasing is that Americans can't seem to live on what they earn. They keep borrowing money for toys (boats, cars, resort vacations, etc.) that they can't afford, don't need, and can't pay for. Credit card debt keeps spiraling upward every year, and the homes people purchase (thanks to creative mortgage products that they don't understand) can leave them one paycheck away from disaster in every direction.

There are seven key factors that financial experts believe have led to the rise in foreclosure rates:

1. *Subprime mortgage programs:* Creative programs that require little or no down payment, interest-only type loan payments, or stated income (what we call "liars' loans") have led people down a path of destruction. Many of these loans were predicated on the fact that property values would continue to rise—and when they didn't, the walls came crashing down. As I write this, more than one out of every five subprime adjustable rate mortgages (ARM) loans are in default around the country.

2. *Weak economic conditions:* With the shift of many manufacturing jobs to Mexico and Asia, employment loss has crippled entire communities. Cities that were reliant on the success of just one or two main industries have had a hard time competing for new job sectors, and the result has been an increase in foreclosure activity.

3. *Predatory lending practices:* They advertise low rates and easy payment terms. They come in to steal the equity of elderly and unsophisticated borrowers with programs that are so usurious, there is no way the homeowner is going to be able to make the payments. It may be for home repairs or a refinance transaction that promises a lot of cash in hand that's too tempting for people to pass up. In the end, interest rates go up, payments become higher than the homeowner's entire monthly income, and the inevitable result is foreclosure.

4. *Low interest rates:* This has been a biggie over the past few years. Low "teaser" rates that sound attractive—until you find out how high and how quickly they can adjust. Low market rates have made access to credit extremely easy, and the increase in two-wage-earner families has made it tempting to get all the house they can. Unfortunately, even a slight bump in the rate or one hiccup in their income results in hard times for the family.

5. *Over extended first-time homeowners:* With Congress's blessing, and lenders as willing accomplices, first-time ownership rates have skyrocketed to an all-time high. New government programs with Federal Housing Administration (FHA), Veterans Affairs (VA), down-payment assistance programs, state grants, and a flood of first-time homebuyer incentives have made the American dream turn into a nightmare for those unprepared. Miscalculating the upkeep on a home, budgeting responsibilities, and increased consumer pricing on goods and services, combined with a low or zero-down payment have left people on the edge. One couple I consulted with was facing foreclosure just because their furnace went out—and there was no money to fix or replace it.

6. *High loan-to-value and debt-to-income ratios:* Twenty years ago, it was common for a homeowner to need at least 10 percent down to get into a new home. It was also required that borrowers not spend more than 28 percent of their income toward their housing payment, and be within 36 percent of their monthly income when their monthly debts were added in. Loan-to-value (LTV) percentages have shot up dramatically, to the point that very few homeowners actually have the 20 percent down payment necessary to avoid mortgage insurance. In addition, automated underwriting practices and subprime mortgages have allowed debt-to-income (DTI) ratios to fly past 36 percent, to 50 percent, 60 percent or even 70 percent in some cases. There just isn't enough monthly income at the end of the month.

7. *Artificial values:* As the economy hummed along, and real estate became increasingly easier to obtain, the natural evolution was for values to go up. It's a simple case of supply and demand. As the number of "qualified borrowers" increased, demand went up and prices grew. They grew so fast in some areas of the country, that double-digit appreciation was considered the norm.

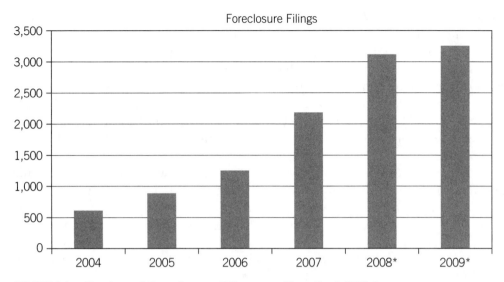

FIGURE 1.1 **Number of Foreclosure Filings per Year (in 1,000s).**
*projected numbers
Source: RealtyTrac.com.

Homeowners treated their homes as ATM machines, and as values continued to increase, eventually the incomes of ordinary homeowners couldn't support the payments, and the "bubble" exploded.

This speculation that was based on artificial values was most prevalent in California and Florida. These areas, with the riskiest lending practices and most rampant speculation, are also the areas with the highest foreclosure rates. Jay Brinkman, the chief economist for the Mortgage Bankers Association, summed it up: "That's clearly the problem. The foreclosure numbers are being driven by the two largest states."

Some cities were hurt worse than others, but we all felt it in one way or another. This left unsuspecting homeowners with artificially inflated values and properties that they couldn't refinance—and couldn't sell. Their only choice left was foreclosure.

Figure 1.1 shows how foreclosure rates have increased in recent years.

Getting Started in Foreclosures

As I mentioned in the Introduction, for me, getting started in foreclosures actually happened by mistake. At the age of 19, I was working for one of the top real estate agencies in Ann Arbor, Michigan, and was showing properties day and night between college classes. I came across this great little two-family unit that needed major rehabilitation. I was cash-poor, but I was young and had nothing but time.

I noticed on the listing card that it was owned by an out-of-state bank—the Bank of Florida. I wondered how they wound up with a little house way up here in Michigan, so I asked one of my fellow realtors. I quickly learned that it was a fore-closure and had been on the market for some time. With nothing to lose, I put in a lowball offer, contingent upon financing. To my amazement, they accepted it right away.

Next, I had to line up the financing. Yeah, right. I was young, in school, and spending any money I had on weekend parties. So again, my broker suggested that I ask the seller to finance the whole thing. He also suggested that I put the property into a Sub-S Corporation (see Chapter 9) because I might want to bring in a part-ner. Again, to my amazement, the bank agreed to finance the entire amount with a 30-year fixed loan, with a five-year balloon payment. I wasn't too sure what that was, but I was ready to do it!

I did have to scrape together $500 for the closing costs, but within 20 days, I had purchased my first foreclosure. I wasn't sure what to do with it, but I was the owner. Then I learned that repairs cost money—money I didn't have. I brought in two partners—my brother Ken, and one of the agents in my office. My brother and I did the repairs, and the agent, Grant, provided the cash. It was a great deal— eventually. It was a long hard learning experience that I'm fortunate didn't turn into a financial disaster. Here's how the numbers broke down:

Purchase price:	$23,000.00
Closing costs:	500.00
Financing (30-yr amortization, 5-yr. balloon, 9% interest)	(23,000.00)
Upfront Cash Investment:	500.00
Rehabilitation costs (materials):	11,250.00
Mortgage payments (14 months @ $185.06)	2,590.88
Mortgage payoff to lender:	22,815.34
Sold 14 months later:	43,000.00
Profit realized:	**$ 5,843.78**

Wow! At the closing, I actually received a check with more digits on it than I had ever seen before. Not bad! My share of the profit was almost $3,000 on a $500 investment. Man, did I have a lot to learn.

I didn't account for my time and labor. Based upon the amount of sweat I had put into the deal, the return wasn't looking all that spectacular. But what I did get was an education. It didn't seem like much at first, but over the years it paid for itself a thousand times over.

 Here are the main points:

1. You probably won't make a killing on your first deal.
2. You will learn a great deal on your first deal.
3. Your time is worth money—figure it into the total expense.
4. Don't let a lack of cash stop you from getting started.

Foreclosures and Short Sales—Neither Illegal nor Unethical

There was nothing illegal or unethical about what I did on that deal. In fact, there is nothing approaching illegal or unethical in any deal I've been involved with, nor will there be with any of your transactions—if you follow your head *and* my advice.

Yes, there are people you will meet who are in dire situations. You will be tested emotionally, and hear some heart breaking stories. You did not cause it, nor can you necessarily fix it. And you don't need to take advantage of it to make a profit. When you are negotiating pre-foreclosure transactions, you should never feel guilty about what you are doing. Quite the opposite. If you don't help out the homeowner, someone else will—and that someone may try and take advantage of the situation.

Many investors become drawn into a situation and are tempted to take advantage of a seller's plight to create a win-lose deal. Don't do it; it will end your career quickly.

Always try to help the homeowner. You are providing a service and should not feel any guilt about doing the deal. In most cases, the bank will end up taking the property back anyway, and you are providing a way for the homeowner to save some face, maybe their credit, and definitely additional heartache. You are saving the bank time and money, and you expect to get paid for your knowledge and experience in solving the problem for both. Nothing I ever suggest or teach in any way should be construed or used for illegal or unethical practices. Do it the right way, and you'll build a great reputation and make some great friends along the way.

What You Need for Success

So what do you need to make this a success and start building a personal real estate fortune? Well, here's my short list for starters:

1. Knowledge or at least the ability to learn
2. Great organizational skills
3. Cash or at least access to people with cash
4. Patience and good listening skills
5. The ability and love of talking to and dealing with people
6. Lots of persistence

If you start with these, the rest will fall into place. A lot of people get tripped up on item 3. Yes, it is a lot easier if you have stacks of cash lying around, and a credit report that's 10 pages long with a credit score of 817. If that's you, you can get started a lot faster, but then you'll just need a "bird dog" to go out and find the pre-foreclosure properties to simply invest your cash in.

In assuming that most of you do not fit directly into that category, I do want to take a moment and be brutally honest with you. If you are broke, unemployed, and have lousy credit, don't waste your time with this book. It will be really hard if not impossible to succeed until you get yourself straightened out.

Another piece of advice for those of you "type A" personalities like me—you will get excited as you read through this book, but don't go out and quit your day job—at least not right away. Foreclosure investing has a wide variety of possibilities, so with a little effort you can quickly decide the best way to build wealth based on your talents and interests. To test your commitment to your success, let's take a little test.

Self-Analysis Worksheet

New investors often ask, "Should you specialize in a particular area?" You can, but you certainly don't have to. Many people specialize in types of real estate that generate positive cash flow: single-family houses, apartments, or rooming houses. Others find a particular niche and focus exclusively on that: rehabs and fixer-uppers, for instance. You can choose to start with one type of property, especially if you're operating with limited capital, and expand into other areas as you generate cash and equity.

The following quiz will help you decide how you can get started based on your financial situation, your skills, and your personal interests. Use it as a guide to determine the best ways to invest in real estate and some of the best investment options based on your individual skills, capabilities, and interests.

1. Do you own your own home?

    Yes: Consider ways to increase the value of your property: renovations, additions, improvements. Remember your home is an investment as well as a place to live—if the improvements you make are attractive to you, they will be to other buyers as well.

    No: Unless you live with your parents and plan to continue living there, the first real estate investment you should make is to purchase your personal residence. If you're paying rent, you're paying someone else's mortgage—plus you don't benefit from the appreciation of the property.

2. Do you have a down payment and good credit?

    Yes: Consider bank financing. You can probably qualify for excellent terms, and in addition you'll build a business relationship with a lender that will be beneficial in the long run.

    No: Look for partners or other nontraditional financing options. (We look closely at other options in Chapter 8.)

3. Do you have carpentry skills?

    Yes: Consider rehabs and fixer-uppers. Instead of paying others to do the work, you can do it yourself—in effect, you'll be paying yourself a wage in addition to increasing the value of the property. Keep in mind, though, that rehabs can take considerable time to renovate—make sure you have that time available.

    No: Focus on buying rental properties, on wholesaling properties, or on other investments where your personal "sweat equity" is not required. Or, find skilled craftsmen who can do the work for you on rehabs or fixer-uppers.

4. Do you like working with people?

    Yes: Consider buying and managing your own rental properties. You'll save on property management fees, and you'll build relationships with local lenders, government officials, and craftsmen. You may even rent to tenants who later will become buyers of other properties you invest in. In addition, you can consider selling your properties yourself instead of using the services of a real estate agent.

    No: If you invest in rental properties, use the services of a property management firm. You'll probably also want to use real estate agents to sell your properties. Landlords have a number of interpersonal dealings with tenants; if you don't like working with people, managing your own properties will be frustrating.

5. Do you have solid financial management skills?

   Yes: Consider handling your own accounting and bookkeeping. You'll have a better sense of the day-to-day state of your business. Alternatively, if your investments are substantial, you'll find you spend a lot of time handling the clerical tasks necessary to run your real estate "empire." At that point, you may decide you're better off handing the clerical duties to someone else while you focus on finding and making great investments.

   No: Educate yourself: attend seminars or take classes. Or utilize the services of an accountant you trust.

6. Do you want (or need) a steady stream of monthly income?

   Yes: Consider income-generating rental properties. Properties with a positive cash flow (meaning your income exceeds your expenses) can provide you with extra income each month. Many investors specialize in investments in rental properties: they increase their monthly income and over time they build equity as they pay down the mortgages on those properties, and as the value of the properties increases.

   No: Consider rehabs, fixer-uppers, lease options, and other shorter-term investments. Buying a house in poor condition, making improvements, and selling it for a profit will generate income, but not on a steady, predictable basis. If your goal is to build wealth instead of increasing cash flow, you can also focus on properties with longer-term appreciation potential.

7. Do you have a source of capital to invest?

   Yes: Use your capital to make down payments and to help you obtain necessary financing. You can also use your capital to finance improvements to your properties.

   No: Focus on investing in properties where limited capital is necessary. Look for little or no money down loans and guard the capital you have closely. Don't sink all of your capital into one property unless you plan to sell the property quickly; otherwise, you won't have capital available to make other investments until that property sells. If you buy rehabs or fixer-uppers, you may have to finance the repairs and renovations using outside financing like credit cards, personal loans, and so on.

8. Is your current income level low?

   Yes: Invest in properties that yield a positive cash flow. If you don't yet own your own house, buy a home that is suitable for renting a room or portion of the home to a third party. You'll lower your monthly expense requirements and can possibly buy a larger home than you could otherwise afford.

No: Invest in properties to build wealth or to make shorter-term profits. Of course, you can still invest in rental properties that generate a positive monthly cash flow, using that cash flow to fund additional investments. You can also rent a portion of your home to a third party if you want to increase your income.

9. Do you like to help other people?

Yes: Buying pre-foreclosure properties is a great way to help others. You can help people stop a foreclosure, possibly find a home they can afford, and you can profit from the transaction at the same time. Or consider buying properties in less-desirable areas; you can provide affordable housing to low-income persons.

No: Keep in mind that helping people can be profitable from a business point of view and also immensely gratifying on a personal level. I like win-win situations; implicit in that premise is that the other party benefits, too.

10. Do you have a real estate license?

Yes: List the properties you purchase. You'll save on commissions when you sell one of your properties.

No: Consider getting your license. In most states, you'll simply need to take a three-month class and pass a licensing test. Once you've passed, you can place your license with a local real estate agency. You don't have to sell real estate full time; many agencies will allow you to simply handle your own transactions. (Of course, you may also occasionally decide to list homes for friends or relatives, generating additional income for yourself.)

Want to Succeed? Set Goals

Most people spend a lot more time *dreaming* about success than they do *planning* for success. Dreaming is simply that—dreaming. Planning requires setting goals and taking appropriate actions to achieve those goals.

Have you heard the saying, "The average person doesn't plan to fail; most failures occur as a result of a failure to plan?" It's true. And setting goals is an important part of planning.

There are two basic ways to set goals. One way is to look at your current situation, decide what you can do, and then set a realistic goal based on the present.

That's okay, but a better way to set a goal is to decide what you want to achieve and then work backward to determine what steps you'll need to take to reach that goal.

For example, if you currently have a full-time job, you might say, "Hmm . . . I have an hour or so a night I can devote to real estate . . . so in six months I might be in a position to buy a pre-foreclosure property." Contrast that approach to the person who says, "Hmmm . . . I'd like to own five rental properties by the end of the year . . . what do I need to do to make that happen? I'll need to get my credit in order, start talking to lenders, start looking for deals, find a contractor who's willing to work with me if repairs are needed, find an agent who might be able to help me sell the properties I buy. . . . So, my short-term goal is to get all those things in place in two weeks."

The difference is critical: The best way to set goals is to decide where you want to be in six months, a year, five years, or more . . . and then develop action plans that allow you to *reach* that goal. You'll have to make changes to your life, but it will be worth it.

Short-Term Goals

Short-term goals are things you can accomplish in less than 12 months. (You can create short-term goals with time frames as short as one day if you like.)

Examples of short-term goals are:

- Own your own home within four months.
- Own three residential rental properties within six months.
- Generate a monthly cash flow of $1,200 within six months.
- Make $8,000 from buying and selling a rehab in four months.

Examples of extremely short-term goals are:

- Interview four real estate agents this week.
- Spend 30 minutes a day looking for suitable properties.
- Inspect five properties a week for possible purchase.
- Meet with four lenders this week.
- Contact 10 sellers per week.
- Place two classified ads per week seeking home sellers.

Long-Term Goals

Long-term goals are tasks you want to accomplish over the next 1 to 30 years. Long-term goals require long-range plans. Your long-term goal could be to retire in 20 years due to the success of your real estate investments; if so, first you'll need to determine how much money you'll need to have, and then set intermediate goals that allow you to reach that level of success. Your long-term goal could be to own $10 million in real estate in 20 years, or to have a positive cash flow from your investments of $7,000 per month.

Here's the key to goal-setting: Your goals are your goals, not someone else's. There is no right or wrong goal—the right goal is the goal that's right for you.

The difference between dreams and goals is that goals are written down. Commit your dreams to writing.

How to Set Goals

Goals are like building blocks: extremely short-term goals support other short-term goals, and short-term goals support mid-term and long-range goals. To determine your short-term goals, you'll have to determine your long-term goals first.

Let's say your goal is to own $10 million in real estate in 20 years. Now you have to get there. You can break that goal down into manageable chunks:

- After 5 years, own $1 million in real estate.
- After 10 years, own $3 million in real estate.
- After 15 years, own $7 million in real estate.
- After 20 years, own $10 million in real estate.

Now you can break that down further:

- After one year, own two properties worth $175,000.
- After two years, own four properties worth $350,000.
- After three years, own six properties worth $550,000.

If you keep breaking your goals down into smaller, more manageable chunks, what seems like an insurmountable task—owning $10 million in real estate—can actually be quite manageable broken into small, achievable steps.

If you work backward from the creation of long-term goals to mid-term and short-term goals, you'll create an action plan that will allow you to reach your dreams. It's not hard to do, and it can be really fun—simply think big, and then work backward to decide what you'll need to do to make your dreams happen.

To make your personal goal worksheet, simply take a pad of paper and put your long-term goal at the top. Then, in outline form, break down the intermediate steps you'll need to achieve. Under those steps, break down the tasks further. When you're done, you should have short-term goals you wish to reach that are no longer than one week in duration—if you allow yourself too much time, you're more likely to procrastinate.

Once a goal or task is complete, check it off your list. You'll enjoy the sense of accomplishment, and you'll stay on track with your action plans.

Remember, you can revise your action plans at any time. If you find an investment that's too good to pass up, you might change your short-term goals. Just make sure you don't change your goals or your action plans due to inactivity—you'll never reach your dreams if you don't take action on a consistent basis. It will take work and effort, but you can do it. Thousands of people are successful real estate investors—there's no reason you can't be, too.

Make Your Goals Happen

Goal setting is fun—but you won't achieve your goals unless you take action. If you set big goals, that's great—but achieving those goals will take time. To achieve your goals, you'll have to manage your time properly. Many people say, "Okay, I set my goals . . . and it looks like I'll need to spend four to eight hours per week meeting those goals. I don't have that kind of time."

My answer to that statement is, "Yes, you do." You simply have to use your time more efficiently. Many of us are busy, but how much of that busy time is truly productive? We're guessing that a lot of it is . . . and a lot of it isn't. If you want to be a successful investor, you have to manage your time well.

The following time management tips will help you increase your productivity without creating additional stress:

- *Find out where you're wasting time.* Many of us are prey to time-wasters that steal time we could be using much more productively. What are your time-bandits? Do you spend too much time surfing the net, reading e-mail, or making personal calls? Track your daily activities so you can form an accurate picture of what you actually do. Remember, just because you're "at" work doesn't mean you're actually working.

- *Create time management goals.* Remember, the focus of time management is to actually change your behaviors. A good place to start is by eliminating your personal time-wasters. For one week, for example, set a goal that you're not going to take personal phone calls while you're working. Or decide that you'll only check personal e-mail at night, after you've finished working.

- *Implement a time management plan.* The objective is to change your behaviors over time to achieve a general goal you've set for yourself, like increasing your productivity or decreasing your stress. So you need to not only set your specific goals, but track them over time to see whether you're accomplishing them.

- *Use time management tools.* Whether it's a written schedule planner or a software program, the first step to physically managing your time is to know where it's going now and to plan how you're going to spend your time in the future. A software tool such as Microsoft Outlook, for instance, lets you schedule events easily and can be set to remind you of events in advance, making your time management easier.

- *Prioritize ruthlessly.* You should end each day by planning the next day. List what you need to get done so when you start work the next day you can hit the ground running. Also be realistic: If you have 20 tasks for a given day, how many of them do you really need to accomplish?

- *Establish routines and stick to them as much as possible.* While crises will arise, you'll be much more productive if you can follow routines most of the time.

- *Get in the habit of setting time limits for tasks.* For instance, reading and answering e-mail can consume your whole day if you let it. Instead, set a limit of one hour a day, for example, for this task—and stick to it.

- *Be sure your systems are organized.* Are you wasting a lot of time looking for files on your computer? Take the time to organize a file management system. Is your filing system slowing you down? Redo it so it's organized to the point that you can quickly lay your hands on what you need.

- *Don't waste time waiting.* From meetings to dentist appointments, it's impossible to avoid waiting for someone or something. But you don't need to just sit there and twiddle your thumbs. Always take something to do with you, such as a number of listing sheets you need to read, an investment that needs to be analyzed, or just a blank pad of paper that you can use to plan your next real estate investment. Technology makes it easy to work wherever you are; your PDA and/or cell phone will help you stay connected.

- *Do the worst things first.* If there are things on your to-do list you don't enjoy, or wish you didn't have to do . . . do them first. Every day you should list what you need to get done—and the first items on your list should be the things you least like to do, or that are the hardest for you to do. Tackle them when your energy level is highest—you'll feel a sense of accomplishment and a sense of relief when they're complete, and you can move on to more enjoyable things.

Ninety percent of success is simply showing up—each and every day. Sure, luck, skill, and timing play a part, but perseverance is a major factor in success.

If you give up, you'll never succeed. If you quit, you'll never succeed. If every day you keep moving forward—making plans, taking small steps, crossing items off your goal sheets and your action plans—then one day you'll look back and realize you've accomplished great things . . . and that you're capable of accomplishing a whole lot more.

Making Contact

As I've already indicated, you can make a lot of money investing in pre-foreclosures, but it'll take some effort. Here's how it will shake out:

> For every 20 properties you analyze, you'll look at 10, write offers on 5, and close on 1. But that also means that for every 100 you look at, you'll end up with 10 properties. Don't worry, the odds get better as you get more experienced in recognizing the real opportunities and discarding the "undoables" faster. But remember—you'll never win by taking advantage of someone.

If after reviewing all the material in this book, downloading the forms, checklists, and worksheets I provide to you at www.ChipCummings.com/Cashing In you still have questions, you can feel free to e-mail me at any time at Chip@ChipCummings.com, or call me directly at (616) 977-7900. I do answer all my e-mail personally and welcome your comments. I also speak at events and do presentations frequently throughout the country, and invite you to stop by and let me know how you're doing. You can find my appearance schedule at www.ChipCummings.com.

Now let's learn more about making money with pre-foreclosures!

CHAPTER 2

Why Most Foreclosure Strategies Don't Work

If you've ever stayed up past midnight, then you've seen the commercials. The endless infomercials and seminars on "How to Make a Billion Gazillion Dollars Part-Time on Foreclosures—with No Money, No Credit, and No Life." It seems like everyone has a quick strategy for taking advantage of the foreclosure market. There is just one problem—they don't work!

Don't get me wrong, there are some good ideas and techniques out there, but if you are looking for a way to get rich quick with little to no risk or cash, I hate to be the one to burst your bubble—it ain't gonna happen.

In my opinion, most of the so-called gurus out there are teaching risky, expensive, and highly competitive techniques. There are risks associated with foreclosure investing, and unfortunately that tidbit got left on the editing room floor.

Let's take a look at some of the most common misconceptions about foreclosure investing, and why this book and my approach are different.

Why Doesn't Everyone Do This?

Simply put—it takes work. Most people don't want to have to work for anything, let alone creating a fortune in real estate. They're looking for the easy route, but that road just keeps taking them down a dead end.

Truth is, anything in life that creates long-term wealth and success takes work. I know it, and deep down you know it, too. Yes, there is a formula, and I can shave years off the learning curve, but you still have to be willing to put forth the effort and time—and just do it!

If you like what you're doing, you'll be more successful at it. It's that simple. If you don't, you won't . . . or you'll hate every minute of it even if you *are* successful. (And who wants that?)

Consider your own personality. Do you enjoy working with people? If you don't, then becoming a landlord probably isn't right for you. (You can still invest in rental properties—you'll just need to factor in the cost of using a property management firm to deal with your tenants.)

Do you deal effectively with stress? If you don't, taking on too much risk might not be the best move for you. You should probably avoid owning large commercial properties, or buying a number of foreclosure properties at one time—at least at first. After you become more experienced, you may find that taking on more risk isn't stressful because you have the capital and the skills and experience to work through problems as they come up.

Then take a look at the time you have available. If you're already extremely busy, buying fixer-uppers thinking that you'll do the refurbishing work yourself probably doesn't make sense. The more work you do yourself, the more money you can make . . . but not if you don't have time to actually *do* the work. If you're already extremely busy, buying rental properties and turning over the day-to-day management to a property management firm may be the right choice for you.

If you're married, does your spouse support your real estate investment interests? Investing in real estate takes time—if your spouse isn't interested or supportive, you'll find it tough to devote the time you need to your investments. If you decide to manage rental properties yourself, you can expect late-night calls on occasion from tenants . . . and if your spouse isn't on board, that can cause *huge* problems. A couple I know owns rental properties and they have a "10-unit divorce rule"—they like to say that if they own more than 10 units, their marriage probably won't survive. Make sure you discuss your goals with your spouse before you get started.

Do you have any mechanical, electrical, or carpentry skills? If you don't, you'll need to pay someone to repair or refurbish your properties. If you have these skills, keep in mind you'll have to make time available to actually do that work.

This all takes work—time and effort. Successful investors don't look for get-rich-quick schemes. They understand that this is a business, just like anything else, and when done correctly, it is a business that can be extremely profitable.

A Note to the Skeptics

Several of you out there are skeptical about your chances of success. Someone you know—a friend, family member, coworker, or even a spouse—may try and talk you out of this "foolishness."

For those of you who are skeptics, please reserve your opinion until you've read the entire book. Does it work overnight? No. Does it work? Yes. I can say that confidently because I have been a real estate investor for more than 25 years.

Ignore what the skeptics say and believe in yourself. You can do it, and with a little help, you'll make some great profits and help a lot of people in the process.

Unlike many other investors out there, I don't see a need to kick someone when they're down or take unfair advantage of another person's unfortunate circumstances. I sincerely try to help people, and if you do the same, you'll enjoy this business a whole lot more.

Why People Fail

But regardless of what I say, most of you reading this will probably fail. But not because the strategies in this book don't work. I travel around the world speaking to thousands of people every year from all walks of life. I provide solid examples and case studies, and provide a road map, but still I can't get everyone to be successful. I've tried, but it just doesn't happen.

I have however, figured out the main reasons why people fail. Here are the top six reasons why most people don't make it:

1. They don't try. I mean really try.
2. They won't read through every section and, therefore, miss critical information.
3. They think they already know it all—start too quick and jump on the wrong deal (and lose money in the process).
4. They skip steps along the way, thinking there's a shortcut.
5. They don't create a win-win situation for everyone in the deal. Greed kills a deal quickly.
6. They try to do it all themselves.

While everything on this list is important, the last item is the one that can accelerate your success the fastest. Nate Martinez (www.NatesHomes.com), a good friend and one of the top realtors in the country with ReMax Professionals, based in Phoenix, sums it up this way: "To be a successful investor in foreclosures and short sales, you need to build a team of specialists. You need people who really understand the foreclosure and short sale process and can negotiate all the twists and turns."

If you recognize the warning signs, and avoid these six traps, then you'll become a proud—and wealthy—graduate! Remember, hard work equals success!

Seventeen Steps to Success

As I mentioned, most foreclosure strategies don't work because they're billed as "get-rich-quick" programs, or fail to fully disclose each step along the way.

Well, after 25 years, I have developed a concise 17-step process of getting into pre-foreclosure properties. And I plan to share it with you—right down to every last detail.

In Part II, we go into detail on each of the steps, but here is the list so you can start thinking about each step in the process. These are in order, and there is no shortcut. So you will need to master each one. Briefly, here they are:

Step 1 *Locate the property.* So where do you start? In Chapter 12, you take a look at how to find the properties that are heading into foreclosure, where and what notices to look for, how to find sellers, and how to get sellers to find you.

Step 2 *Contact the owner.* In Chapter 13, you learn the best way to reach the owner, and what to say once you get their attention.

Step 3 *Verify the initial data.* Chapter 14 reveals how to get to the real story on the situation and make a decision quickly as to whether the deal even makes sense.

Step 4 *Conduct an investigation.* Also known as doing your homework! Chapter 15 teaches you to become a super sleuth. Learn the 12 types of key searches, and 16 types of liens.

Step 5 *Inspect the property.* Next you learn how to thoroughly inspect a property—inside and out. What to look for, what to say, and what not to say!

Step 6 *Estimate the value.* Chapter 17 shows you how to calculate the value of your investment, and why you never pay retail. Learn the four simple steps to arriving at the real value of the property.

Step 7 *Analyze your costs and profits.* None of this makes any sense unless you can make a profit. Discover how to accurately estimate repairs, renovation, and holding costs, and how to arrive at your offer price.

Step 8 *Negotiate with the owner.* There are six rules when negotiating with owners. Chapter 19 walks you through the process, and shows you how to create a win-win situation that gets everyone what they want.

Step 9 *Negotiate with the lenders.* Chapter 20 shows you exactly what you need to know in order to negotiate with lienholders, and how to get rid of subordinate liens.

Step 10 *Negotiate with attorneys and trustees.* Attorneys and trustees will be involved in the transaction, so Chapter 21 takes a close look at getting to the right people, and how to how to get them out of your way.

Step 11 *Negotiate the short sale.* Times are tough, and lenders are in a dealing mood. Chapter 22 teaches you how to set up, calculate, and structure a short sale for the homeowner, and how to present it to get lender approval.

4 **Step 12** *Negotiate the purchase.* Nothing happens until the owner agrees to sell the property to you. Chapter 23 focuses on what to say, how to prepare a purchase agreement, and how to protect yourself along the way.

5 **Step 13** *Protect your interests.* Once the deal is set, Chapter 24 explains how to protect your new property before the closing and how to avoid last minute surprises—like an undisclosed, unrecorded lien.

6 **Step 14** *Close the deal.* Chapter 25 focuses on the closing—before, during, and after. What to do, who to use, and when and where you actually get control of the property.

7 **Step 15** *Fix it up.* There will be repairs—sometimes, lots of repairs. Do you repair or replace? What should you start with, and how much will it cost? Chapter 26 outlines an eight-step repair plan.

8 **Step 16** *Sell it (or rent it).* It's only fun if you make a profit. So Chapters 27, 28, and 29 look at the specifics of making sure that you make money on your investment.

Step 17 *Do it again!* If you've followed the steps correctly, you'll be excited to try it again. Each deal is different, and a fortune is waiting right around the corner.

Three Phases of Foreclosure

As I mentioned in Chapter 1, there are three stages of foreclosure. You will quickly learn how to recognize which phase the property you are looking at is in. The further into the process you get, the lower the profit margin there is.

Here is a quick look at the three phases of the foreclosure process:

1. *Pre-foreclosure stage:* This is the period between when a homeowner misses a payment, and when the lien is sold at public auction or by the trustee.

2. *Public auction stage:* This is the time between when the auction takes place and the redemption period is over.

3. *Post-auction stage:* This is the stage after the redemption period, when the lender takes possession of the property.

Avoid the Last Two Phases

The first stage is where you want to focus your energies. Yet many people will continue to tell you that there is great money in all phases of foreclosures. Having bought properties at all different points in the process, here is why I disagree.

During the public auction stage, there has been a lot of attention brought to the property, and the owners have been beaten up and are worn out. Buying at this stage is both risky and competitive. Here are 14 things that most people don't know about public foreclosure auction sales:

1. *All sales are final.* If you are the high bidder, you are expected to pay almost immediately, and there is no recourse if the property or title has problems. There could also be environmental problems such as mold, oil leaks, or asbestos. It is truly bought "as-is, where-is," and the old saying "buyer beware" comes to mind very quickly. Pretty risky.

2. *The property could be redeemed by the owner.* Even though you are the high bidder, in several states, the redemption period could upset your plans when the owner comes into some unexpected cash, sells the property during the redemption, or refinances out of their situation. This situation is too uncertain.

3. *You can't inspect the property prior to the sale.* Even if you got a look inside several weeks ago, the property may have been stripped, or systems and utilities may have been shut down. Without an on-site presale inspection, you're literally going in blind. This is really dangerous.

4. *You must have cashier's check and/or verified funds to bid.* Financing options are not available, and you almost always have to go in with a cashier's check or a bank Letter of Credit.

5. *It's an auction.* If you've ever been to an auction, you know that the bidding can get competitive, and people get caught up in the moment. This is no different, and properties can easily go for more than they're worth sometimes. It can be very expensive.

6. *There could be collusion between the bidders.* In a few instances, I have witnessed prearranged bidding partners who have gotten together ahead of time to negotiate their bids, blocking out others, or splitting up multiple properties.

7. *The property may not be insurable (aka trashed property).* We are not talking about the lawn being overgrown here. Insurers are concerned about properties that have been stripped and trashed, or that have extensive claims against them. They will check the C.L.U.E. system for previous claims, and can deny coverage to riskier properties. This is too big a gamble.

8. *May not be able to get satisfactory title insurance.* Most title insurers will not cover claims resulting from flawed chain of title due to the foreclosure process. Exceptions will be built into the policy, and problems will have to be settled with a "quiet title" action that can be expensive and time consuming.

9. *Terms of the sale are nonnegotiable.* There is no back-and-forth negotiating because the procedure is set by state law. Try negotiating with the sheriff or the court sometime!

10. *No leveraging—simply cash.* One of the greatest benefits of owning real estate is the ability to leverage the investment. Since financing is not an option at an auction, your cash gets tied up very quickly, and possibly for a long time.

11. *Property could be occupied by really cranky people.* Homeowners who have been foreclosed on are usually very emotional and stressed out at this point in the game. If they are still around, getting them out could be a dangerous proposition.

12. *There could be environmental problems or other health/safety issues.* Without being able to visit and research the physical property, there may be hazardous substances on the property, a leaking oil tank in the basement, an old pool or dry well, a sink hole, or a variety of other safety issues. There is no seller disclosure for properties purchased at auction, so this risk alone doesn't make it worth it.

13. *The foreclosure process could have been flawed.* Any slight misstep along the way, and an attorney will have the process restarted. A break in the chain of title, missed notices to lienholders, incorrectly filed paperwork, or any number of errors could throw a wrench into the whole proceeding—and leave you picking up the pieces and starting from scratch.

14. *Doesn't extinguish tax liens or IRS liens.* As most people know, the IRS always gets the last laugh. No different here because a federal tax lien stays with the property, giving the IRS another 120 days to redeem the property for tax settlements.

Statistics from ForeclosureRadar.com show that about 96 percent of all public auction properties revert back to the lender. Are there deals out there? Yes, but they take a lot of work—and luck—to get. Not my cup of tea.

Properties that are purchased during the post-auction stage are also riddled with problems. First, almost all properties are listed with real estate agents, and at regular retail prices. That makes it a little hard to make a profit. Due to the recent rash of foreclosures, you may come upon "wholesale auctions" where banks are offering hundreds of properties. While good deals can be found, there are many pros at these things, and you're likely to end up over-bidding.

Banks are required to market these properties this way by law, and to try to get the highest possible retail value for the asset.

At this point, the property may have already been fixed up, and the lender has taken their loss. They are under no pressure to wheel-and-deal, and most properties end up selling for within 10 percent of the asking price.

Here are the seven biggest reasons why you can't make any money with lender-owned properties:

1. Properties are sold through agents at retail—fair market prices; you just can't get a good deal paying retail.

2. All sales are final—could end up in a position with hidden defaults, such as environmental, lead-based paint, asbestos, and so on without recourse. No seller disclosure is necessary on these properties either, making it hard to know the true condition of the property.

3. Must have verified funds or have been preapproved with closing in 30 days or less. They are not in a negotiating mood most of the time, and so you must be able to close the deal on a tight time schedule.

4. Hard to inspect the property—many systems may have been turned off (gas, electric, water, etc.) making it hard to identify system malfunctions or repair costs.

5. Lenders are not very flexible on terms, conditions, and contingency clauses. There are exceptions, but as a general rule your negotiating skills will go to waste here.

6. Property may have been vacant for a long time. Properties that sit vacant start to have all sorts of problems—and small problems undetected turn into larger problems.

7. Title insurance could contain exclusions from prior auction process, leaving you vulnerable to claims. A break in the title could still have you filing a quiet title action just to be able to transfer the title later on.

Pre-foreclosure Is the Best Stage to Invest

Purchasing properties during the pre-foreclosure stage offers you several advantages. First, there is less competition—since most investors get involved at the public auction stage, you will be able to operate and negotiate with the owner in a more comfortable environment.

It's far easier to work directly with the owner as opposed to an attorney or the trustee of the lender, and you have more time to put together a successful deal. There are more options that you can explore with the homeowner, and the costs are generally lower.

Another big plus is that there is no redemption period, so the deal becomes final right away. With the negotiation taking place earlier, you also get more time to conduct your research, and have the luxury of conducting a thorough property inspection. The property is usually in better condition as well.

Pre-foreclosure Risks

There are risks involved in pre-foreclosure investing as well. Owners at this stage are usually quite emotional, or in a state of denial—and only want to sell at the retail price.

Dealing with these types of homeowners can be complicated and stressful and then just as you get a deal negotiated, they can change their mind. In fact, because of the confusion surrounding the ordeal they are going through, many of them do exactly that.

You will also encounter owners who misrepresent or falsify information. Priorities sometimes can be a little mixed up, and owners may think they are smarter than you. That's where Chapter 15 on doing your homework will come in handy.

There are also legal issues and liabilities that face an investor purchasing a foreclosure directly from a homeowner. Because you will be purchasing properties at less than market value, your actions could be seen as taking advantage of the distressed homeowner. We look at how to protect yourself from that in Chapter 23.

However, for all the risks involved, you still have the chance to help out a great number of people, and make good profits along the way.

CHAPTER 3

Down Markets: The Easiest Time to Capitalize and Make Money

Most people tend to stay away from buying real estate when the market is down. Not the savvy investor! During a down market, there are more properties available, and the market becomes more competitive for sellers, actually driving prices down.

This presents a great opportunity for investors to make deals and build some quick equity. Let's take a look at how market factors affect our potential profits.

Good Markets Versus Bad Markets

To start, let's clear up the difference between a good market and a bad market. When the economy is experiencing problems and real estate values are depressed, inventories start to climb and marketing times swell. Right now, according to the National Association of Realtors®, the nationwide average marketing time for a house is approximately 11 months. That's the highest it's been in over 20 years. This would be described by most people as a "bad real estate market."

When the market is good, prices are stable or rising, there is a steady balance between supply and demand, and there are far less options in the marketplace for buyers. Properties usually are sold within three to four months, and sales prices are typically within 93 to 97 precent of the asking price.

Don't be fooled though; foreclosures happen every day of the week, all over the country—in good times or bad.

Why a Down Market Is Better

The market cycles represent an inverse relationship for investors. When the market is down and demand decreases, prices drop. This leads to increased competition for sellers, especially among people going through foreclosure.

Most of my better deals have come during so-called down markets, although the exit strategy needs to be adjusted. Flipping properties is not as lucrative during these times because profits are more geared toward long-term rentals and equity build-up.

Understanding Foreclosure Statistics

There is another over riding rule, and that is that all real estate is local. Just because California, Florida, Nevada, Michigan, or Arizona are experiencing high rates of foreclosures doesn't mean the entire state are. There are plenty of markets where the overall numbers of foreclosures are up, yet certain cities, and pockets of neighborhoods are doing extremely well and sales prices don't follow the state numbers. To illustrate how some areas are able to buck the trend, look at Figure 3.1.

Why Foreclosures Happen

You need to understand what is behind a foreclosure to help you identify solutions for the homeowner and ways to negotiate creative agreements. Here are the most common circumstances that set a foreclosure in motion:

- *Divorce:* Approximately half of all marriages end in a divorce. Who keeps the house and who pays for the house—and whether the house is even affordable any longer—can be a major issue. Unfortunately, in many instances, people lose perspective, pure spite takes over, and common sense disappears. (In fact, the cost of the divorce itself can even be the main cause of foreclosure.)

- *Health problems:* Unexpected illnesses or injuries can cost a homeowner thousands in medical bills, and the rising rate of uninsured Americans leaves fewer people with a safety net. When a medical emergency occurs, mortgage payments are sometimes understandably seen as less important, at least in the short term.

- *Job loss:* Losing a job is also a common cause of foreclosure. As unemployment rates increase, foreclosure rates naturally tend to rise. But even during

	Foreclosure Rate%	Median Sales Price	% Change
California	+197.78		
San Jose	+343.32	$755,000	−12.7
San Francisco	+203.94	684,900	−19.1
Florida			
Orlando	+247.94	223,500	−15.7
Miami	+112.86	310,100	−19.3
New York	+61.66		
NYC Metro	+66.19	498,500	−10.8
Albany	+276.60	198,400	+3.5
Illinois	+57.99		
Chicago	+58.30	257,600	−9.0
Decatur	+61.66	94,200	+6.0
North Carolina	+57.97		
Raleigh	+64.10	213,200	−5.3
Charlotte	+25.45	210,300	−2.9
Texas	+40.47		
Houston	+83.86	153,400	−1.0
El Paso	+2.77	137,700	+4.1

*12 month period as of Q2 2008
Source: RealtyTrac.com and National Association of Realtors®

FIGURE 3.1   Foreclosure Rates versus Average Sales Price

booming economic times, some companies lay off employees, transfer, consolidate, or just plain go out of business.

- *Predatory lending:* Irresponsible, greedy, or poorly trained loan originators can "sell" a homeowner on a loan that sets the homeowner up for failure. This is one of the causes of the mortgage meltdown that started in 2008.

- *Soaring cost of living:* When pay increases fail to keep up with inflation, homeowners may not be able to keep up. We have seen sudden increases in property taxes, insurance premiums, and fuel costs—without comparable increases in personal income.

- *Death:* If the sole wage earner dies, the likelihood increases that the family will lose their home in foreclosure.

- *Taxes:* Some mortgage programs do not include tax escrow accounts, and it becomes easy for a homeowner to fall behind. In these cases, the lender can call the loan due and accelerate payments to avoid a tax-lien sale.

While financial irresponsibility is a common cause, as you can see, death, job loss, medical expenses, and divorce are also common reasons for a property foreclosure. Sadly, bad things do happen to well-meaning, otherwise financially responsible people.

Understanding the Market and Market Trends Is Important

On Wall Street, investors are taught to "buy low and sell high" and to watch for trends to create profits. In real estate, it is just as important for investors to recognize trends in the market, and the reasons behind those trends.

Whether the trend is going up or going down, there are only two forces that drive the trend—economic or speculation.

In an economic-driven trend, consumer income and expense factors are controlling the property values and marketing times. Bad employment leads to fewer qualified borrowers, increased rentals, and increased foreclosures. In this type of trend, investors should be looking for more long-term strategies, with better pricing.

In a speculative-driven market, consumers are hungry for real estate, and better economic times lead to greater demand, shorter marketing time, and higher sales prices. The play for the investor in this type of market is more short-term gains, with better opportunities to flip the property for a quick resale.

Because every market is different, it is up to you to research the demographic and geographic make-up of your consumers in your marketplace. Research what properties are moving in your area. Stay on top of trends through your local real estate association, chamber of commerce, or visitors and convention bureau. They can provide statistics that help you decide in what areas and what types of properties to invest in.With the credit crisis that started in 2008, including bank failures and government bailouts, market trends indicate that real estate investors will enjoy unprecedented opportunities well into the year 2010.

CHAPTER 4

Everything You Need to Know about the Foreclosure Process

N ow let's get down to the terms and details of the foreclosure process that you need to know. This chapter helps you get a handle on the players, documents and clauses, and exactly what happens along the way.

Security Instruments

When a loan is made, either residential or commercial, the property is put up as collateral to secure repayment. To secure the lien against that collateral, two types of security instruments can be used:

1. Mortgages
2. Deeds of trust

A mortgage involves two parties: A *mortgagee* who is the lender and a *mortgagor* who is the borrower. The borrower (mortgagor) signs a note and a mortgage, which is held by the lender (mortgagee) until the loan is paid off.

A deed of trust involves three parties: the *trustor* who is the borrower, the *beneficiary* who is the lender, and a *trustee* who is a neutral third party. The borrower (trustor) signs a note and a deed of trust that conveys title to the lender (beneficiary), which is held in trust by the neutral third party (trustee) until the note is paid in full.

States primarily use one method or the other, but some states use both security instruments. Check the list in Chapter 6 to determine which document is used in your state. This is important for the foreclosure process used in your state.

Copies of security instruments can be found on Fannie Mae's web site here: https://www.efanniemae.com/sf/formsdocs/documents/secinstruments/.

Two Types of Lenders

Real estate loans that are secured by a mortgage or a deed of trust are provided by two types of lenders:

1. Institutional lenders or
2. Private lenders.

Institutional lenders include banks, mortgage lenders, mortgage bankers, credit unions, federally insured depositories, and some pension funds, REITs, or insurance companies.

Private lenders include everyone else—individuals, businesses, private companies, associations, or investment groups.

You need to recognize what type of lender you are dealing with because that will have a direct effect on how you approach and structure the deal.

Types of Real Estate Loans

In addition to the type of lender, you need to determine the type of loan that is being foreclosed on. There are seven types of real estate loans:

1. *Conventional:* These are the most common type of residential loan and are typically purchased or eligible for purchase through the two large government-sponsored entities known as Fannie Mae and Freddie Mac.

2. *Subprime:* These are residential loans that do not fit the requirements of Fannie Mae or Freddie Mac. Also called nonconventional, these include stated-income, no documentation, or limited asset type loans. These loans can have a variety of loan terms and higher interest rates and adjustments, and many do not include tax escrow accounts.

3. *Federal Housing Administration:* These are residential loans that are guaranteed and insured by the Federal Housing Administration (FHA). Typically used for first-time homebuyers, they feature a low down payment, and market interest rates.

4. *Veterans Affairs:* These are residential loans that are guaranteed and insured by the Department of Veterans Affairs (VA), available to veterans and service members. These feature zero down payments and low market interest rates.

5. *Rural Development:* These are also residential loans that are guaranteed and insured through the U.S. Department of Agriculture (also known as RD loans). Provided for properties located in rural areas, these loans offer 100 percent financing and attractive interest rates.

6. *Hard money (private):* These are residential or commercial loans provided by private parties. They include a wide variety of interest rates and terms, and typically are more expensive to borrowers.

7. *Commercial:* These institutional loans are provided for residential properties of five units or more, or any other type of commercial structure.

Senior Lien Versus Junior Liens

It is also critical that you are able to distinguish between senior and junior liens. One of the rules of foreclosure investing is to *never* bid on a junior lien.

The senior lien, or first mortgage, is the one that was recorded first in time/date sequence at the county recorder's office.

Second, third, or fourth liens are called junior liens, and their position is strictly determined by the date and time of when the security instrument was recorded.

A mortgage document that was recorded on January 17 would have a senior position over one that was recorded against the property on January 21. In this case, the first one would be called the first mortgage or senior lien, followed by a second mortgage, and so on.

Mortgage Lender Versus Mortgage Broker

When dealing with mortgage entities, you want to get to decision makers. It helps to understand the roles of the two types of mortgage entities:

1. A *mortgage lender* is a licensed entity who has its own funds or access to funds to directly lend to a borrower.

2. A *mortgage broker* is a licensed individual or company who is permitted to initiate loan applications and represent the programs of many different mortgage lenders to borrowers. Mortgage brokers earn a fee directly from the lender or the borrower, or a combination of the two.

Even though a mortgage broker may have initiated the original loan for the borrower, they will not be of any help in negotiating or tracking down the current loan information with the lender.

Controlling Loan Covenants

Because most residential loans are conforming loans that are controlled by Fannie Mae and Freddie Mac, the documents used are fairly standard. In any security instrument, there are three clauses (or covenants) that control the rights of the borrower during foreclosure. They are:

1. Due-on-sale clause

2. Borrower's right to reinstate

3. Acceleration

The due-on-sale clause (also known as Section 18) is what provides the lender with the right to call the loan due and payable if there is a transfer of ownership in the property.

The borrower's right to reinstate (also known as Section 19) is the covenant contained in the security instrument that allows the borrower to pay all the delinquent payments, fees, and costs to reinstate the loan and bring it current.

The acceleration clause (also known as Section 22) spells out the lender's right to accelerate the amounts due under the terms on the note.

Due-on-Sale Clause

The due-on-sale clause allows a lender to accelerate the loan and make it due and payable in 30 days if the ownership or beneficial interest of the property is transferred. It reads as follows:

> **18. Transfer of the Property or a Beneficial Interest in Borrower.** As used in this Section 18, "Interest in the Property" means any legal or beneficial interest in the Property, including, but not limited to, those beneficial interests transferred in a bond for deed, contract for deed, installment sales contract or escrow agreement, the intent of which is the transfer of title by Borrower at a future date to a purchaser.
>
> If all or any part of the Property or any Interest in the Property is sold or transferred (or if Borrower is not a natural person and a beneficial interest in

Borrower is sold or transferred) without Lender's prior written consent, Lender may require immediate payment in full of all sums secured by this Security Instrument. However, this option shall not be exercised by Lender if such exercise is prohibited by Applicable Law.

If Lender exercises this option, Lender shall give Borrower notice of acceleration. The notice shall provide a period of not less than 30 days from the date the notice is given in accordance with Section 15 within which Borrower must pay all sums secured by this Security Instrument. If Borrower fails to pay these sums prior to the expiration of this period, Lender may invoke any remedies permitted by this Security Instrument without further notice or demand on Borrower. (*Source:* Fannie Mae)

Take a closer look at paragraph two—it states that the "Lender may require immediate payment in full." This is an optional step, and one we will test later on and use to our advantage. But you need to know if the homeowner's loan contains this provision.

The only way to know if a mortgage security instrument contains this clause is to look for it. While most standard mortgages contain the clause exactly this way, many others do not. We discuss this clause and its application in more detail in Chapter 8.

 Make sure to ask the homeowner for a copy of his or her mortgage, note, and/or deed of trust, and review it for these three clauses.

Reinstating Loans

Even after a default, deep into the foreclosure process, the borrower still has a right to reinstate the loan. Reinstatement means paying all delinquent amounts owed, including past due payments, interest, penalties, fees, and legal costs.

For most government loans, a borrower can reinstate right up until the date of the public sale. For conventional loans, most lenders will allow reinstatement up until a few days prior to the sale. Here is what the actual clause states:

19. Borrower's Right to Reinstate After Acceleration. If Borrower meets certain conditions, Borrower shall have the right to have enforcement of this Security Instrument discontinued at any time prior to the earliest of: (1) five days before sale of the Property pursuant to any power of sale contained in this Security Instrument; (2) such other period as Applicable Law might specify for the termination of Borrower's right to reinstate; or (3) entry of a judgment enforcing this Security Instrument. Those conditions are that Borrower: (1) pays

Lender all sums which then would be due under this Security Instrument and the Note as if no acceleration had occurred; (2) cures any default of any other covenants or agreements; (3) pays all expenses incurred in enforcing this Security Instrument, including, but not limited to, reasonable attorneys' fees, property inspection and valuation fees, and other fees incurred for the purpose of protecting Lender's interest in the Property and rights under this Security Instrument; and (4) takes such action as Lender may reasonably require to assure that Lender's interest in the Property and rights under this Security Instrument, and Borrower's obligation to pay the sums secured by this Security Instrument, shall continue unchanged. Lender may require that Borrower pay such reinstatement sums and expenses in one or more of the following forms, as selected by Lender: (1) cash; (2) money order; (3) certified check, bank check, treasurer's check or cashier's check, provided any such check is drawn upon an institution whose deposits are insured by a federal agency, instrumentality or entity; or (4) Electronic Funds Transfer. Upon reinstatement by Borrower, this Security Instrument and obligations secured hereby shall remain fully effective as if no acceleration had occurred. However, this right to reinstate shall not apply in the case of acceleration under Section 18.

Acceleration

When the borrower is in default on the note, the acceleration clause provides the lender with the right to call the balance on the loan due and payable right away. We discuss this in more detail in Chapter 8, but here is what the clause, also known as Section 22, states:

22. **Acceleration;** Remedies. Lender shall give notice to Borrower prior to acceleration following Borrower's breach of any covenant or agreement in this Security Instrument (but not prior to acceleration under Section 18 unless Applicable Law provides otherwise). The notice shall specify: (1) the default; (2) the action required to cure the default; (3) a date, not less than 30 days from the date the notice is given to Borrower, by which the default must be cured; and (4) that failure to cure the default on or before the date specified in the notice may result in acceleration of the sums secured by this Security Instrument and sale of the Property. The notice shall further inform Borrower of the right to reinstate after acceleration and the right to bring a court action to assert the nonexistence of a default or any other defense of Borrower to acceleration and sale. If the default is not cured on or before the date specified in the notice, Lender at its option may require immediate payment in full of all sums secured by this Security Instrument without further demand and may invoke the power of sale and any other remedies permitted by Applicable Law. Lender shall be entitled to collect all expenses incurred in pursuing the remedies provided in this Section 22,

including, but not limited to, reasonable attorneys' fees and costs of title evidence.

If Lender invokes the power of sale, Lender shall give notice of sale to Borrower in the manner provided in Section 15. Lender shall publish and post the notice of sale, and the Property shall be sold in the manner prescribed by Applicable Law. Lender or its designee may purchase the Property at any sale. The proceeds of the sale shall be applied in the following order: (1) to all expenses of the sale, including, but not limited to, reasonable attorneys' fees; (2) to all sums secured by this Security Instrument; and (3) any excess to the person or persons legally entitled to it.

Types of Foreclosure Actions

When the borrower does default on a residential or commercial loan, there are two different processes that are used to foreclose on the property:

1. Judicial process
2. Nonjudicial (or trustee) process

The specific type of process used in your state can be found in the table in Chapter 6.

Judicial Process

The judicial process involves the court system and is used by about half the states in the country. The lender (plaintiff) files a legal complaint against the borrower (defendant) and any other lienholders of record. A *lis pendens*, which means suit pending, is also filed to let the whole world know of the impending court action. This is what sets off the feeding frenzy of investors and contacts to the homeowner.

The borrower then typically has between 15 and 30 days to respond to the lawsuit and present a defense. Usually there is none, and the court simply rules for the plaintiff lender and orders the property to be foreclosed upon and sold at public auction to satisfy the claim.

The public foreclosure auction is then advertised and the property is sold to the highest bidder, which is usually the lender. After any redemption period, the high bidder is awarded and issued a *sheriff's deed* to the property.

Nonjudicial Process

In a nonjudicial foreclosure process, the court action is skipped thanks to a power-of-sale clause in the security instrument. A Notice of Default is filed with the county office by the lender or beneficiary in the case of a deed of trust.

A date is set for the trustee sale, which must then be advertised in the legal news or newspaper of record in the county where the property resides. Again, there is a sale to the highest bidder, and after any redemption period, a trustee's deed is issued to the winning party.

Identifying Your State Process

One of your first assignments is to identify the process used in your state. In Chapter 6, there is a table that indicates the actions used in each state, as well as which security instruments are used and the redemption periods.

Terri Murphy, the CIO of U.S. Learning, Inc., has been in the real estate and foreclosure industry for over 30 years. As a top realtor and financial analyst, she handled foreclosure transactions for Freddie Mac. Terri states that, "One of the most important things an investor can do to save time, money, and headaches is to make sure they know the foreclosure laws and process in their state. Lenders don't want to deal with inexperienced rookies."

Since things do change periodically, I recommend that you do a little research and become familiar with each of the steps used in your area. Go to the library and get a copy of the legal newspaper to see what type of information is included in the foreclosure notices.

As you've probably guessed, your best bet is to get started before there is any type of public notice. In Chapter 12, we take a closer look at strategies for getting to the seller early *before* the competition becomes fierce.

How the Process Is Stopped

Equally as important is to understand how the foreclosure process is stopped. There are several ways a borrower or lender can stop or stall the entire sequence of events, which could affect your timing on a purchase of the property:

- *Reinstatement:* The borrower can pay back any delinquent amounts at any time prior to the public auction or trustee sale, and reinstate the loan.
- *Forbearance:* The lender and borrower could enter into what's called a forbearance agreement, which allows the borrower additional time to bring the loan current or make other payment arrangements.

- *Bankruptcy:* If the borrower files for bankruptcy at any time prior to the auction, or during the redemption period, the process grinds to a halt until the bankruptcy court has a chance to review the matter.

- *Note modification:* The lender has the right to alter the terms of the note to make it easier for the borrower to make the payments. While the borrower has to agree to the terms, such modifications are becoming more common with the drastic increase in foreclosures. The interest rate, payment amount, terms, and even converting an adjustable rate loan to a fixed rate loan can be modified to keep the borrower in the home. Remember, a lender does not want to foreclose—it's usually the last option to protect his or her interest. So keeping the borrower in the home saves him or her money in the long run.

- *Short pay:* Different from a short sale, a short pay allows a borrower to pay off a lender for less than is owed, but they remain in the property. Usually done in refinance situations, this is still cheaper for the lender than a full-blown foreclosure, but is rare because it's hard for the borrower to qualify for any type of refinance anymore.

- *Repayment plan:* Similar to a note modification, the lender and borrower agree to a new payment plan without altering the terms of the note. This is a great option for the lender because the foreclosure option is still readily available if the borrower doesn't follow through on the new payment schedule. The most common initial option, this can involve payments added to the end of the loan, biweekly payments, or lower payments for a period of time until the borrower gets back on their feet again.

- *Deed in lieu of foreclosure:* Similar to a borrower crying "uncle," they simply sign over the deed to the lender without having to go through the drawn out foreclosure process. Great for the lender, but obviously short circuits the time available for a borrower to find alternative solutions. If the homeowner really doesn't want the property, this saves time and aggravation for everyone involved.

CHAPTER 5

Everything You Need to Know about Foreclosure Properties

You don't want to own every foreclosure property. This sounds obvious, but sometimes beginning investors try too hard to make every deal work. Most deals won't—that's just the nature of the game. In this chapter, we take a look at how to size up a property in five minutes or less. When you're looking at lots of properties, you can't afford to spend too much time weeding out the bad deals.

Determining the Stage of Foreclosure

The first thing you need to do is to figure out what stage of the process the property is in. Some properties are obvious by their appearance, but many will be in the final days of the redemption period, and look like a showcase home. It may even still be listed for sale with a real estate agent, hoping for one last miracle buyer to walk through the door.

So how do you figure out where in the process they are? If you haven't spotted it listed in the legal news, then a few simple questions will do the trick. When speaking with the homeowner or real estate agent, ask the following questions to determine the status:

- Is the property subject to any current or recent foreclosure action?
- Has a public auction already taken place, or what is the sale date?
- Is the property currently in a redemption period, and when does it expire?

The answers to these questions will tell you volumes. If the auction has already taken place or it's in a redemption period, your opportunity has already passed. I will typically pass on these properties because there's just not enough profit in the deal. If there was, an investor would have already won the bid at the auction phase. The exception is if the property has been sitting around for a very long period of time.

Make a Quick First Assessment from the Curb

If the answer to the second question is no, then you need to make a quick curbside assessment. What they say about first impressions is usually true. If there is serious visible damage to the exterior, such as a sagging or collapsing roof, missing siding, broken windows, and so on—then walk away. This is typically an indicator of what you'll find inside, and it won't be pretty.

Is the property occupied? If it appears abandoned, then internal systems such as water, electric, heat, and gas may have been disconnected, leading to serious and expensive repairs. I can tell you how bad a house gets after sitting through a couple of winter months in Michigan if it has not been properly winterized.

Assess the Neighborhood

In addition to the subject property, drive around the neighborhood. Look for other obvious foreclosures or abandoned properties. What's the condition and upkeep of other homes on the street? Remember, you need to be able to resell or rent out the home, and if nobody wants to drive down the street, they'll never step foot into your property—no matter how nicely the repairs have been done.

While driving around the immediate vicinity, also look for the following:

- *Trash:* General neglect of the neighborhood.
- *Schools:* Location and quality of the school district.
- *Shopping:* Is it nearby and convenient? Discount stores or new upscale retailers?
- *Construction:* This is a sign of investment in the area. Any new buildings or major renovations?
- *Crime statistics:* Local police departments can tell you what has been reported in that area. In my area, this information is even online in almost real-time.
- *Other properties for sale:* Look to see what the other competition is. Are there lots of homes on the market, and how long have they been for sale? There's usually a reason if everyone's leaving.

Evaluate the Investment Potential

A good neighborhood assessment will instantly get your mind running. As you get more used to this strategy of driving around, you'll find that you can quickly evaluate any potential in the property. You'll subconsciously be deciding to rent it or flip it. You'll have a good idea of the retail price range, and what your general bottom-line number will be in order to make a profit.

This ability will come in time, but start out by making notes. Initially, try to make an appointment to view any homes for sale on the street, or drop by some open houses on a Sunday afternoon. Then start by working the numbers backward. I begin with a general retail price, then subtract 7 percent for sales commissions, another 5% percent for a below-market sale, and 10 to 15 percent for repairs. Then I subtract off my required profit margin, and I'm left with a rough down-and-dirty estimate of acquisition. Here's how it might look:

Retail sales or listing price:	$150,000
Marketing and sales commission:	(10,500)
Quick sale incentive:	(7,000)
Repairs and renovation:	(22,500)
My minimum profit:	(10,000)
Maximum acquisition:	$100,000

This means that unless I can get the property for $100,000 or less, it won't make sense to pursue it. Is a 10 percent return good enough? Sometimes yes, and sometimes no. But make sure you add it in. The numbers will vary depending on your quick neighborhood and property curbside assessment, but this assessment helps weed out a lot of properties right up front.

We take a much more detailed look at calculating your costs and profits in Chapter 18, but it's important to be able to size up a property quickly.

Conducting Thorough Research

Profits and costs aside, they will mean nothing if you can't get the title to the property or get sidetracked for a year thanks to an unforeseen roadblock. Although it's impossible to eliminate every possible problem, you can avoid most by doing thorough research on the property and its history.

One property I purchased had been vacant for over a year, and as a result, the local ordinance required it to be reinspected by the city to be recertified for occupancy. It didn't meet the new current code requirements, and as a result I ended up spending a lot more time and money than planned. This could have been avoided with a simple phone call to the building department.

Most information will be easily obtainable, but some will require a bit more detective work. In the end, you don't want surprises that end up killing your deal—or costing you thousands to fix.

In Chapters 14 and 15, we look at how to independently verify property facts and information, get straight answers from lenders and lienholders, and conduct a very detailed search on the property.

CHAPTER 6

Navigating State Foreclosure Laws and Regulations

U
nlike many other real estate transactions, foreclosure purchases will sometimes be put under the microscope, and you will find yourself subject to a
wide variety of state and sometimes even local laws and regulations.

Even when you're trying to do things right, the rules can work against
you, so it's only natural that you need to become aware of the basic foreclosure laws that apply to you. One of my favorite web sites for finding regulatory
compliance information is the U.S. Foreclosure Network (www.usfn.org) which
is run by mortgage banking attorneys. They hold seminars and training events,
and under their "Publications and Products" link is a *Foreclosure Reference Desk
Guide* that has state-by-state regulations. It's an invaluable tool, and a bargain
for only $45.

Finding State Statutes Online

If you are going to play the game, it's a good thing to know the rules. There are
regulations in all 50 states regarding the foreclosure process. Although there is not
space to dive into each one separately in this book, I want to give you a head start
as to where to look.

Listed next, you will find the corresponding statutes for every state. I recommend that you go to your state government web site, and download or print off a
copy of the statutes listed. It makes for good bedtime reading.

State	Statute
Alabama	§35-10-1
Alaska	§34.20.090
Arizona	§33.807
Arkansas	§18-4-49
California	§2924
Colorado	§38-37-113
Connecticut	§36a-785
Delaware	§25-16
Florida	§702.01
Georgia	§44-14-161
Hawaii	§667-1
Idaho	§6-101
Illinois	§15-10 1 & 12-122
Indiana	§32-29-7
Iowa	§654.1
Kansas	§60-2410
Kentucky	§381.190
Louisiana	§2631
Maine	§6321
Maryland	§7-105
Massachusetts	§3-244
Michigan	§451.401
Minnesota	§508.57
Mississippi	§89-1-55
Missouri	§443.320
Montana	§71-1-228
Nebraska	§25-2137
Nevada	§107.020
New Hampshire	§479.22
New Jersey	§2A-50-2
New Mexico	§48-7-7
New York	§1401 (repeal 7/09)
North Carolina	§45
North Dakota	§32-19-01
Ohio	§2323.07
Oklahoma	§46
Oregon	§86.010
Pennsylvania	§1141

Rhode Island	§34-11-22
South Carolina	§15-7-10
South Dakota	§21-47-1
Tennessee	§35-5-501
Texas	§51.002
Utah	§57-1-14
Vermont	§4528
Virginia	§55-59.1
Washington	§61.12.010
Washington, DC	§42
West Virginia	§38-1-3
Wisconsin	§846.01
Wyoming	§1-18-101

Reference provided by http://law.justia.com

Remember that these can and do change periodically, so stay on top of any changes that affect your states foreclosure process, and any forms or disclosures that might be required.

State-by-State Foreclosure Guidelines

To help you get started researching your state's specific guidelines, Table 6.1 includes the type of foreclosure process used, the type of security instrument used, and whether a Notice of Default (NOD) or *lis pendens* is required.

TABLE 6.1   State-by-State Foreclosure Process

State	Type of Process	Type of Security	Notice of Default
Alabama	Both	Both	Not mandatory
Alaska	Both	Both	Varies by area
Arizona	Nonjudicial	Both	None
Arkansas	Both	Both	Mandatory
California	Both	Both	Mandatory
Colorado	Both	Deed of Trust	None
Connecticut	Judicial	Mortgage deed	None
Delaware	Judicial	Mortgage deed	None
Florida	Judicial	Mortgage deed	None
Georgia	Both	Both	None

(Continued)

TABLE 6.1 (*Continued*)

State	Type of Process	Type of Security	Notice of Default
Hawaii	Both	Both	Possible
Idaho	Both	Both	Mandatory
Illinois	Judicial	Mortgage deed	None
Indiana	Judicial	Mortgage deed	None
Iowa	Both	Mortgage deed	Mandatory
Kansas	Judicial	Mortgage deed	Mandatory
Kentucky	Judicial	Mortgage deed	None
Louisiana	Judicial	Mortgage deed	None
Maine	Judicial	Mortgage deed	Mandatory
Maryland	Judicial	Both	None
Massachusetts	Both	Both	None
Michigan	Both	Both	None
Minnesota	Both	Both	Mandatory
Mississippi	Both	Both	Mandatory
Missouri	Both	Both	Mandatory
Montana	Both	Both	None
Nebraska	Judicial	Mortgage deed	Mandatory
Nevada	Both	Both	Mandatory
New Hampshire	Nonjudicial	Both	Mandatory
New Jersey	Judicial	Mortgage deed	Mandatory
New Mexico	Judicial	Mortgage deed	None
New York	Both	Both	None
North Carolina	Both	Both	Mandatory
North Dakota	Judicial	Mortgage deed	Mandatory
Ohio	Judicial	Mortgage deed	Mandatory
Oklahoma	Both	Both	Mandatory
Oregon	Both	Both	Mandatory
Pennsylvania	Judicial	Mortgage deed	Mandatory
Rhode Island	Both	Mortgage deed	None
South Carolina	Judicial	Mortgage deed	None
South Dakota	Both	Both	None
Tennessee	Both	Both	None
Texas	Both	Both	Mandatory
Utah	Both	Both	Mandatory
Vermont	Both	Both	Mandatory
Virginia	Both	Both	Mandatory
Washington	Both	Both	Mandatory
Washington, DC	Nonjudicial	Both	Mandatory
West Virginia	Both	Both	Mandatory
Wisconsin	Both	Both	None
Wyoming	Both	Both	Mandatory

State-by-State Process Timelines

Table 6.2 lists the approximate length of the foreclosure process, the approximate redemption period (which can vary depending on circumstances, such as abandoned properties, natural disasters, or notification requirements), and any requirements for posting the Notice of Sale (NOS).

TABLE 6.2   State-by-State Foreclosure Timelines

State	Process Period	Redemption Period	Notice of Sale Requirements
Alabama	60–90 days	12 months	Posting; advertise
Alaska	90 days	12 months; none for nonjudicial	Posting; advertise
Arizona	90 days	None	Posting; advertise
Arkansas	90–120 days	12 months; none for nonjudicial	Posting; advertise
California	120 days	12 months; none for nonjudicial	Posting; Record; advertise
Colorado	45–180 days	75 days residential; 180 days agricultural	Mailed; advertise
Connecticut	60–150 days	By court	Attorney publish
Delaware	210–300 days	none	Mailed; Posting; Advertise
Florida	150–180 days	none	Advertise
Georgia	60–90 days	none	Mailed; advertise
Hawaii	180 days NJ; 330 days Judicial	none	Mailed; advertise
Idaho	150–180 days NJ; 330 days Judicial	12 months; none for nonjudicial	Mailed; advertise
Illinois	300–360 days	90 days	Mailed; advertise
Indiana	150–270 days	none	Personal delivery; advertise
Iowa	120–180 days	Varies	Mailed; posted; advertise
Kansas	12–24 months	90–180 days	Advertise
Kentucky	180 days	12 months	Advertise
Louisiana	60–270 days	none	Personal service; advertise
Maine	180–210 days	90 days	Advertise
Maryland	60–90 days	By court	Mailed; advertise
Massachusetts	75–90 days	None	Mailed; advertise
Michigan	90–420 days	180–365 days	Posting; advertise
Minnesota	120 days	6–12 months	Personal service; advertise

(Continued)

TABLE 6.2   (*Continued*)

State	Process Period	Redemption Period	Notice of Sale Requirements
Mississippi	90–120 days	none	Posting; advertise
Missouri	21–45 days	0–365 days	Mailed; advertise
Montana	150–180 days	none	Posting; mailed; advertise
Nebraska	120–180 days	none	Advertise
Nevada	120–180 days	12 months; none for nonjudicial	Posting; mailed; advertise
New Hampshire	90 days	12 months; none for nonjudicial	Mailed; advertise
New Jersey	90–270 days	10 days	Posting; mailed; advertise
New Mexico	120 days	9 months	Advertise
New York	210–450 days	none	Advertise
North Carolina	90–120 days	10 days	Posting; mailed; advertise
North Dakota	90–150 days	180–365 days	Mailed; advertise
Ohio	150–210 days	none	Advertise
Oklahoma	90–210 days	none	Advertise
Oregon	150–180 days	12 months; none for nonjudicial	Advertise
Pennsylvania	90–270 days	none	Posting; mailed; advertise
Rhode Island	90–270 days	none	Mailed; advertise
South Carolina	150–180 days	0–30 days	Posting; advertise
South Dakota	90–150 days	60–120 days	Mailed; advertise
Tennessee	60 days	0–720 days	Advertise
Texas	30–90 days	none	Posting; mailed
Utah	150 days	By court; none for nonjudicial	Posting; advertise
Vermont	90–270 days	180–365 days	Mailed; advertise
Virginia	60 days	none	Mailed
Washington	120 days avg.	12 months	Recorded; mailed; advertise
Washington, DC	30–60 days	none	Posting; mailed; advertise; mayor
West Virginia	60–90 days	20 days	Mailed; advertise
Wisconsin	90–290 days	180–365 days	Varies
Wyoming	60–90 days	90–365 days	Advertise

i   There is a more detailed list of this information located at the end of the book.

California Foreclosure Statutes

The state of California has specific regulations designed to protect homeowners. Make sure to read up on Home Equity Sales contract (CA Code Section 1695) and laws covering foreclosure consultants (CA Code Section 2945).

Both of these can be found online at www.stop-foreclosure-info.com/civil-code-1695.html and www.stop-foreclosure-info.com/civil-code-2945.html.

Your Legal Responsibilities

You are not expected to be an attorney, but you do need to know the laws that govern the way you operate. Remember, ignorance is not a defense!

While we're on the topic, you should also NEVER pass yourself off as an attorney (unless you are one!). Doing so is not only stupid, but is illegal as well. Never advise someone against consulting with an attorney, and do not make or recommend legal decisions on behalf of any homeowner you are dealing with. Due to the foreclosure crisis that started in 2008, many states have enacted specific laws concerning "foreclosure rescue" businesses and "loan modification" specialists. Be sure to check your state web site for updated regulations.

CHAPTER 7

How to Avoid Foreclosure Fraud Scams

There is nothing worse than taking advantage of someone when they're down. Foreclosures are hard enough on people, but there has been a huge increase in foreclosure fraud scams as well. The Federal Bureau of Investigation indicates that the number of fraud reports jumped nearly 700 percent over the past four years, with more than 47,000 cases in 2007 alone. According to the Department of Justice, fraud is now a multibillion dollar problem.

Part of your responsibility in dealing with homeowners is to alert them to possible fraud schemes. While you can't necessarily protect them, you can make a point of educating them about what to watch out for.

Common Foreclosure Scams

There are two types of real estate fraud: fraud for property and fraud for profit. Foreclosure scams are mostly designed to get the property from the homeowner. The most common one is called the *Quit-Claim Deed Scam*.

Scammers promise to help troubled homeowners avoid foreclosure and improve their credit ratings. As part of the process, they convince the borrower to sign a quit-claim deed and other documents that transfers the title over to a third-party purchaser, just for a year, promising to use the equity to pay down the debt.

The money is never used to make the payments, but instead transferred to the scam artist while the foreclosure proceeds against the homeowner. Several other variations of this scam are widely used as well, leaving unsuspecting homeowners vulnerable to a double whammy.

One of the first things I do is put homeowners on alert. This educates them as well as positioning me in a more positive light for possible negotiations later on. I refer them to two web sites to learn more about mortgage fraud schemes:

- www.freddiemac.com/avoidfraud
- www.freddiemac.com/avoidfraud/fraud_schemes.html#rescue

As an investor, you want to maintain a professional image and avoid possible scams or the appearance of scams at all costs. Educating the homeowner is the first step, but I also offer personal and business references to the homeowner, and ask that they check them.

Become a member of your local chamber of commerce and the Better Business Bureau to establish a sense of security for your customers (who are the homeowners and your tenants), and write articles for your local paper or trade journal to help establish professional credibility.

Another requirement I use to help prevent fraud is to ask for picture identification from all the owners and representatives that I come in contact with. I offer mine to them as well, and mention that this is for their protection.

Ultimately, your best preventative measure against you falling into a fraudulent transaction will be the quality of the research you do on the property (see Chapter 15). Do your homework—it pays off.

Avoid Equity Skimming

As defined by federal law (Public Law 100–242 of 1987), equity skimming occurs when an individual or business willfully engages in a pattern of acquiring properties secured by home loans insured, guaranteed, or made by the government, failing to make payments that become due on those loans within one year subsequent to the purchase, or diverting rental proceeds from the property for personal use.

Equity skimming is illegal and expensive because fines can run up to $250,000 and can come with a ticket to federal prison for up to five years. Definitely not worth it!

In a typical pre-foreclosure property equity-skimming scheme, the property is purchased "subject to" the existing loan, then resold without making payments on the first loan. Sometimes it's even refinanced without the knowledge of the owner; that is, until the foreclosure goes through and the homeowner is left picking up the pieces—and without any equity left.

Use a Licensed Servicing Company

To avoid even the appearance of impropriety, and to keep everything above-board, when entering into any kind of installment sales contract or land contract with an owner, I recommend using a qualified, licensed servicing company.

These companies will act as a neutral third party, collecting payments and dispersing them to the appropriate parties, and furnishing a yearly report to everyone. This is a great way to go and puts everyone at ease with respect to the accounting of funds. It also protects you from an equity-skimming charge.

I also strongly recommend that when entering into a land contract or installment sales transaction, that you also have all transfer documents signed and held in escrow by a trustee. The last thing you want is to pay on a contract for years, only to have a problem getting the borrower to sign—or not being able to even track the borrower down.

One lady I met had been making payments for over 10 years on a land contract, only to find out that the titleholder had added a lien and was being foreclosed on. She had to pay off the original owner's foreclosure just to get clear title after 10 years. Make sure you use a servicing company.

Many banks offer this service, but here are a few nationwide loan servicing companies:

- Note Servicing Center, Inc, www.SellerLoans.com
- Reliable Loan Servicing, www.ReliableLoanServicing.com
- Midland Loan Services (commercial loans), www.MidlandLS.com

Reputation Is Everything

You will quickly discover that in the world of foreclosure investing, reputation is everything. Always act in an honorable, upfront, honest, and reputable fashion. If you are ever asked to do anything that seems questionable, or are tempted to save time or money, but it seems fishy, don't do it.

Make sure to properly disclose all aspects of the transaction to the homeowners, and make sure they understand their options. When I present an offer to someone, I actually go so far as to read each paragraph with them and explain the meaning. I don't want any confusion or bad feelings generated from a simple misunderstanding.

You've heard the old adage that success in real estate is based on location, location, location. Well, in the world of foreclosures, success is based on disclosure, disclosure, disclosure!

CHAPTER 8

Financing Solutions for Foreclosure Properties

I hate walking into a store and finding something I really like, only to discover that I left my wallet at home. That's sort of what you'll feel like when you find a good foreclosure deal, only to find out you have no way of paying for it.

Before you start looking at any foreclosures, you need to have your financial ducks in a row. This chapter discusses the different types of financing options, and tells you how to prepare yourself for getting the money to fund your investments.

Show Me the Money

Okay, let's cut to the chase. You will need to have access to cash to buy pre-foreclosures. It doesn't have to be yours, but it has to be available when you need it. Let's start by taking a brief look at the types of loans that might be available to you for financing your investment.

Residential loans are used for one-to-four-family-unit dwellings. Properties that have five or more units fall under commercial financing and a completely different set of guidelines. Here are the six types of loans for residential properties:

1. *Conventional:* Or sometimes called conforming loans, these are loans provided by mortgage lenders, banks, or other financial institutions that are purchased by Fannie Mae or Freddie Mac. There are loan limits, and standardized requirements for the property and the borrower. The advantage is a ready access to funds at relatively low interest rates. Disadvantages for investors include strict qualifying guidelines, lower available loan to value (LTV) (usually 75 percent), and higher closing costs.

2. *Nonconforming:* These may be referred to as subprime loans. They are provided by various mortgage lenders, mortgage bankers, and finance companies. These loans are more attractive to investors because they allow higher LTVs and more variety with payment terms, borrower qualifications, and property requirements. Downside is slightly higher interest rates and costs, and constant change of program availability and qualification requirements. Even with the mortgage meltdown of 2008, when most sub-prime and nonconforming loans were eliminated, there are still several lenders that offer these types of loans. You have to look harder, but they're out there.

3. *Federal Housing Administration:* Loans insured by the Federal Housing Administration (FHA) are great for owner-occupied properties. If you are looking to get into your first home, and pursuing a foreclosure, this allows as little as a 3.5% down payment, regular market interest rates, and normal closing costs. For purchasing properties that need major renovations, take a look at the 203(k) program. Investors can only get involved with FHA financing if the government (Department of Housing and Urban Development or HUD) is the seller. This option is usually unattractive because this means the property has already gone through the foreclosure process and come out the other side. Some special programs are available to investors as well, such as their REO program.

4. *Veterans Affairs:* Loans through the Department of Veterans Affairs are a good deal for veterans and members of the armed services. Qualifications and availability vary depending on length of service, but allow for zero down payment, low interest rates, and reasonable closing costs. All costs can be paid by the seller, allowing a veteran to get into a home for no money down. The downside is that the program is for owner-occupied properties only. Investors may be able to assume VA loans—see later in this chapter for details.

5. *Rural Development:* Rural development (RD) loans, sometimes called RECD loans, are insured by the U.S. Department of Agriculture. These are limited to owner-occupied as well and are only available on properties located in designated rural areas at 100 percent LTV.

6. *Private lenders:* This is always a good choice for investors because the possibilities are endless. Individuals or small investment groups have capital they want to invest for short periods of time. I have a group of doctors that I use for short-term financing on projects that I plan on flipping, or properties that can be rehabbed and then refinanced later on (typically no sooner than 12 months). Sometimes referred to as "hard money" lenders, these loans come with higher interest rates and costs, but if the cash flow works or you need a quick cash investment, it's good to have a few of these in your back pocket.

Very few people have the contacts and resources to be able to get their hands on $7 million in cash within a week. If the situation was right and I had to, I've developed the connections to do just that. After some experience and networking with various lenders, you'll be able to do the same.

Very Important

Fannie Mae and Freddie Mac

Fannie Mae, or the Federal National Mortgage Association (FNMA), is a quasi-government agency created to insure the free flow of money and financing availability for financing residential real estate. They do this by purchasing mortgage debt from lenders, and packaging and reselling the debt as securities on Wall Street. Since the meltdown of 2008, the U.S. government is much more heavily involved in the regulation of Fannie Mae, and the types of loans they are able to purchase. More information can be found on Fannie Mae at their web site, www.FannieMae.com.

Freddie Mac is the kissing cousin of Fannie Mae and serves the same purpose in the marketplace. While their lending criteria, structure, and missions are quite similar, they do have slightly different lending guidelines. You can find out more about them at www.Freddiemac.com.

Since these agencies make up the conforming loan market, there are strict guidelines for investors to be able to obtain financing. You will be limited to 75 percent LTV, and financing will not be available for properties that need major rehabilitation work.

As an investor, you also need to be aware that currently, you are limited to four properties (excluding your personal residence) financed by Freddie Mac at any one time, and currently 10 properties with Fannie Mae. This limitation is per borrower, so it applies even if you are a co borrower on other properties. Be careful, as rules are being tightened as I write this, so check their web sites for updates.

Raising Cash

As I mentioned earlier, you will need to have access to cash. Before going out and building a war chest full of dollar bills, understand that there is a difference between *constructive debt* and *destructive debt*. I would never suggest that you borrow money from or tap into your retirement fund without having a written plan for your investment. Likewise, I would never suggest you go out and invest your life savings, or your last pay check on any real estate investment. You *always* need to have a personal nest egg of at least six months' reserves in readily accessible (liquid) cash in case you need it. If you're not there, then stop everything and "don't pass go" until you are. As you start to assemble your list of cash resources, here are some ideas of where to look:

- *Personal funds:* What liquid assets do you have immediate access to? This includes checking and savings accounts, retirement funds, CDs, stocks and bonds, investment accounts, and other negotiable securities.

- *Personal loans:* Look for ways to access funds through auto loans, signature loans, or loans from family members or friends. Home equity loans or lines of credit allow you to tap into funds as needed, and may even qualify for a tax deduction.

- *Government loans:* Grants and government loans are available for properties located in distressed areas, rehabilitation projects, and certain ethnic or minority groups. Community reinvestment loans are available under certain circumstances, and many of these programs are severely underutilized.

- *Hard money:* Private investors and investment groups are a great source of investment capital. You can run a small classified ad in an investment newspaper or the financial section of your local paper. I have had success finding small investors through attorneys, CPAs, and financial planners. They deal with people looking for good investment returns, and once you have established a track record, it gets easier to go back with new deals. I found my first investor right in my office, but have located several great contacts through small classified ads.

- *Unsecured lines of credit:* Credit cards are a great source of instant cash, and I keep several just for that reason. They can charge fairly hefty fees to access the money, but I only pay if I use the money, and it's available within just a day or two.

- *Grants:* Federal government agencies, local community groups, economic development agencies, local and state housing agencies, and even companies provide grants for real estate development projects. If you have located a deal inside a designated target area, redevelopment zone, or tax renaissance district, there could be grant money available for the asking. This takes a bit of research, but is well worth the effort because most of these are zero-interest loans or outright grants.

- *Sale of assets:* Do you have any nonperforming assets that are collecting dust? Vehicles, boats, snowmobiles, or long-forgotten coin collections. Jewelry, art, or other collectibles can fetch some pretty good money when you need some start-up capital.

Assuming a Loan

FHA Loans

Federal Housing Administration loans that were placed on properties on or before December 14, 1989, are fully assumable by anyone without any qualification requirements. You can pay an assumption fee and simply take over the payments.

For loans closed after that date, assumptions can only be done by owner-occupants, and income and asset verification is required. Investors are not permitted to assume these loans. However, you could assume the loan as an owner occupant, then move out at a later date. The initial FHA loan requires the borrower to sign his intent to occupy the home for a 12-month period. There is no such requirement on an assumption, so the time frame has never been established, but make sure you do move into the property. They will check driver's license records, tax returns, utility bills, and postal records to see if you ever occupied the property, and if you never had the intent, they'll prosecute you for fraud.

VA Loans

Veterans Affairs loans that were placed on properties on or before March 1, 1988, are also fully assumable by anyone without qualification requirements. You can pay an assumption fee and start making payments. After that date, a due-on-sale clause was instituted that requires the approval of the VA for assumption. Investors can assume these loans, subject to a $300 fee and half of a 1 percent funding fee, and qualify for the loan. But there is another way to get around this clause, which I'll illustrate a little later.

Conventional Loans

Most conventional loans are non assumable. Only adjustable-rate mortgages allow assumption, and even then it is subject to qualification. Almost all conventional mortgages contain the due-on-sale clause that is violated when any transfer of ownership or beneficial interest takes place. Fortunately, this happens every day. I'll explain how to take advantage of this later.

Private Party Loans

There is no set standard for assumptions of loans made by private parties. There may be a due-on-sale clause, and it might have been left out. When I negotiate private party loans, I always insert an assumption clause allowing me to transfer the loan, but this is not the norm.

The only way you are going to find out if a loan can be assumed, or if there is a due-on-sale clause, is to examine the loan documents. In your initial meeting with the homeowner, you will want to have the opportunity to examine all the loan documents, including the mortgage and note or deed of trust.

Taking Title "Subject to"

Taking title to a property by purchasing it "subject to existing liens" is different from assuming the loan. In an assumption, the loan is actually put into your name, or at least the lender is put on notice. Purchasing a property "subject to" is paramount to trying a simple assumption without telling anyone. But it usually doesn't work.

Since the loan is already under heavy surveillance due to the foreclosure, the lender is easily tipped off if anything unusual happens. A sudden reinstatement written off of someone else's checking account, and subsequent payments made by someone other than the borrower will certainly draw attention. A bigger problem is insuring the property. As soon as the insurance clause is changed, the lender is notified, and they will more than likely accelerate the loan due to the change in beneficial interest.

Lenders also catch on when address changes for the borrower are picked up by the post office, on notifications, or year-end statements. Unless you are prepared to pay off the loan once it is accelerated, I would avoid this strategy.

Violating the Due-on-Sale Clause

This is easily one of my favorite strategies, and not just because I'm a rebel! First, please understand that there is nothing illegal about violating a due-on-sale clause. It simply gives the lender the *option* of calling the note due and payable, and triggers the acceleration clause. When a due-on-sale clause is breached, the lender has three options:

1. Call the note due and payable
2. Foreclosure on the loan
3. Do nothing

I personally like option 3. The loan is already in foreclosure, so number 2 is sort of a moot point. They could exercise their acceleration rights under Section

22 of the security instrument, but in over 25 years, when testing this clause, I have never had had a lender call the note due.

Here's why: the lender is only concerned about getting paid. If I have brought the loan current, and continue to make the payments, then they are satisfied. They have bigger problems to worry about at that point. There are two ways to assume a non assumable loan:

1. Send a certified letter to the Loss Mitigation Department indicating that you would like permission to assume the loan on the borrower's behalf. Include personal financial information and give them permission to run a credit report. Ask for a reply in writing, and promise that you will send them a cashier's check immediately to bring the loan current.

2. Send a letter to the bank informing them of your intent to assume the loan. I send it certified mail so I have proof that they have been notified, then begin making the payments. I have yet to have a lender refuse to take my money!

Either way, I like this option better than the risk of taking on a property "subject to" a lien because I have communicated my intent with the lender. Again, most of the time they will not care, as long as they have a qualified borrower on the hook for the loan.

On properties that have a current VA loan, you can also avoid triggering the due-on-sale clause by purchasing the property on what's known as a land contract or installment sales contract. The VA specifically addressed the option for owners to sell their property this way in their published handbook (H26-94-1) in February 1994, Chapter 1, Subsection 1.14(j), which states:

> **j. Sale Agreements Not Subject to 38 U.S.C. 3714.** A sale on an installment contract, contract for deed, or similar arrangement in which title is not transferred from the seller to the buyer is not considered a "disposition" of property and therefore does not require prior approval by VA or the loan holder. However, the holder should caution any borrower considering a sale in this manner that he or she remains liable for repayment of the loan under such an arrangement.

Working with Other Investors and Partners

One of the easiest ways to get started, especially when you don't have much cash, is to use partners, or team up with other investors. This is how I got started years ago: I provided the deal, and the sweat—and they provided the cash. It was a great marriage! But just like any good marriage, it takes the right people to make it work. Here are some of the pros and cons of working with partners:

Pros

- You each bring different assets to the transaction.
- You get access to needed capital and renovation funds.
- The risk is spread out among several people.
- Experience and perspective is brought to the decision-making process.

Cons

- Profits are shared among several people.
- Difference of opinions can hinder progress.
- Too many "chiefs" can cause a war.

If you decide to enter into a partnership, it is imperative that you have a written agreement. The agreement can be simple, but should contain the following elements:

- Clearly define the roles and responsibilities of each partner.
- Create the partnership on a "per property" basis.
- Decide in advance how much will be spent on repairs, and determine a dollar amount that when exceeded, requires the approval of all partners.
- Indicate the partnership percentages and who will receive the tax benefits from the transaction.
- Include a clause that provides the other partners with "first right of refusal" on any other partner's equity position. *Question*
- Decide how "ties" will be settled when disagreements arise (and they will!).

In defining the roles of each of the partners, it is possible to have simply *equity partners* who provide cash, or *working partners*, and the splits do not have to be even.

You can also "sell" the tax benefits in a property as well. There are many investors in the marketplace who are looking for tax advantages that properties provide and will sign up as a partner just to purchase the tax benefits.

For larger partnerships, or more formal arrangements, I suggest you form a Limited Liability Corporation, or LLC (see Chapter 9). This will provide for better protection from personal liability and greater tax advantages.

Planning for Contingencies

No matter how well you plan, there will always be unexpected things that come up. It is important that you carefully estimate your total cash needs, and then add a little! In estimating your total cash requirements, you will need to figure in the following costs:

- Purchase price of the property
- Financing costs, including closing costs on the loan
- Assumption fees or lienholder payoffs
- Monthly holding costs—loan payments, interest, property taxes, insurance, and utilities
- Property repair costs—typically 10 to 15 percent of the purchase price
- Marketing costs for selling or renting out the property
- Emergency or contingency funds

I always set aside an emergency fund of six months worth of payments just in case. I rarely have had a need to dip into those funds, but I sleep better at night knowing that they're there.

Another contingency plan you need to have in place is for disposition of the property—always have a Plan B. If you intend to sell the property, what if it doesn't sell in three months, or six months—what will you do? If you decide to rent it out, what if you don't find a tenant for six months? Have a plan in place.

Where to Start

So now the big question—when it comes to the financing, where do you start? As I mentioned at the beginning of the chapter, you need to have your financing options in place before you go out and start looking at properties. But you'll need to take a hard look at some other areas as well.

Financial Abilities

If you find it hard to balance your checkbook, investing in real estate will be harder for you. You'll need to understand the basics of personal and mortgage finance and have a general understanding of taxes and other accounting issues. If you don't, that's okay—you'll just have to be willing to hire professionals to help you.

You can also take basic real estate classes at most community colleges. Some people even take the real estate agent preparatory class (a class that's required for prospective real estate agents) in order to gain knowledge about real estate investing. You don't have to become a real estate agent if you take the class, but it's a great way to look at the ins and outs of real estate.

Personal Credit

Your credit rating will seriously impact your ability to get financing . . . and to get financing on the best terms possible.

If you have poor credit, your financing options may initially be limited as you work to repair your credit. But all is not lost: you can still qualify for owner financing, you can assume a mortgage, or you can qualify for financing targeted to individuals with poor credit.

Getting and maintaining an excellent credit rating is critical to investment success because you can get better terms and rates and you can more easily leverage your properties. If you have poor credit, you can still invest—people do it every day—but you'll have to be more creative (or accept less favorable terms).

☞ Get copies of your credit report! Lenders will check your credit before they do anything else, so you will want to know exactly what's on there. Contact the three major credit bureaus:

1. Experian (888) 397-3742, www.Experian.com

2. TransUnion (800) 916-8800, www.TransUnion.com

3. Equifax (800) 685-1111, www.Equifax.com

Or you can go to www.AnnualCreditReport.com, which is a site sponsored by all three bureaus that allows you to order a "merged" credit report like the lenders get. Pay the little extra to receive your credit scores.

Carefully review the reports for any errors or outdated information, and get them fixed right away.

To understand how credit scores work, and to find out what your score means, go to www.MyFICO.com.

Build Your Financial Foundation

If your goal is to be a successful real estate investor and to build wealth, you'll probably have to change some of your priorities.

If you want to build wealth, you'll need to be willing to do the following:

- *Cut your spending and increase your savings.* Eliminate "nice to" or "want to" spending and stick with "have to" spending.

- *Improve your credit rating.* At the very least, pay your bills on time and meet your financial obligations.

- *Start looking closely at the real estate listing in your local papers, as well as at any sales flyers or brochures from local real estate agencies.* Over time, you'll develop a keen sense of your particular real estate market.

- *Start looking at properties that interest you, even if you have no intention of buying.* You'll start to get a sense of what's available, and you'll also meet local real estate professionals—and hopefully find professionals you're comfortable working with down the road.

- *Talk to a lender about your investment goals and see what type of financing you qualify for.* Don't wait until you're ready to make an offer to find out if you even qualify for a loan under terms you can accept.

Your Debt-to-Income Ratio

Lenders evaluate the total amount of debt you have in relation to your income. If the ratio is too high, they'll be unwilling to loan you money. (You can still explore seller financing options, though.)

Decreasing your debt-to-income ratio can help you qualify for better loan terms. How do you decrease that ratio? Pay off existing debt. If you need to decrease the ratio quickly, consider selling some assets and using the proceeds to pay off an existing debt, or to simply get out from under the debt. Do you have a boat in the driveway you almost never use? Sell it. You'll get more enjoyment from profiting from your real estate investments than you will from an occasional ride on your boat.

The Down Payment

While it's possible to invest without putting any money down, in most cases, you'll still need cash for closing costs and other initial expenses. Plus, you'll need some cash in case of emergencies.

Keep in mind that mortgage terms for investment properties aren't as liberal as for owner-occupied properties. Why? Investment properties carry more risk. (Owner-occupants are more likely to take care of the property than renters.)

If you have available cash, great! If not, there are still options to generate cash. You can sell assets. You can borrow against a 401(k) plan. You can seek funding from friends or family who wish to be partners with you.

You can even go so far as to generate cash using your credit cards, but understand the risks involved. The interest rates tend to be high and you'll increase your debt-to-income ratio, making it harder for you to borrow money . . . unless, of course, you quickly flip your first investment, pay off the credit cards, and use leftover profits to finance your next investment.

Here's my best advice: start accumulating cash now—even if it's not your own. Cash is king, and access to cash can make even the most complicated deals go smoothly.

Put your personal finance package together.

Get copies of your last two years federal tax returns, W-2 earnings, 1099 statements, K-1 statements, corporate or partnership returns (if self-employed), two months worth of bank statements, and a list of income and assets.

Many investors even go so far as to complete the standard loan application (1003 form) ahead of time, which you can find online at www.efanniemae.com/sf/formsdocs/forms/1003.jsp.

Build Lending Relationships Now

Grab a copy of your credit report and make an appointment with a loan officer at your local bank (bring your own copy so the loan officer won't have to pull one; that way you'll avoid a new credit inquiry on your credit report). Show the loan officer your report and discuss your interest in real estate investing.

The loan officer will review your credit and tell you what types of financing you currently qualify for. He or she can also give you advice about what you can do to qualify for better terms, bigger loans, and so on. The easiest way to learn about what types of financing you can qualify for is to ask a person who evaluates potential loan candidates every day.

Now make an appointment with a local mortgage broker and do the same thing. You may get the same answers; you may not. Regardless, you'll be learning, and in effect you'll receive free advice and guidance. Best of all, you'll walk away with a good sense of what you need to do to strengthen your financial position, improve your credit, and what types of properties and investments you can make through traditional financing means.

You'll also establish rapport with local loan professionals, and who knows—you may find a new member for your investing team.

Contact and interview three mortgage brokers.

Ask what types of loan programs they offer, and what their experience is with investors. Ask for and check three recent references, and verify their licensing and credentials with your state licensing division.

CHAPTER 9

Getting Serious about Being a Foreclosure Investor

I n the Introduction, I promised to tell you the truth, and this chapter is no exception. So, let's start with this:

> Successful foreclosure investing takes time and effort—*considerable* time and effort. You'll need to do your homework. You'll need to stay on top of every detail. You'll need to work harder than the next person to succeed.

Isn't that true about success in any profession? Now let's take a look at how to take this new profession seriously.

Foreclosure Investing Is a Business

Never forget that you are in this to make money. Making a profit is more than just being able to sell properties for more than you buy them for, it means running a business, and running it well. Business profits can be attained in one of two ways— you either bring in more than you spend, or spend less than you bring in.

Keep your expenses low. There is no need to rush out and buy the fastest computer, new forms, or expensive software for your business. I operated for years with basic supplies, a hand-me-down printer, and nothing more than Microsoft Word and Excel. Come to think of it, not much has changed!

But your attitude MUST change. This is not a hobby, even though most people treat it that way. What I mean by that is that they spend a lot of time buying a couple of properties, devote hundreds of hours to repairs that should have been completed in two days, make a couple of grand—and think they are a serious investor.

Start by separating yourself from the crowd. A lot of your success in this business depends on you. Take some time to analyze your strengths, admit your weaknesses, and think if this is really for you. Begin by asking yourself the following questions:

- Do people like you and feel comfortable being around you?
- Do you enjoy talking to people you've never met before?
- Are you a good listener?
- In stressful situations, can you be diplomatic without taking sides?
- Do you like to solve problems and enjoy working on puzzles?
- Are you good at basic math and do you understand cash flow?
- Can you be brutally honest and tell the truth even when others may not want to hear it?
- Can you handle disappointment and frustration?
- Can you handle it when others fail?

If you answered yes to these questions, then you're on the right track. But everyone has different strengths and weaknesses. When you're first starting out, your best bet is to play to your strengths and let others help you where necessary. Let's talk about how to set yourself up as a true professional investor.

Becoming a Professional

My parents always said that if you want to be successful, you better look the part. I'm not talking just clothes, but in the way you act, the tools you use, and the way you organize your business.

Organize Your Mobile Office

You will be spending a lot of time on the road, and that means your car will become an office. To operate on the road, you will need to have the following items with you at all times:

- Laptop computer (preferably with wireless Internet access card)
- Cell phone
- Portable file folder with:

- Property worksheets and checklists from this book
- Purchase agreements
- Inspection forms
- Portfolio with letter-size pad to take notes
- Financial calculator (I use an old HP 12C)
- Tool kit with basic hand tools and a tape measure
- Work gloves
- A *good* quality flashlight

Make sure that you have a small notebook for tracking your mileage as well.

Marketing Yourself

You will also need some basic marketing tools for promoting your business. While there are lots of ways to spread the word about being a real estate investor, I will only focus on the basics because I don't want you spending a lot of cash up front. Save it for investing.

Business Cards

You can order basic business cards for less than $30 from any office supply store. You can also get some for free on the Internet at www.VistaPrint.com.

They don't need to be fancy, but they need to include your name, business mailing address (P.O. Box or mail drop box will work fine), cell number, and the words "available days, nights, and weekends." You can use the title of "Real Estate Investments," but do *not* put the word foreclosure anywhere on the card—people could be too embarrassed to keep it or pass it out to friends.

Letterhead

You do not need fancy letterhead and envelopes. I use standard copy paper that I run through my color printer. Envelopes should be standard #10 white, with a simple return address label. Again, do not put the word foreclosure anywhere on it. You want prospects to open it, don't you?

Call Capture System

You will also need a telephone management system known as a call capture system. This will allow you to receive calls from anyone, anywhere, with a toll-free number. If anyone calls and hangs up, you will capture their number and can call them right back. It also works as an answering system and a call forwarding system so that prospects can press a button and immediately be forwarded to your cell phone.

☝ This call capture system will also be used for marketing your properties, and I describe how to use it in more detail in Chapter 29. I have developed a custom system that you can find at www.CCUCallCapture.com.

Creating Your Marketing A-List

They say that you are six people away from knowing everyone in the world. I've never tested the theory, but I only want you to try it two or three people deep. Set aside an hour or two, and start writing out a list of everyone that you can think of who might come in contact with anyone who's in financial trouble, or an organization that represents groups of people. I like to go through the Yellow Pages and look for specific professions that I can use for referral sources. You need to come up with at least 100 names, addresses, and phone numbers. Here's a list to help you get started:

- Real estate attorneys
- Foreclosure attorneys
- Divorce attorneys
- Bankruptcy attorneys
- Probate attorneys
- Financial planners
- Accountants
- Loan officers
- Pawn shops
- Second-hand stores
- Housing centers
- Family or marriage counseling centers
- Homeowners associations
- Churches
- Business and social clubs
- Community and service organizations

Once you have a list, make it a point to call and speak with 20 contacts per week. You can use Microsoft Outlook or an Excel spreadsheet to keep track and manage your contacts. It will take an average of six to seven contacts before they are comfortable sending you a referral—most people will give up after two or three, and miss the referral.

Setting Up Your Office

Your office doesn't have to be fancy—after all, you'll be spending most of your time on the road. But you do need to have at least a little corner to call your office. Here are some of the details you'll need to address:

- *Home office space:* Specify a specific location or room of the house as your office, and you may be eligible for a tax deduction. For more information of what the IRS rules are, go to www.irs.gov/publications/p587/index.html.

- *Checking account:* You need to establish a separate account for your investment business. This is not only for tax and accounting reasons, but will help you stay on budget. If you get into managing several rental properties, it may also be easier to have a dedicated account for each of the larger properties.

- *Business expenses:* The easiest way to track business expenses is with a dedicated credit card. The major companies (American Express, VISA, MasterCard, etc.) will provide detailed quarterly and yearly statements that will make your expense tracking a lot easier. Make sure all expenses are paid either with a credit card or business check, or for supplies purchased online, I also use a PayPal account (www.Paypal.com).

- *Auto expense records:* Make sure you document all mileage used for business purposes. This becomes a direct tax write-off at the end of the year, and with the cost of gasoline, you'll need the deduction.

- *Accounting records:* You will want to track all of your accounting on your computer system. I use Peachtree Accounting software, which allows me to track properties individually within the system, but Quickbooks works just as well. These systems will also print checks directly on your computer, so I never miss filing an expense.

- *Record keeping:* You will need a filing cabinet, with a sealable, expandable, Pendeflex folder for each property. These files will become large at times, and you need to keep them separate.

At the end of the year, I transfer the files to a large envelope to file them away.

I recommend that you store all important documents, such as deeds, title insurance, property insurance, and tax records, in a safe deposit box, or at least a fire-proof safe.

To Hire or Not to Hire?

One question I get frequently is about hiring assistants and helpers. The easy answer is—don't! Now don't get me wrong, I do have a staff and a great assistant who has been with me for over 15 years—but for the new and average investor, you don't need the payroll, payroll taxes, unemployment, workers comp, and all the paperwork that comes with each of those things.

For all your repair and renovation work, you will be hiring independent contractors. If they are individuals, and you pay them more than $600 in any year, you will need to provide them with a 1099 form at the end of the year.

Once you get big enough and need some office or accounting assistance, then you can look into getting a virtual assistant. They can be located anywhere in the world, and they can get the work done just as efficiently. Some resources you can check into include:

- International Virtual Assistants Association, www.IVAA.org
- Tasks Every Day, www.TasksEveryDay.com

Forming a Legal Business Entity

Another decision you must make is how to protect you and your family in your new venture. There is a certain amount of liability and risk associated with real estate investing, including the property repairs, contractors, not to mention the legal side of the transactions. What happens if disaster strikes? What if a prospective purchaser of one of your units slips and falls? You get served with a lawsuit.

I had a woman slip and fall on the ice on one of the driveways of a property that was for sale. Her claim? After the fall, she said could only speak Spanish. I was not even there, but was served with a lawsuit for not keeping the walkway clear. Once she realized the property was owned by an LLC with limited assets, she dropped the suit.

Whether you are an individual or one of many partners, you need to form a layer of protection between your business and your family. Setting up a corporate structure does just that, as well as provide several tax benefits along the way. You have four options here:

1. Limited Liability Corporation (LLC) limits your exposure to risk. If someone takes legal action against the corporation, your personal assets are protected. This is the best solution for most investors.

2. A Chapter S corporation (S corp) also limits your exposure to risks and allows for pass-through taxation (unlike a C corp). With pass-through taxation, the corporation's profits pass through to your individual income tax return, avoiding double-taxation (in which both you and your corporation are taxed). Only individuals, not other business entities, can have ownership in an S corp, up to a maximum of 75 shareholders.

3. A Chapter C corporation (C corp) also limits your personal liability, but I don't recommend going the C corp route for most real estate investors. A C corp exposes you to double-taxation, which can really take a bite out of your profits.

4. The general partnership is my least favorite because it provides little if any liability protection. Don't bother.

All necessary forms and instruction booklets are available at www.irs.gov/formspubs/article/0,,id=98171,00/.html, and I recommend that you discuss your options in more detail with your accountant or attorney (which you will have as a result of building your team in Chapter 10).

Shaking Off "First Time Jitters"

The first time you do anything new, you're nervous. Uncertainty of exactly what to say, what to do, how to analyze a deal, what forms to use, and dozens of other excuses keep people from taking their first steps—and keep them from building a future for themselves and their families.

No, you're not going to learn this overnight, but there are things you can do to keep the butterflies to a minimum. First, you need to dress the part. No, not in a suit and tie. I recommend going with business casual, but don't overdress. Don't show up at a property in a brand new Lexus or BMW, but a $50 beat-up clunker won't cut it either.

Never place a sign on your vehicle that advertises "foreclosures" or "I buy houses"—that will just get you a cold shoulder or a door slammed in your face.

Always be courteous and professional in your approach and conversation, and even if it's your first time—don't sweat it. You are still more knowledgeable than the homeowner since you've taken the time to read this book.

There's one last thing we need to cover before we get into the nitty-gritty, and that's what we will do in Chapter 10—we will build a solid team around you.

Build Your Foreclosure Dream Team

I f you expect to build a fortune through real estate foreclosures, you're going to need help. Not just contractors or loan officers, I'm talking about a real team of professionals who you can count on to help you build your success—your own dream team.

First, you will try to do everything yourself and fly solo. This is normal. You won't want to share any of your "secrets" with possible competitors, or look foolish if you make a mistake. Loosen up—you will make mistakes (we'll just try to limit them), and nobody will steal your ideas or deals—only you know all the pieces to the puzzle.

By finding key professionals and getting them in your corner, you'll have important experience to rely on, and be able to delegate responsibilities that will allow you to go and find more deals. You need to start building your team by recruiting the right players.

Recruiting the Players

The most important member of my team, my number one fan, is my wife Lisa. When things are going great, she is there to share the joy, and when it's bumpy, she makes the ride a little less painful. So your first recruit needs to be your spouse or significant other.

If your spouse is not on your team, it will make your new foreclosure career a true uphill battle, and one that will eventually wear you out. Share your plan and ideas with your spouse first, and make sure you have his or her support. I would strongly advise against pursuing your dream if you don't have that person's full support and blessing. It also wouldn't be much fun. Here are some of the other team members:

Real Estate Agents

Next you need to find some good real estate agents for your team. Just like any other profession, real estate agents have specialties. Some concentrate on listings, others on sales. They could focus on first-time homebuyers or resort properties on the lake. Still others specialize in working with foreclosures and foreclosure investors. Those are the ones you're looking for.

Mark Baragar, a top agent with ReMax in Grand Rapids, Michigan, has over 14 years of experience, many of which has been dealing with foreclosures, desperate sellers, and investors. Mark suggests that for investors, "The best qualifier is to seek out agents who have a lot of that type of inventory. Agents are starting to catch on, but there is a wide gap in that level of expertise. There are a lot of little tricks of the trade, and you can't afford to waste a lot of time with someone who is just learning the ropes."

There are several ways to find the names of possible agents to interview. The easiest way is to check out your local newspaper on a Sunday, and read the ads—focusing on the ones that are listed in the investment section, mention foreclosure, or concentrate on the type of properties you are looking for. Come up with five to seven possible names, then prepare a letter like the one in Figure 10.1.

This letter is designed to find serious agents who can help you find properties, and sell the ones you end up purchasing. If you narrow down the list to active investment-savvy agents, you'll get a positive response from the majority who receive this letter.

Then interview them just like you would any job prospect. Develop a short list of questions such as:

- How long have you been a licensed agent?
- What types of properties do you primarily list and sell?
- What geographic areas do you primarily operate in?
- Do you have a sample marketing package I could review?
- How do you obtain most of your business?
- What are your fees, and can I see a list of the services you provide to property owners?

This should give you a good idea of their qualifications, and an opportunity to see if their personality is a good fit. Select one or two agents to work with initially, then expand as necessary later on. Add them to your team, and go to work on other key professionals.

(date)

(name)
(company)
(address)
(city, state, zip)

Dear (name),

My name is (your name), and I am a real estate investor specializing in foreclosure properties. You were recommended to me as an experienced agent in the area, and I have two main reasons for contacting you.

First, most of the investment properties I acquire are not held as rentals, but rather rehabilitated and resold in the marketplace. I am looking for a reputable and experienced agent such as yourself to market and represent my properties, and am willing to pay standard commission rates.

Second, if you have a seller who is facing a foreclosure situation, I would be interested in reviewing the property to see if it meets my investment objectives. Please understand that as an investor, I am only interested in looking at properties that reflect discounted wholesale pricing opportunities.

I would be interested in speaking with you to discuss the opportunity of working together to create a win-win business relationship. Please feel free to call me at (your number), or e-mail me at (your e-mail) at your earliest convenience, so that I can find out more about you and your services. Thank you for your time, and I look forward to speaking with you in the near future.

Sincerely,

(your name)

Figure 10.1   Sample Letter to Real Estate Agent

Appraisers

You need to connect with one or two good appraisers that can provide quick estimate of values, indicate market trends, and provide quality property appraisal reviews. Call one or two in your area and make an appointment to meet with them for a half hour, or send them a letter similar to the one used for real estate agents. They know what's going on in the market, what properties are actually moving, and more importantly—what features and characteristics of a home are getting the most attention from buyers.

(date)

(name)
(company)
(address)
(city, state, zip)

Dear (name),

My name is (your name), and I am a real estate investor specializing in pre-foreclosure properties. You were referred to me as an experienced attorney in the area, and I have two main reasons for contacting you.

First, I am looking for a qualified and experienced individual who can assist me with my real estate transactions. I need someone who is familiar with foreclosure real estate contract law and transaction closings.

Second, if you or any of your associates have individuals who are facing a foreclosure situation, I would be interested in reviewing the property and circumstances to see if it meets my investment objectives. Please understand that as an investor, I am only interested in looking at properties that reflect discounted wholesale pricing opportunities.

I would be interested in speaking with you to discuss the opportunity of working together to create a win-win business relationship, as I also speak with many homeowners in distress looking for qualified legal counsel. Please feel free to call me at (your number), or e-mail me at (your e-mail) at your earliest convenience, so that I can find out more about your firm and the services you could provide to me. Thank you for your time, and I look forward to speaking with you in the near future.

Sincerely,

(your name)

 FIGURE 10.2   Sample Letter to Attorneys

Attorneys and Trustees

You need to find a good real estate attorney. Not one who took care of your friend's divorce, or works criminal trials—but a specialist in real estate.

Call or write a letter of introduction to a few, and interview them as a candidate for your team. You are looking for someone who is familiar with foreclosure procedures, title insurance law (including what are known as "quiet title actions"), and specializes in real estate transactions. You don't need someone who charges $300 an hour, but don't skimp here because they will earn their keep the first time you run into a problem. Figure 10.2 is a sample letter you can use.

Mortgage Broker

Good financial people are hard to find, but you need one on your team. A mortgage broker will be able to provide a variety of loan programs from several different lenders, and stays on top of the ever-changing market. You want someone who is familiar with investor loans and has several years experience working with conventional, subprime, and government loans.

Use a sample letter like the one in Figure 10.3 to introduce yourself, and set up an appointment to interview at least three brokers.

Once you have met one or two mortgage brokers who you feel comfortable with, make sure you check their references and credentials. Go online to your state licensing division to make sure they are licensed. Check the Better Business Bureau and chamber of commerce for membership and complaints. Plug their name (and their company name) into Google, Yahoo!, and MSN search engines, and see what comes up—if it is several lawsuits, then it's time to recruit new team members.

Also take time to check their membership in organizations such as the National Association of Mortgage Brokers (www.NAMB.org), and the Mortgage Bankers Association (www.mbaa.org). You want long-term players that are committed to their industry, and to your success.

Accountant

Certified Public Accountants (CPAs), financial planners, bookkeepers, and accountants can all be a great source of leads both for foreclosure properties and for investor partners. More importantly, you will need someone to keep track of your properties, expenses, and all that extra profit you'll be racking up. Off-the-shelf tax preparation software isn't going to cut it anymore. You won't need a major CPA firm, but spend some time speaking with a few good accountants and find someone who will fit with the rest of the team.

Title Company

Title agents and their closing staff are a real key to your success. Foreclosures are different from normal real estate transactions. There will be last minute phone calls with lenders and attorneys, frantic and emotional sellers, and different paperwork, filing, and payoff requirements. They need to be familiar with how foreclosure transactions work, and available to answer questions for you as they come up on insuring the title transfer and lien discharges.

(date)

(name)
(company)
(address)
(city, state, zip)

Dear (name),

My name is (your name), and I am a real estate investor who specializes in purchasing fore-closure properties. You were referred to me as an experienced mortgage broker in the area, and I have three main reasons for contacting you.

First, I am looking for a qualified and experienced individual who can assist me with the financing of my real estate properties. I am in need of someone who is experienced specifically with investment property loans, and has access to several different wholesale investors (both con-forming and non conforming) for purchase and refinance transactions.

Second, if you or any of your associates know of individuals who are facing a foreclosure situation, I would be interested in reviewing the property and circumstances to see if it might fit my investment objectives. Please understand that as an investor, I am only interested in looking at properties that reflect discounted wholesale pricing opportunities.

Third, since most of the properties I acquire are rehabilitated and then resold, I need some-one available to provide financing to my purchasers (mostly conventional and FHA transactions).

I would be interested in speaking with you to discuss the opportunity of working together to create a win-win business relationship, as I also speak with many homeowners in distress looking for financing options. Please feel free to call me at (your number), or e-mail me at (your e-mail) at your earliest convenience, so that I can find out more about you, your firm, and the loan programs and services you could provide to me. Thank you for your time, and I look forward to speaking with you in the near future.

Sincerely,

(your name)

  FIGURE 10.3   Sample Letter to Mortgage Broker

Call and ask to interview a manager at one of the local title companies. I use First American almost exclusively, and for a list of their agents nationwide, go to www.FirstAm.com. Most people are unfamiliar with what a title company actually does, and the wide variety of services they can offer. For the purpose of your team member, you want someone who is there to answer questions and close your trans-actions smoothly and quickly.

Home Inspector

You will be conducting all the initial inspections of properties you visit, but as you successfully negotiate a purchase, you need to have a professional inspector on your team to go through the property. This is not to pick apart every little detail of the house and all the cosmetic blemishes, but rather to look for major structural or support system problems, and help you estimate the repair costs. You don't want to get hit with a $6,000 bill for fixing a support wall that you thought just had a small crack in it.

Find someone who can do a complete inspection (heating, plumbing, electrical, structural) and is licensed and insured. I recommend that you make sure they are a member of the American Society of Home Inspectors. You can find one at www.ASHI.org.

Contractors, Subcontractors, General Contractor

Other important members of your team will be experienced contractors and subs. You may be able to handle the small basic stuff, but when it comes to replacing drywall, pouring cement, and putting on a new roof—these are tasks better left to the pros. Find companies and team members in the following specialties:

- Major electrical work
- Major plumbing repairs
- Heating and cooling systems
- Drywall replacement and repair
- Roof replacement
- Basement and cement repair
- Carpet installation

Many of these team members will change over time, and you will meet some of the best ones when you are in the middle of an emergency. If you are skilled and qualified in any of these areas, then consider doing the work yourself, but be careful—it is easy for time to slip away, and your holding costs and the loss of marketing time will add up quickly. Stick to your best and highest use—finding and negotiating deals.

Only for major projects that involve more than four to five subcontractors should you start considering hiring a general contractor. For most projects, you can easily manage the work schedule and oversight or the repairs and renovations.

Now let's go find some foreclosure investment properties.

FINDING AND INVESTING IN FORECLOSURES

Now that you have a solid foundation and an understanding of the pre-foreclosure market, it's time to put your business in gear, and go make some money. In Part II, I go through the actual process of finding fore-closure properties, and you learn how to deal and negotiate with owners, attorneys, lenders, and trustees, and how to analyze each property.

By the end of Part II, you'll also know how to find every detail of the property and homeowner's situation, compute the property value (and the profits!), and get yourself to the closing table.

To start, let's take a look at my tried-and-true 17-step process.

CHAPTER II

The 17-Step Process

I n this chapter, we discuss the process involved with pre-foreclosure investing, including an explanation of terms you must become very familiar with. I lay out my 17-step process, with details to follow in subsequent chapters. It is vital that you establish an overhead "helicopter" view of all stages involved in these pre-foreclosure transactions. Let's lift off.

Declaring a Loan in Default

You've probably seen that most embarrassing red-lettered notice attached to the window of a home approaching foreclosure. It's hard to miss. This notice indicates that the homeowner has not made payments as agreed, and a terrible chain-reaction is underway.

Before you see that bold notice, several things have happened behind the scenes. First, the homeowner has missed a number of payments; the lien is about to be sold at public auction, which is then followed by the lender taking official possession of the property.

When payments have not been made within the agreed monthly deadlines, a lender declares a loan to be in default. Although technically in default the day after a payment is due, the lender usually doesn't actively start the default process until at least three months of payments are missed. The lender can wait an additional 90 days or more to move forward with taking possession. As an investor, you (the potential buyer) must quickly assess where the home is in the process. The sooner you move, the more favorable the odds are for a successful transaction.

In Chapter 2, we talked about all of the steps, and the pros and cons involved with the default process. The bottom line is this: when the public finds out, it's over. What I mean by this is that the real money is made in "private"—prior to auction and all the marketing campaigns of so-called foreclosure tours. This is an industry where research pays off big, and a trip to the courthouse, a conversation

January 21, 2009

John A. and Sally B. Homeowner
1155 Treetop Lane
Wilkens, NY 10034

Dear Mr. and Mrs. Homeowner,

Our records indicate that you are currently PAST DUE for your mortgage payment in the amount of $1566.09. If you have recently sent your payment, please accept our appreciation. If not, you must bring your payment current within 30 days of this letter, including any additional late fees and costs.

You may send your payment in the form of money order or Certified Check for the full amount due to: Bank of New York, 1300 Boston Rd., Yonkers, NY 10014.

Acceptance of less than the total amount due and payable, which includes but is not limited to, principal and interest, late fees, and all other outstanding charges or costs, does not waive our right to demand the entire balance due and payable under the terms of your mortgage agreement.

If you do not bring your loan current within 30 days of the date of this letter, the Bank of New York will accelerate the entire amount due under the terms of your mortgage agreement, and may institute legal action to foreclose on the mortgage, which may result in the forfeiture and sale of your property. We may also have the right to obtain a judgment against you for any deficiency amount still due after the home is sold.

You have the right to bring your loan current after legal action has been initiated, as well as prepare a defense against this action as you see fit. We wish to work with you to resolve this problem as quickly as possible, and help you bring your account current.

Please contact Ms. Susan Collector at (212) 555-0099 as soon as possible so that we can assist you with this situation.

Sincerely,

Walter P. Lender
Loss Mitigation Specialist

FIGURE 11.1   Sample Letter to Homeowner

with the clerk, and a daily perusal of the local newspaper classifieds and legal notices page can make a huge difference.

It all starts when the homeowner receives a letter worded something like the one in Figure 11.1. If this letter doesn't elicit action from the homeowner to solve the problem, the chain-reaction continues.

Foreclosure Notices

Next, a foreclosure notice is published in the legal section of the local newspaper in the county where the home is located. The foreclosure notice is also posted on the property itself in a very obvious manner. This posting will generally take place some time after the third mortgage payment is missed.

The courthouse can be considered your business partner. All filings take place there and are wide open for public viewing. Your local county Register of Deeds office can point you directly to where specific foreclosures notices are published, and it isn't a bad idea to subscribe to the newspapers that regularly carry this information (which is not usually your regular local paper). This is a low-cost way to stay informed on a weekly basis, and a small price to pay for potentially valuable information.

Be organized; keep good records of those properties you have marked to be of potential interest. The notices will change frequently, so you should update your database to represent the most recent legal notices. I keep track of everything by property address—not by the owner's name. It's easier to monitor the progress this way.

When flagging the houses to watch, make sure you record all the very valuable information contained in the notice itself, including case reference number, insertion date, county where the home is located, city, subdivision, legal lot number, name(s) of homeowner(s), the lender, interest rate, attorney listed, auction date, redemption period, and anything else of value.

Remember, as a real estate investor, you must first and foremost approach each transaction or potential transaction as a business, not a hobby. Gather all the pertinent information so that if and when it is time to move forward, you have stayed on top of everything worth knowing and can concentrate on making a solid offer.

Notice of Lis Pendens

As an investor, a *lis pendens* notice is also your friend (Figure 11.2). The term stands for "suit pending," and it acts as a loud bullhorn to inform the public of a formal, written notice against a particular property. Used in judicial foreclosures, this notice must be filed with the clerk of court in the county where the property is located. The public records filing serves two important purposes: it first provides the owner of the real property an opportunity to address any valid or invalid claims, and second it notifies all interested buyers that the property is involved in a potentially damaging legal action.

It is important to remember that a lis pendens notice in and of itself does not represent a validated charge against a property title, but rather a cautionary flag that a lender or individual has made such a claim that must be proven in court.

IN THE CIRCUIT COURT OF THE 6TH JUDICIAL CIRCUIT, IN AND FOR DADE COUNTY, FLORIDA

GENERAL JURISDICTION DIVISION

CASE NO: CV-08-53321

ABC MORTGAGE CORPORATION

PLAINTIFF(S)

VS.

JOSEPH A. HOMEOWNER AND SALLY B. HOMEOWNER, JOINTLY AND SEVERALLY, ASSIGNEES, LIENHOLDER OR, CREDITORS, TRUSTEES AND ALL OTHER PARTIES CLAMING AN INTEREST AGAINST TENANTS IN POSSESSION

DEFENDANT(S)

NOTICE OF LIS PENDENS

1. TO: The above named Defendants, **AND ALL OTHERS WHOM IT MAY CONCERN:**

2. **YOU ARE NOTIFIED** of the institution of this action by the Plaintiff against you seeking to foreclose the Note and Mortgage encumbering the described property and the decreeing of a sale of the property under the direction of the court in default of the payment of the amount found to be due the Plaintiff under the Note and Mortgage, and for other, further and general relief set forth in the Complaint.

3. The property involved is that certain parcel, lot or unit situate, lying and being in DADE County, Florida, more particularly described as follows:

LOT 211 AND 212, WATERFORD HEIGHTS SUBDIVISION, ACCORDING TO THE PLAT THEREOF AS RECORDED IN PLAT BOOK 07, PAGES 53 OF THE PUBLIC RECORDS OF DADE COUNTY, FLORIDA

Dated at Dade County, Florida this 17th day of December 2008.

ARNOLD ATTORNEY

Law Offices of Wicker, Wicker & Smith, P.C. Attorney for Plaintiff

111 S. Main St., Suite 1400

Wilkens, FL 30003 (222) 555-1313

Bar #009445

FIGURE 11.2 Sample Notice of Lis Pendens

Notice of Default

In nonjudicial foreclosure actions, lenders do not have to file an actual lawsuit, and so a notice of default (NOD) is used instead of a lis pendens filing (Figure 11.3 on page 98). Generally speaking, when a homeowner receives a notice of default, bad things follow. Receiving such a notice basically says to the owner, "Act now or forever lose your house." Consider the NOD as the first step in formal foreclosure proceedings.

A NOD also serves as a last chance for the owner to bring his account current before a lot of extra costs are added, and the lender will usually give him about 90 days for this to be accomplished—although many homeowners are not aware that there is still time after receiving this notice to make things right. Many valuable days can be wasted sitting in an emotional black hole instead of working toward a solution to save the property.

The real estate investor must remain aware of this tendency of the homeowner to slip into denial and become immobile, taking no action. This is the time for you to research, strategize, and implement your pre-foreclosure strategy.

Foreclosure Tracking Worksheet

Figure 11.4 on page 99 is the main worksheet that I use to hold all of my valuable data on the foreclosure. You will be able to keep track of property information, property owner, lien holder's information, important dates, and amounts outstanding. In addition, other critical information you need to track and keep organized as you assess the most favorable situation for your investment will all be listed in one place. I place this in a three-ring binder, sorted by property address, to maintain a comprehensive picture of all vital statistics, and place any additional notes (phone calls, etc.) on the back.

This form is also downloadable on my web site at www.ChipCummings.com/CashingIn/.

Publishing Foreclosure Notices

When a lender starts the process of foreclosure, whether or not a NOD is required, what the publication requirements are, and how long the redemption period is (if any), along with all the other important elements of the foreclosure stage can vary from state to state. You the investor must stay abreast of applicable laws in your local community. Remember, this is a business, so know your business. You can find a detailed outline of state-specific foreclosure practices in Chapter 6. Become very familiar with the rules that apply to you, or you'll get burned.

NOTICE OF DEFAULT

Joseph A. and Sally B. Homeowner
123 Treetop Lane
Anywhere, N.Y. 11223

Walter S. Scott, Esq. as trustee (or beneficiary) under that certain deed of transfer in trust executed by _Joseph A. and Sally B. Homeowner,_ as Trustor, _to ABC Financial Bank_ , as Trustee and _HMS Wilson_ , as beneficiary, dated _January 1, 2005_ , recorded in Book _05-1222_ , Page _221_ of official records in the office of the County Recorder of _Wexford_ County, State of _New York_ , hereby give(s) notice that a breach of the obligation for which such transfer in trust is security has occurred, the nature of said breach being the failure to _pay the principal sum due, together with interest, fees and costs_ , and that the Trustee (or beneficiary) elects to sell, or cause to be sold the trust property in order to satisfy said obligation.

NOTICE:

YOU MAY HAVE THE RIGHT TO CURE THE DEFAULT DESCRIBED HEREIN AND REINSTATE THE MORTGAGE OR DEED OF TRUST. SECTION _904-A_ OF THE CIVIL CODE PERMITS CERTAIN DEFAULTS TO BE CURED UPON PAYMENT OF THE AMOUNTS REQUIRED BY THAT SECTION WITHOUT REQUIRING PAYMENT OF THAT PORTION OF PRINCIPAL AND INTEREST WHICH WOULD NOT BE DUE HAD NO DEFAULT OCCURRED. WHERE REINSTATEMENT IS POSSIBLE, IF THE DEFAULT IS NOT CURED WITHIN _30 DAYS_ FOLLOWING THE RECORDING OF THIS NOTICE, THE RIGHT OF REINSTATEMENT WILL TERMINATE AND THE PROPERTY MAY BE SOLD.

TO DETERMINE IF REINSTATEMENT IS POSSIBLE AND THE AMOUNT, IF ANY, NECESSARY TO CURE THE DEFAULT, CONTACT THE BENEFICIARY OR MORTGAGEE OR THEIR SUCCESSORS IN INTEREST, WHOSE NAME AND ADDRESS IS _____ AT _____. ANY FAILURE TO COMPLY WITH THE PROVISIONS OF THIS SUBDIVISION SHALL NOT AFFECT THE VALIDITY OF A SALE IN FAVOR OF A BONA FIDE PURCHASER OR THE RIGHTS OF AN ENCUMBRANCER FOR VALUE AND WITHOUT NOTICE.

Dated: _____   _____

                              (Trustee or Beneficiary)

FIGURE 11.3   Sample Notice of Default (NOD)

FORECLOSURE TRACKING WORKSHEET

PROPERTY INFORMATION
Property Address: _____
Tax ID: _____
Legal Description: _____
Assessed Value: _____
Date of Last Assessment: _____

LIEN INFORMATION

Homeowner(s) Name: _____

Warranty Deed Name(s): _____

Original Lender's Name: _____

Original Lender's Address: _____

Current Lender's Name: _____

Current Lender's Address: _____

Purchase Price: _____ Mortgage Amt: _____ Interest Rate: _____

Original Loan Date:_____   Assumable? ☐ Yes ☐ No   ☐ 1st ☐ 2nd

Loan Type: ☐ Conventional ☐ Non-Conf ☐ FHA ☐ VA ☐ Private ☐ HELOC or H/E

Monthly Pmt: _____   Principal: _____   Interest: _____

                                 Taxes: _____   Insurance: _____

Date Recorded: _____   Liber: _____   Page: _____

FORECLOSURE INFORMATION

Foreclosure Case #: _____ Date Filed: _____

Lender's Attorney: _____ County:_____

Address/Phone: _____

Unpaid Principal Balance: $_____ Total pmts in arrears: $_____

Total interest, late charges, and legal fees: $_____

Total amount needed to cure: $_____

Mortgage Sale Date: _____ Redemption Period: _____

Homeowner Desire: ☐ Sell   ☐ Keep   Property: ☐ Listed   ☐ Abandoned

FIGURE 11.4 Foreclosure Tracking Worksheet

Either way, a notice has to be posted for public access, and usually most states require an advertisement in a local publication with notices spread out over several weeks. But again, this is what attracts the sharks—so get started early.

Accessing Foreclosure Notices

Once an investor decides to seek pre-foreclosure investments, they usually have no idea of where to start, or where to find and access the notices. This is not uncommon. Learning where notices are being filed and recorded, and which agency to visit and who to speak to can certainly be frustrating.

There is a little-known secret to finding out what you don't know—ask! Remember the people working in the local country courthouse or government agency are there to help. They may not always act like it, but they are there for the public use and are paid by you, the taxpayer.

Being a successful real estate investor requires that you also be a person of discernment, able to sense what will and won't work with a variety of individuals. Personal people skills are a real plus. Your ability to gain favor with the "gatekeepers at the courthouse is crucial to your success. You must learn who to ask what, when to ask, and how to ask. Your life will be much easier when you do.

I can remember when I first started investing in pre-foreclosure properties, there was a lot of information that I needed from the courthouse and one particular woman in the office seemed to know everything I needed to know. I had a plan. Although being nice may seem very obvious, it still works like a charm. After speaking to this lady for a while, I decided to send her a beautiful bouquet of flowers as a way of saying, "thanks for your help." When I did that, my life instantly became easier. The next time I visited the courthouse, the word had spread like dust in a windstorm.

Everybody was talking about the roses I sent and total strangers were walking past me smiling. The red carpet was out, and you would have thought I'd written a check for a million dollars. Ironically, the flowers that cost less than $20 actually brought me more than a million dollars worth of transactions through that one office. Lesson: don't ignore the obvious, be nice and good things will happen.

The information you need from the local court is simply the latest lis pendens or NOD filings. Remember, the court is where the process begins. Before a notice has arrived at the property, before the sign is posted on a window, everything is first filed at the courthouse.

Once you have gotten the legal notices either in person or online, you can then access more details of the distressed property and quickly make a decision whether to move forward to the next stage or to wait for another opportunity.

Foreclosure Reporting Services

If you've ever stayed up watching television way past your bedtime, you've probably seen ads marketed as "Foreclosure Experts" or "Advanced Foreclosure Listing Services." Well, in my opinion, there are several problems with these "services." The best way I can describe it is in the form of a question: How much would you pay for yesterday's newspaper? If you have a fireplace, you may pay a few pennies for the extra newspaper to start the fire, other than that, old newspapers are pretty worthless.

This is very descriptive of the information obtained through a foreclosure notice service. Once it has been listed in a public format, it is old news, worth absolutely nothing. The key to pre-foreclosure investing is beating the information to the press. That is your edge—that is your advantage. Most people will not take the time to do the research needed to take advantage of news that's not widely known yet. But you will, and that is where 97 percent of your success stories will be found.

How Lenders Handle Delinquent Loans

Before the lender can take any pre-foreclosure actions, the borrower obviously must first be in default on the loan. The lender must notify the borrower, and provide ample opportunity for the loan to be brought current.

(i) Foreclosure proceedings don't happen immediately because lenders generally wait until a loan is at least 90 days past due before heading down that path.

For the lender, foreclosure is costly, time consuming, and not a preferred option. It is very true that lenders don't want to sit on a handful of homes. They want their money—not the property.

Once foreclosure proceedings have begun, a runaway train is . . . well running away. Back mortgage payments combined with fees, legal costs, and interest becomes a toxic soup. It is very difficult for the owner to bring all of these items up to date while preparing for the next mortgage payment just around the corner.

After missing several payments, the lender officially recognizes they have a delinquent note on hand. They will usually start the foreclosure process by appointing a trustee or attorney to record the NOD with the county recorder. This generally provides the homeowner with a solid 90 days to get his financial house in order, or lose his house. Once this time has expired and the property has not been brought current, the lender (or the court) will set a foreclosure sale date.

(*i*)   The foreclosure is not automatic. I know a woman in Ohio who was delinquent for over a year, and was still waiting for the lender to foreclose. They hadn't even filed yet, and she was still maintaining the property for them.

Once a delinquent loan has gotten to this stage, things can move pretty fast. An auction date is set and scheduled—usually at the courthouse. This auction will be conducted by a representative of the court (sheriff's office), the trustee, or an appointed attorney.

The Real Key to Success

The real key is timing. Not only does the early bird catch the worm, but the earlier worm eats before the bird is on the hunt.

One of the best ways to know you are late to a possible property is when you learn of it through some public means. If you find a property through research that is not yet in the public domain, then the clock may very well still be in your favor.

Pre-foreclosure investors have to have a sixth sense about the status of a home, its condition, and the possible problems the homeowner are about to face. Although it takes time, with enough practice and commitment you will develop a feel for what is a high probability deal and what properties will be a waste of your time, effort, and money.

Homeowners whose loans are delinquent can be very difficult to find. After all, they aren't necessarily interested in letting you know how close they are to being on the street. Embarrassment, combined with the emotions of their family, and disappointment and discouragement in their situation, leads them to adopt very secretive actions. This is when you must take an action that will garner an equal and opposite action.

If you are seeking a method of finding distressed owners in the early stages of delinquency, provide them with a method to remain secret, unnoticed, and a way of keeping their dignity intact. A good method is to place a classified ad that targets property owners who are very close to foreclosure. You may ask a simple question: "Need help paying your house payment?" or "Call me if you want to avoid foreclosure." See Chapter 12 for some examples. There are a number of well-placed phrases, but the bottom line is to throw out a line and you'll be pleasantly surprised by what you may catch.

In Chapters 12 though 25, we take a detailed look at each of the steps necessary to build your fortune. Just to refresh your memory, here are my 17 action steps to get from A to Z:

Chip's 17 Steps for Successful Investing in Pre-foreclosures

Step 1—Locate the property.

Step 2—Contact the owner.

Step 3—Verify the initial data.

Step 4—Conduct an investigation.

Step 5—Inspect the property.

Step 6—Estimate the value.

Step 7—Analyze your costs and profits.

Step 8—Negotiate with the owner.

Step 9—Negotiate with the lenders.

Step 10—Negotiate with attorneys and trustees.

Step 11—Negotiate the short sale.

Step 12—Negotiate the purchase.

Step 13—Protect your interests.

Step 14—Close the deal.

Step 15—Fix it up.

Step 16—Sell it (or rent it).

Step 17—Do it again!

CHAPTER 12

Locating the Right Pre-foreclosure Properties

One of the biggest challenges in pre-foreclosure investing is finding the right opportunities. This can be difficult because many times the difference between a good and a great opportunity can be very small. This is why doing your research and doing it well is the most certain strategy to avoid wasting your precious time, much less your precious money. In this chapter, we discuss how to locate properties nearing foreclosure, and how to filter out the losers—quick and fast.

Finding Pre-foreclosure Opportunities

Train your eye to pick up desperate sellers. The newspaper is an incredible resource for finding pre-foreclosure opportunities. You can find out when a paper publishes legal foreclosure notices by simply calling the paper and asking. This information is all public, so you are well within your rights to request their publishing schedule.

The classifieds section is also very revealing. Look for ads with words such as "Motivated," "Desperate Sellers," "Must Sell," or "For Sale by Owner." Each of these terms are really saying, "Make me an offer, I am desperate, Call me today!" Take full advantage of such situations. In the end, you can create a win/win scenario where the seller needs to move the home and you need to buy for very little money.

Here are keywords in newspaper ads (or Craig's List at www.CraigsList.com) that could trigger a pre-foreclosure buying opportunity:

- Must sell
- Motivated seller
- Below market price
- Below appraised value
- Divorce situation
- Foreclosure
- Loss of job
- Transferred
- Death
- Illness
- Nothing down
- 100% financing
- Owner will finance
- Best offer

Bankruptcies are not a secret, but they can provide some great buying opportunities. They are public knowledge with record trails everywhere. When someone declares bankruptcy, the official Receiver notifies their creditors—from utility companies to land registries to credit agencies.

You can find bankruptcy notices in the local and national newspapers, or directly at the court. Think about this, if a person has gotten to the point of filing for bankruptcy, things have gotten pretty bad. Such a filing stays on your credit records for 10 years and generally it is a last resort. This creates a profile for negotiation if the person is in a home, trying to get out of a home, or is about to be foreclosed. The only difference will be that the bankruptcy court will have to approve the sale. Keep up with the local bankruptcies in your area. You can find many opportunities there.

Similar to a bankruptcy, divorce filings and decrees are public knowledge. A divorce is a legal action and naturally must be filed in court with official documents. Just as you can find someone's records of marriage, you can also find the record of divorce. The financial fallout from divorce can be monumental, and so can the bitterness and long negotiations. Divorce is an opportunity but a tricky one. You must be extra detailed and diplomatic when you are seeking to purchase property from someone going through a divorce.

One of the biggest challenges, according to real estate expert Terri Murphy, is that you have to "negotiate evenly with both sides. Bring them options to get it settled, not just more bad news." She loves working with divorce situations—to get leads, she just goes around asking people if they're happy—or not.

In divorce situations, you may not be getting the entire story; in fact, it's almost guaranteed that you're not. There are three sides to every divorce, his side, her side, and then the truth.

Strongly consider hiring an attorney to wade through court filings to make sure there isn't a judgment out there or one currently being argued that may upset your entire bid or purchase. Divorce can create a great pre-foreclosure opportunity, just beware of the many possible dangers.

There are also many specific foreclosure web sites. They all claim to provide in-depth, first-to-know information to their subscribers. While many are absolutely good for nothing, some can provide a few decent items. The key to the web sites is to use them only as a supplemental source for ideas—never as a single source of information. Many of the sites claim they will make you $20,000 as you sleep, and even more when you wake up! Yeah, right.

Some sites to visit:

- foreclosureradar.com
- all-foreclosure.com
- foreclosure.com
- foreclosurefreesearch.com
- realtytrac.com

One of your most effective secret weapons is the friendly real estate agent. Full-time agents show, look at, sell, and buy homes for a living. No matter how much research you do, you will not be able to replace the information you will gain from an agent that lives and breathes this stuff.

Find an agent and create a partnership—remember agents are in business to make money, this isn't a hobby for them either. Many times, agents are the first to know when a homeowner is in trouble, long before papers have been filed and long before anyone in the public domain has a clue. Agents are in and out of neighborhoods all day, they know many of the neighbors, they know the rumors, small talk, and gossip—all of which is very valuable. Remember, we make money from acting on information early so we need to know everybody who knows anything we don't know. Network, network, network!

 It's not what you know, it's who you know—or better yet, who they know!

Sometimes it's good to just take a step back and look at all the elements involved in pre-foreclosure filings, notices, and the like. Ask yourself the question: Who has to do this? Who has to do that? And where do they go to do it? The answers to these questions will render just about every contact you need to stay on top of valuable information that gives you an edge.

For example, no legal proceeding against a homeowner can take place without an attorney. Lesson: Partner with an attorney. No foreclosure can take place without the lender pushing it forward. Lesson: Become friends with a local lender who can tell you what is about to happen and where. The same applies for probate court and any other official body that handles proceedings. Remember, the obvious holds all the secrets. Simply let people know what you are looking for, be professional, be nice, and be precise with your words. You'll be surprised how much information people will give you if you know how to ask.

Get to know all the players because word-of-mouth is still the most valuable, revealing form of data gathering. People like to talk. Give them somebody to talk to.

Most people don't ask for the fear of not being told. That isn't what a pre-foreclosure investor does. We are in the business of making money from pre-foreclosures. We ask, we search, we knock, and we win. The goal is to find that homeowner one payment away from foreclosure. If you look hard enough, you will find them all over the place because multiple lenders are just waiting to pull the trigger on the process, find these people and their lenders.

In this business, timidity is punished and boldness is rewarded. Keep this in mind if you are ever shy about approaching someone.

How to Find Foreclosure Notices

Local publications are still a great way to find potential investments. Although being published indicates it isn't "new," you can still find great opportunities if you are a good investigator.

As we discussed earlier, networking will get you everything you need. Get to know the people at the Register of Deeds offices. All types of information are kept in this office. The Register records all real estate deeds, deeds of trust, financial statements, mortgage information, cancels claims made against property, and so on. They will make copies for citizens who request public information . . . on and on. Again, this is very obvious, but powerfully relevant. Try to get on the e-mail or mailing list for the Register of Deeds office.

The Best Types of Property to Buy

When you think about where to buy, do just that, think about it. You are making an investment of time and money. Don't take unnecessary chances. Single-family homes still reign if you are playing the odds of what is most likely to resale for a profit. It is a good idea to concentrate on neighborhoods within miles of where you currently live.

You need to be able to ride by frequently at day and at night. Watch for signs of crime, or areas that are consistently unkempt. Look for vagrants, or any element that may endanger your value. This is your money so measure twice before you cut!

Take a clue from neglected neighborhoods and neglect them. I also stay away from high-end neighborhoods. Concentrate on the bread-and-butter, working class communities where people get up and actually go to work every day. You must play the middle, the torso of the market.

You want neighborhoods that have an obvious sense of pride. If all the houses around the one you are looking at have uncut grass 10 feet high, leave and find another property. When you drive by properties, you should be met with affirmations, not questions. Use online zip code searches to help you narrow down the options. Find homes in a certain price range, located in certain counties, zoned for certain schools. This information alone can bring you closer to a profile worthy of your time.

Finding the Sellers

With today's technology, finding sellers has never been easier. There are numerous online chat rooms, electronic classifieds, MySpace, and Facebook-type sites where people post everything about everything. You can even locate distressed owners on YouTube. Simply search for "House for sale Atlanta," or whichever city you need. Also search for the terms, "Motivated seller, reduced home for sale," or "Real estate for sale." You will get multiple hits from people trying to sell for various reasons.

You can also utilize people-finder sites if you need to locate sellers who have moved out that haven't left any contact information. Some of my favorite sites for locating lost people are:

- ZabaSearch.com

- FindingPeople.com

- TheUltimates.com

- People-Search.com

- AnyWho.com

Letting Sellers Find You

Sometimes it is easy to forget that sellers are looking for us, too. Thousands of homeowners around the country are thinking right now, "I wish there was someone to take this house off my hands." So you have to ask yourself, "Am I easy to find?" They won't look long.

Even with the advent of the Internet, desperate people still go to the newspaper. Call it habit or whatever, it is still a fact. At 2 AM, they are looking at the classifieds because they can't sleep. You need to have an ad for them. One that simply tells them you are the one they are looking for. Ads like this work: "We buy houses," "Can't make your next house payment? Call me" or "Don't be foreclosed, if you want to sell now, I want to buy now." Distressed owners will call. Figure 12.1 shows a couple of ideas for some quick, inexpensive but effective classified ads.

Facing Foreclosure?
I Can Help!
Call (101) 123-4567 - Confidential

Trouble with Mortgage Payments?
I Can Help!
Call (101) 123-4567 - Confidential

Can't Afford Your House?
I Can Help!
Call (101) 123-4567 - Confidential

Cash Paid For Home in Foreclosure!
7 Day Closing!
Call (101) 123-4567 - Confidential

FIGURE 12.1   Ads That Attract Desperate Sellers

When prospects call, you need to make sure they can reach you. Even desperate sellers have a limit and will not continue chasing you down. I use a call capture system that is only about $20 a month and has a toll-free number that captures the number of the caller. It also allows them the option, with the touch of a button, to be forwarded to me directly. Whether they reach me immediately or I call them back, contact is crucial. You must be reachable, and you must be reachable now. I love technology, and this thing works wonders. Learn more about the system I use at www.CCUCallCapture.com.

CHAPTER 13

How to Properly Contact and Interact with Homeowners

A large part of your success will be based on your ability to read people. If you can quickly discern what to say to whom, at what time, and for how long—you will have more success than you can imagine.

people are terrible communicators. Those who are good communicators are much more successful in getting deals done, and in building strong relationships with sellers. When seeking out properties, you must follow common sense first—and business sense second. There are entire academic studies on the theory of "first things." This basically says people give more credibility to what is first than what is second. Your job is to beat everyone to the punch, be first in line, and then more often than not, you'll be the first to eat.

Remember, you're there to solve a problem, not present a new one. Communicate like a problem solver, not an investigator. There will be rejections, and a lot of them, but rejection is like gas for your car—you can't get anywhere without it.

In this chapter, we discuss communication, common sense, and how to better handle your emotions—and manage theirs.

Why Direct Mail Works Best

When a homeowner is in distress, a ringing phone becomes a sound you don't want to hear. The very thought of picking up the phone sends distressed people into panic. The lesson? Don't call!

If there is anything that is more disturbing than a constantly ringing phone (mostly from bill collectors and creditors), it is the unexpected knock on the door. Be wise; engage in communication from a distance. Distance is good. It reduces pressure and allows people to think. It's also cheaper for you, and sorts out the "wanna-bes" who are in denial. Distance can also keep things more professional and keep emotions at bay that otherwise would spill out if you were standing face to face.

Ideally, you want the homeowner to contact you. The very act of him or her picking up the phone to call gives you the immediate advantage. This is why I like direct mail so much—it gets the homeowner involved. Yes, you have to send out quite a few pieces, and the response may be proportionally minimal—but this is a numbers game. Direct mail responses are *quality* responses and give you a higher probability of doing a deal. Plus, with my Excel tracking sheet, computer mail merges make it easy to send out hundreds of pieces at a time.

When you send out mail, never send anything that remotely resembles a bill. Remember, that is their problem—they can't pay their bills. If your letter looks like another bill, you have just wasted a stamp because it's going in the trash. Also, never put the word "foreclosure" on the envelope. Think about it this way— imagine you were up all night trying to think of a way to get more money to keep your house, and then went to the mailbox the next day. What would you want to see? What type of mail would prompt you to open it? Probably one that looked more personal, and a bit more sentimental as opposed to corporate junk mail. Homeowners in this situation are seeking relief—emotional and financial relief.

You are selling relief, so package your mail accordingly. I use first class mail, regular stamps, computer typewritten on plain copy paper printed with a color logo, and plain envelopes. No bells and whistles, just straight down the middle. Another reason I do this is you don't want to publicize their problems to anybody. If they think your piece of mail just alerted the mail carrier to their problems, the door will be shut to you forever. Respecting people's privacy is good for business.

Don't be afraid to address the individual with "Dear Mr. (Homeowner's name)." One thing to remember is that the general practice of credit collection is designed to degrade a person while asking for money. This is a terrible philosophy and violates everything about human nature, but nevertheless they continue to do it. We are going to respect human nature and never call someone by his or her first name until we've established a relationship. Use the appropriate courtesy titles of Mr., Ms., or Mrs. every time. Bill collectors are notorious for not using courtesy titles, so it never hurts to be respectful and it might be just what you need to start a dialogue. Finally, sign the letter personally (blue ballpoint) with your name, not the name of your business.

Mailing letters in a format that escalates in tone and urgency can be a very powerful tool. You'll get different responses at different stages, but the key is to send them out consistently and match the tone with the elevation of the homeowner's situation. Study the sample letters that follow. Where you live will determine how frequently you send the letters out. Some states have redemption periods longer than others. For example, if a redemption period is six months, then you want to spread your letters out evenly, maybe even add a couple more that are similar in tone. Shorter periods require a more "rapid fire" attack.

Homeowners respond best to letters offering to relieve emotions, rather than letters based on logic.

(i)   Presenting a spreadsheet of how you are going to make their financial situation better is of no help. Presenting a letter detailing how you understand what they're going through and how you can realistically reduce stress is the way to go. Be firm, serious, and stress the magnitude of what they are about to experience.

Track your letters in an Excel spreadsheet. This is a great organizing tool because you can track what letter went to whom on what date. Once you have several potential situations at the same time, you are going to need to make sure you don't miss anything.

One of the biggest mistakes well-meaning investors make is assuming they can write as well as they speak. Writing is a very different skill set. Most of the greatest speakers in history didn't write their own speeches.

Unless you are a writer with proven success from your copy, *do not* write your own letters. You'd be better off hiring a journalism student from your local college to compose the text. Again, writing effectively is a skill set all unto itself; don't discount the skill required to do it.

Six Letter Approach

To illustrate how important and effective good communication and letter writing is to your success, I have included a series of six letters in Figures 13.1 through 13.6 as samples. These letters have been very carefully worded and tested to elicit specific responses and hit a nerve with the homeowner. The methodology is to be clear about your objective, be consistent, be increasingly serious, and present yourself as the solution each time in every letter. You'll notice that the tone changes as the homeowner gets deeper into trouble.

Figure 13.1 shows how we start the ball rolling.

Send Figure 13.2 as soon as the NOD or *lis pendens* is filed.

Figure 13.3 should go about a week later.

Figure 13.4 should be sent about one to two months prior to the auction date.

Figure 13.5 should go out one month prior to the auction date.

And finally, two weeks prior to the auction date they should receive Figure 13.6.

If the homeowner is able to get out of trouble without your help, I like to send a congratulations letter like the one in Figure 13.7. I never want to see someone

(date)

(name)
(company)
(address)
(city, state, zip)

Dear (name),

I am sorry to hear that your mortgage lender has filed a lawsuit and begun the foreclosure process. As you may know, this means that if you are not able to bring your mortgage payments current before the scheduled foreclosure sale, your home will be sold at auction, and you will be evicted.

The lender is only interested in getting their money, and if you are dragged through this process, you will receive nothing from the sale. It will destroy your credit, prevent you from getting a new mortgage, and will affect you and your family emotionally, not to mention financially for years to come.

You could possibly sell the home yourself, or with the help of a real estate agent, but the market is tough right now, and homes in this area are taking months to sell. Despite what you may have been told, there may still be some other options that are available to you.

I specialize in helping people who are in foreclosure. I am committed to making sure that homeowners such as yourself in this situation are aware of all of their alternatives, and are not taken advantage of by people trying to make a quick buck at your expense. I am very familiar with the foreclosure process in the area, and can assist you in looking at all the options – some of which may include your being able to stay in your home, or at least delay the process to give you more time to search for a solution.

If you are interested in getting out of this situation, I invite you to call me today at (your number) so we can set up a time to get together to discuss your options in more detail. In certain circumstances, I can also make you an immediate offer to buy your house for cash, with a closing in seven days. I would also take care of all the transaction details and closing expenses, at no cost to you. That would stop the foreclosure, save your credit, and I can even provide assistance in finding you a new home in which to start over.

Either way, please call me right away. Don't lose your home because you are too ashamed to ask for advice. The worst thing you can do is nothing, as the clock is now ticking, and if you ignore the situation, you will lose your home and be evicted.

I look forward to hearing from you so we can talk about your options.

Sincerely,

(your name)

Figure 13.1   Letter to Homeowner #1

(date)

(name)
(company)
(address)
(city, state, zip)

Dear (name),

I am writing to you again, because unfortunately, your financial situation is now a matter of public record, and you are starting to run out of time. Your mortgage lender has filed an action that, in just a short while, will lead to a public auction in which the new owner will have the Sheriff's Department evict you from your home.

Additional expenses are starting to pile up, and your options are getting slimmer. The lender is only concerned about getting their money at this point, and not about your wellbeing.

As I mentioned in my last letter, I specialize in helping people who are in foreclosure. I am committed to making sure that homeowners in this situation are aware of all of their alternatives, and not taken advantage of. You may not think that you have many choices, but you do.

You need to call me right away at (your number) to set up an appointment to get together. I can make you an offer to purchase your house today (for cash), with a closing in seven days. I will take care of dealing with your lender, the transaction details and closing expenses, all at no cost to you. That would stop the foreclosure and save your credit. I can even provide assistance in finding you a new home as well.

Again, the worst thing you can do is nothing, as the clock is now ticking, and if you ignore the situation, you will lose your home.

I look forward to hearing from you so we can talk about your options, and start to put this nightmare behind you.

Sincerely,

(your name)

P.S. – You will start hearing from a lot of people trying to "help" you out, but please be careful as there are many scam artists out there. I am a professional, will provide references, and will bring in attorneys and title closing specialists for both of our protection.

 FIGURE 13.2   Letter to Homeowner #2

(date)

(name)
(company)
(address)
(city, state, zip)

Dear (name),

I am very concerned about your situation!

This is my third letter, and I have not heard from you yet. If you do not bring your mortgage payments current very soon, your home will be sold at a public foreclosure auction sale, and soon thereafter, you will be evicted.

Please do not continue to ignore the situation, or think that you can just leave or trash the house and the problem will go away. It won't. Those types of reactions could lead to civil or even criminal liability, and the repercussions will only get worse.

You can still salvage the situation! You need to call me right away at (your number) to set up an appointment to get together. I can make you an offer to purchase your house today (for cash), with a closing in SEVEN days, but YOU need to make the first move. I will take care of dealing with your lender, the transaction details, including the proper transfer of title and closing expenses—all at no cost to you. That would stop the foreclosure, save your credit, and get you out of this mess. I can even provide assistance in finding you a new home!

Please call me directly at (your number) today. I can help you, but time is running out. I look forward to hearing from you so we can start to get this situation cleared up for you.

Sincerely,

(your name)

P.S. – The Sheriff's auction and sale of your home has been scheduled and posted, and the process is now REALLY hard to stop. If you want to save what's left of your credit and avoid a public auction and eviction, doing nothing is NOT an option! Call me TODAY so we can get the foreclosure stopped before it's too late.

 FIGURE 13.3   Letter to Homeowner #3

(date)

(name)
(company)
(address)
(city, state, zip)

Dear (name),

We are getting down to the wire, and almost out of options. In less than 60 days, your home will be sold at a public foreclosure auction, and the high bidder will have you evicted by the county Sheriff's Dept.

By now you should understand that when this happens, you will receive nothing from the sale. Not one dime. The lender does not care about you, only about getting their money as quickly as possible. But you can still do something.

I have the knowledge and resources to help you, but you need to take the first step and call me as soon as possible. I have seen the effects of foreclosure, and what it does to people and their families. It's not a fun time that you're going through right now, and I know that firsthand. But you can still take control of the situation and save some of your credit—and a little of your dignity. We can stop this foreclosure within the next week.

You need to call me NOW at (your number) to set up an appointment so I can make you an offer to buy your house today. I can get you cash within seven days, and take care of your lender, take care of the paperwork, all the transaction details, and even the closing expenses—all at no cost to you. That will stop the foreclosure and get you out of this mess.

But you have got to do something RIGHT AWAY! I have helped lots of people in this type of situation, and I want to help you too. But if you continue to ignore this, you'll be out of options, and out on the street.

Please call me directly at (your number) today. I look forward to hearing from you so we can start to get this situation cleared up for you.

Sincerely,

(your name)

P.S. – People in your situation are commonly in a state of denial about what's going on, but the clock is still ticking, and you don't have a lot of time left. Call me now so I can help you.

 Figure 13.4   Letter to Homeowner #4

(date)

(name)
(company)
(address)
(city, state, zip)

Dear (name),

As a foreclosure specialist, I hate to see what happens to people at times like this. You are now within 30 days of the public foreclosure auction of your home, and I haven't heard from you. I am sure the stress is building, but it doesn't have to be this way.

This is my fifth letter to you, and you are aware of the consequences of what's going to happen to you and your home. The lender is anxious to get the property back, as it has already cost them a lot of money in losses. Losses that they will pin on you! It is getting more expensive every day, and you will feel the effects for years.

I don't want to see you lose everything during this foreclosure—you don't have to! As I've told you in my previous letters, I am a specialist in foreclosures, and help people to GET OUT OF THEM! I can still help you do the same—but you need to call me.

My direct number is (your number). You will deal with me personally, confidentially, and I can make you an offer and get you cash within seven days. I will take care of dealing with the lender, take care of the paperwork, all the transaction details, and even the closing expenses. It won't cost you a dime, BUT you need to call me right now!

Time is very short, and you need to put this nightmare behind you. I look forward to hearing from you so we can start to get this foreclosure stopped.

Sincerely,

(your name)

P.S. – Doing nothing is NOT an option! After the public foreclosure auction sale, they will then immediately start the process of evicting you from your home. Call me TODAY so we can get this stopped!

 FIGURE 13.5   Letter to Homeowner #5

(date)

(name)
(company)
(address)
(city, state, zip)

Dear (name),

The time has come, and frankly, I am concerned for you. I wanted to try to reach you one last time, but this is my final letter, for as you know, the foreclosure auction on your home is just days away.

Your home will be sold to the highest bidder, and you will be evicted by the Sheriff's Dept. Are you really ready for what's coming? I doubt it. Most people crumble under the pressure, as this is a financially and emotionally devastating process that will haunt you for years.

Why? You don't have to go through this! There is still a very small window of opportunity to act, but you must call me immediately at (your number). I have the resources to assist you, and as I have mentioned to you several times, can make an offer to buy your house for cash and close within seven days. This will stop the foreclosure auction so it won't show up on your credit, and will protect you from further public embarrassment and humiliation.

I will deal with the lender and other secured creditors, have my attorneys and the title company prepare all the documents and process the closing—all at no cost to you. I will even assist you in relocating to a new home. But the time to act is NOW.

This is my final request that you call me directly at (your number) so we can get this foreclosure auction stopped, and prevent you from being evicted.

Sincerely,

(your name)

P.S. – Trashing, stripping, and abandoning the property may make you feel better, but it doesn't make the situation go away, and will subject you to further problems. Don't make the situation worse. Call me today!

 FIGURE 13.6   Letter to Homeowner #6

(date)

(name)
(address)
(city, state, zip)

Dear (name),

    Congratulations! I was pleased to see that you were able to reinstate your mortgage and stop the foreclosure process!

    I know that this has been a tough time for you and your family, and I hope that everything is back on track for you. Foreclosures aren't fun, and as a foreclosure specialist, my first priority is to try and see that people are able to remain in their homes and get the problem solved.

    If you still have questions, or if you or anyone you know faces a similar situation in the future, please feel free to call me at (your number). I have enclosed a few business cards, and am happy to assist in any way that I can.

    Again, congratulations for getting this behind you, and I wish you the best in the future!

Sincerely,

(your name)

FIGURE 13.7   Congratulations Letter to Homeowner

lose their home, so it is a nice way of saying "whew!" I enclose a few business cards, and invite them to call me with any questions they might have in the future, as well as refer any friends and acquaintances that might have questions or problems regarding their mortgages. I get referrals on occasion using this strategy.

When the Phone Rings

Okay, letters have been sent and you get the call you've been waiting for—now what?

    When the homeowner calls, this is your opportunity, and maybe your only opportunity, to seal the deal. Be courteous, yet professional. Avoid emotional conversations at all cost. This takes practice and experience, but your tone, your answers, and the length of your answers has a lot to do with setting the standard for productive personal dialogue.

Homeowners will try to negotiate over the phone—don't. All you want to do is get some basic information and set the appointment. You want this to be a conversation about substance, and as soon as the substance is over, so should the phone call. Stay clear of discussing how much this is affecting their family, recent sicknesses, health care bills, and the like. Your job is to move forward with your plan—not engage in family counseling.

Don't negotiate over the phone! Get the information, and get the appointment!

You need to know how much they owe, when the last payment was made, whether they have filed bankruptcy, if they have officially listed the house for sale yet, how much equity they have, how much they think they can sell it for, and other key info. Stick to substance!

Last, ask when you can get together. You need to get in front of them ASAP.

To see how the initial conversation should go, study the sample phone script shown in Figure 13.8.

First, Try to Help

Help me help you . . . in the end helps everybody!

When a homeowner is far behind in payments, many times they can't see the forest for the trees. Emotions are blinding. Before offering to take the home off their hands, make sure they have explored all the other available options. The point is to be a resource for relief. If there is a way the homeowner can save the home and it isn't you, guess what? You still win! If they ever get in trouble again, you'll be the first one they call. Many deals aren't done the first time around. Your first contact may just establish to them that you are a knowledgeable willing resource. You never know where your profit will come from down the line.

You want to explore the homeowner's assets and family resources with them. Walk them through the thinking process. Make sure that every possible financial source is tapped out. This does two things; it allows you to estimate the seriousness of this situation while showing the homeowner the same thing—how serious this is. By the time you've spoken about all options and you're the only one still standing, they have actually made your argument for you. Again, it's a win-win scenario.

Make sure the owner has explored reinstating the loan, forbearance agreements, refinancing, and so on—everything possible to keep their home from foreclosure. You can probably tell that you must strike a nice balance between what

This is a sample script that can be used during your FIRST communication with the homeowner. When you speak with them, have your Homeowner Profile Worksheet (Form 14.1) ready to fill out!

IF THEY CALL YOU:

HOMEOWNER: Hello, can I speak with (your name)?

YOU: This is (your name), can I help you?

HOMEOWNER: Yes, this is (their name), and I am calling about the letter you sent me.

YOU: Yes, thank you for calling (their name), I am a foreclosure specialist, not a real estate agent, and I contacted you to see if I might be able to help you out . . .

IF YOU CALL THEM BACK:

YOU: Hi, this is (your name), and I appreciate you calling me back regarding the letter I sent you. I know it's a rough time you're going through right now, and you're being contacted by a lot of people. Despite what they tell you, there are several options available to you. I am a foreclosure specialist, not a real estate agent, and I contacted you to see if I might be able to help you out . . .

YOU: To start, can I ask you a few basic questions about your situation? I promise that everything will remain strictly confidential.

ASK KEY QUESTIONS AND FILL OUT HOMEOWNER PROFILE WORKSHEET

Ask the key questions to weed out the "undoable" deals quickly. If the situation is a lost cause, politely explain that in this situation it does not appear that you can be of any assistance. Suggest that they speak with legal counsel about their situation, and wish them well.

If the deal has possibilities, then continue as follows:

YOU: I know you are anxious to get this problem solved, and I would like the opportunity to come and meet with you and view the property. When is the earliest you would be available – do you have time later today, or would tomorrow be better?

(*Make the appointment!*)

 Figure 13.8   Initial Telephone Script

profits you—and what profits the homeowner. Think of it this way, whatever profits the homeowner through your purchase or your advice, actually profits you. You are setting yourself up as a specialist, and you'll sleep better at night knowing you're doing the right thing.

i At the end of the day, people in distress know other people in distress. The person you keep out of foreclosure becomes your free marketing representative. They will spread the word.

The letter in Figure 13.7 has the positive attitude that must be presented when you keep a homeowner from foreclosure. If you come in positive and leave positive, you will be viewed as a positive option. That's good business any day of the week!

Now let's discuss gathering the key information on the property.

CHAPTER 14

Verifying Critical Property Information

It would be nice if everyone involved in a transaction was honest and had perfect memory recall. Unfortunately, that's just not the case in most real estate deals. This is even truer if the homeowner has lived there for many years. When large public corporations buy smaller companies, they do what is called *due diligence* on the company being purchased. This involves a very thorough examination of all of the company's historical and business records. They send in a team of auditors to go over the books for years back. It's the only way they'll move forward with the huge amounts of money at stake.

You are the corporation in this case. The purchase you're about to make isn't for billions of dollars, but it is certainly enough of a chunk of money to deserve your own due diligence. Your research must be very thorough and you don't have the luxury of taking months to do it. To get on track, stay that way, and finish in a time frame that will hopefully work for the lender, you must have a plan and follow it.

If, after the initial conversation, you can see that there is potential in the deal, then we need to go hunting for facts. We start with fact-gathering at its most basic level . . . interviewing the homeowner.

Getting the Facts

This experience sort of sums up what most homeowners are thinking: years ago, as I arrived at a property to inspect, I walked up to this guy's house and he immediately ran out and asked me, "How much will you give me for my house?" I said, "About $600." In total shock, he exclaimed "What?" I quickly replied, "yes, $600—because that's the value of the front door, and that's all I've seen so far." He laughed, and that started things off on the right note.

Owners want quick information based on sketchy details. As investors, we want to take our time and gather all available data in order to make a solid assessment.

Your first step, as I mentioned, is to set up a meeting with the homeowner in person. Be courteous but professional, and be sure that they understand that it might take a while, and to set aside the time necessary (usually one to two hours). If their home is full of family so that there isn't a quiet place to meet, it might take a little longer, but meet them right there at the property.

i The kitchen table is the best place to meet, negotiate, and talk. It's their comfort zone, and you'll be able to get more information from them.

If that's not possible due to travel or it being tenant-occupied, then pick a neutral place like a nearby restaurant. This is second choice, however, because they may end up without some documentation that's tucked in a drawer somewhere at home.

I do not schedule appointments or pursue transactions with people who are addicted to drugs or alcohol, or who have serious mental health issues. If there are those warning signs, I'm outta there. Not only is it going to be an uphill fight to get negotiations done, but their agreements and actions might be deemed unenforceable later on.

If you are a woman, use some common sense and do not meet total strangers at their property at night or in a questionable environment. Meet in a public location, or go during daylight hours.

It is human nature to forget things, and this is especially true in situations like this one. You don't know this person very well at all, and yet you are asking highly personal financial questions. It is stressful for both of you. Go in with a list of questions so that you do not have to call them back to ask something you forgot. I carry extra interview sheets with me, and pull one out to fill out with the homeowner. Figure 14.1 is a copy of my suggested sample interview sheet. You can download this in Word format off my web site, which allows you to modify it if you want.

Owner Information

Get all of the contact information for the owner. Mailing addresses, phone numbers at home, work and their cell phones are important. You are not sure of the time line for the transaction, nor their plans, so if possible, get some contact information for relatives and friends. If the deal takes longer than anticipated, the

HOMEOWNER PROFILE WORKSHEET

HOMEOWNER INFORMATION

Homeowner Name(s): _____

Address: _____

Home Phone: _____ Work Phone: _____ Alt Phone: _____

Marital Status: ☐ Single   ☐ Married   ☐ Divorced   # of Kids:_____ Ages: _____

Occupation: _____ Employer: _____

Referral Source: _____ Why did you call? _____

LOAN INFORMATION

Warranty Deed Name(s): _____

Lender's Name: _____

Lender's Address: _____

Loan Balance: $_____ Interest Rate: ___%   # of Months Behind: _____

Loan Type: ☐ Conventional   ☐ Non-Conf   ☐ FHA   ☐ VA   ☐ Private   ☐ Other

Do you have any: ☐ Second Mortgages   ☐ Tax Liens   ☐ Mechanic's Liens

What is your estimate of the value?   Source? _____

Monthly Pmt: $_____ Principal: _____ Interest: _____

Home in foreclosure? _____ Sale Date: _____ Redemption Period: _____

Why are you in foreclosure? _____

HOMEOWNER ACTION STEPS

Have you been in foreclosure before?   ☐ Yes   ☐ No Listed it for sale? ☐ Yes ☐ Yes

Have you ever filed bankruptcy?   ☐ No   ☐ Chapter 7   ☐ Chapter 13

Bankruptcy Details: ☐ Currently in   ☐ Discharged on: _____

Others you have consulted: ☐ Lender   ☐ Attorney   ☐ Realtor
                                       ☐ Accountant   ☐ Others:

What was their advice?

What would you like to happen?

Best Resolution: ☐ Cash Buy ☐ Finance ☐ Assumption ☐ Short Sale ☐ Rental ☐ Other

FIGURE 14.1   Homeowner Profile Worksheet

homeowners could end up moving out suddenly. Don't be left with a disconnected phone number as your only contact.

Financial Information

If you are helping homeowners prepare the hardship letter (see Chapter 22), then the owner information will need to be quite extensive, and you will want documents to back up every bit of it. You'll need to ask about:

- All credit card bills and their current payment status
- The status of their first mortgage payment, how far in arrears, contact information for the lender
- All junior liens, equity loans, or home improvement loans
- The current payment status of all of these loans, copies of the documents, and contact information for the lenders
- Any delinquency letters they have received for possible loss mitigation contact information
- Medical bills and their payment status, delinquent notices
- Divorce decree—if it is part of their financial situation
- Children's college loan information if they are guarantors, and so on

I want to have as clear a picture of the situation as possible—the 5 "W's"— What's the status and nature of the property, where is their pressure coming from, why they're at this stage, when they have to take action, and who all is involved.

To do that, I use a Property Loan Worksheet like the one in Figure 14.2.

Property Information

There will probably be a trip or two to the county records for this step, but first let's see what you can do to make your job easier by getting information from the homeowner. When you set up the interview appointment, ask them to get together every document they have that pertains to the ownership of the property. They may need to go to a safe deposit box, so give them a little bit of notice. Ask them to make copies for you, or offer to make copies and get them the originals back (immediately). Everything they can give you will be one less document you'll have to pay to have printed at the records office.

PROPERTY LOAN WORKSHEET

Property Address: _____

Lender's Name: _____

Lender's Address: _____

Loan Officer's Name: _____

Loan Officer's Phone #: _____

Loan Account #: _____

Original Loan Date: _____ Loan Amount: _____ Interest Rate: _____

Loan Type: ☐ Conventional   ☐ FHA   ☐ VA   ☐ Private

Assumable?:   ☐ Yes   ☐ No

Monthly Pymt: _____   Principal: _____   Interest: _____

          Taxes: _____   Insurance: _____

Date Recorded: _____   Liber: _____   Page: _____

Unpaid Principal Balance: _____ Total Payment in Arrears: _____

Total Interest, Late Charges, and Legal Fees: _____

Total Amount Needed to Cure: _____

Mortgage Sale Date: _____   Redemption Period: _____

Prepare one worksheet for each lien

Notes: _____

_____

_____

_____

_____

Figure 14.2   Property Loan Worksheet

Prompt their memory by asking them to dig up everything they can, including:

- Original deed copy
- Plat or survey
- Title insurance policy
- Any lien documents they received
- Tax bills
- Insurance policies

Here is where you can get into trouble by trusting the honesty or memory of the homeowner. They are under a great deal of stress, and it could just be that they forgot a mechanic's lien from a few years back. You will be making a trip to the county records office with the information you get from the homeowner, including their letter authorizing you to gather information, and you will research the court records for the property. Get all recorded documents pertaining to the home that you do not already have. Don't try to read them at the courthouse, take them home so that you can take your time. You don't want to miss any claims against the property at this stage.

Sometimes, as hard as it is to believe, homeowners will leave information out. Check everything yourself.

Property Condition Information

If there have been any recent repairs or remodel work done, get all the paperwork you can on them. There could be a lien involved, but you also want to know about any past problems that could relate to current value. Have any major defects been identified? In many cases, the homeowners may have tried to sell the property on their own or with a ealtor. Were there any potential buyers who went far enough to get an inspection? If so, you want a copy of the inspection if the owner has one. You also want the contact information for the potential buyer because they might be a candidate for a future purchase from you. Remember, you don't know where your profit will come from.

Major defects could be anything from large slab cracks to roof damage that will require a replacement. You want any paperwork or inspections that mention these things. It might just make you change your mind about doing the deal at all, or at the very least, change your offer price to reflect repairs you'll need to make. Information is king—respect it as such!

You might want to get the owner to go online and order a Home Seller's Disclosure Report from Choice Trust or C.L.U.E. Only the homeowner can order it. It is a report of any claims or questions that have been recorded by home insurers. If there has been damage to the home that resulted in discussion with the insurance carrier or a claim, this report will disclose it. It will give information on the resolution and any payments made.

 The C.L.U.E. web site can be found at www.choicetrust.

Securing Loan Information

Before you begin to contact lenders and lien holders, get a signature from the homeowner(s) authorizing you to do so. Figure 14.3 is a sample of a borrower authorization form I use.

Contact the senior lien holder first. This is the first mortgage holder, and the one that typically will be deciding whether a foreclosure will go forward, how fast, or whether a short sale will happen. Then contact all junior lien holders. Use the same procedure with each, letting them know the situation and negotiating with them as to settlement of their claims, considering the situation of the borrower.

Of course, negotiating with junior lien holders will be a bit different, as many will be losing all or most of their investments, which are subordinate to the senior lender. The key is that you must end up with a clear picture as to how much is likely to be forgiven and what may be left to pay to liquidate the claims. I shoot for a 60 to 80 percent discount to start.

Let's talk about Estoppel. This is a legal doctrine that simply means someone agrees not to come to court later to make a claim that contradicts a previous legal decision or a previous statement of fact. What we want to do is get the lender(s) to state their claim(s), so that there is evidence in case their claim later tries to get bigger.

I prepare an estoppel letter or form (Figure 14.4), and have all borrowers sign it. I want the lender to provide the terms of the loan, balance, penalties, interest, and any other claim they are making as to their compensation. This provides a statement that makes it more difficult to make changes later on that can damage our position.

Many times, the lender will simply print out a computer version of their own mortgage balance information sheet, and that will usually have the same information on it.

Dealing with Private Lenders

What if I'm not dealing with a Citibank or Bank of America? Then the approach is a bit different. Private lenders could be anyone from a relative or a friend, to the

(date)

(lender rep. name, position)
(lender)
(address)
(city, state, zip)

RE: Mortgage Loan #_____ ;

Dear (name),

    I hereby authorize you to release any and all information regarding my loan, including payment history and balance information to (your name, address, phone). Here is the necessary information:

Borrower Name _____

Loan Number _____

Property Address _____

City, State, Zip _____

    Thank you for your prompt assistance and attention in this matter.

Sincerely,

(borrower signature)
(borrower name)

 FIGURE 14.3   Borrower Authorization Form

previous owner who did owner financing or took a second mortgage for part of the proceeds of the sale of the home. It could also be a single investor or a group of investors who pooled their resources to fund home mortgages.

    The process isn't really any different, just the party on the other end of the negotiation—and the negotiation tactics used. A payoff means a lot more to John C. Noteholder than it does to Bank of America. There's a certain personal attachment to the balance, so they're usually easier to motivate. Figure 14.5 is sample information release and Figure 14.6 is a sample estoppel letter if you're working with a private lender.

(date)

(lender rep. name, position)
(lender)
(address)
(city, state, zip)

RE: Mortgage Loan #_____;
     Borrower Name: _____

Dear (name),
     Please complete the following information (or a printout containing the same) and transmit it via fax to (your name) at (fax number), or by e-mail to (e-mail address) as soon as possible.

Original Loan Amount: $_____ Current Principal Balance: $_____

Principal/Interest Payment: $_____ Accrued Interest & Late Fees: $_____

Taxes/Insurance Payment: $_____ Legal Fees & Penalties: $_____

Total Monthly Payment: $_____ Interest Rate: _____%

Type of Loan: ☐ Conventional   ☐ FHA   ☐ VA   ☐ Other

Date of Original Loan: _____ Payment Due Date: _____

Current Escrow Balance $_____

Total Amount In Arrears $_____

Total Amount Needed to Reinstate This Loan $_____

This Is True and Accurate as of: _____

Signed: _____

Phone:_____

Thank you for your prompt assistance and attention in this matter.

Sincerely,

(borrower signature)
(borrower name)

 FIGURE 14.4   Lender Estoppel Letter

(date)

(lender/party name)
(address)
(city, state, zip)

RE: Property Address: _____;

Dear (name),
    I hereby authorize you to release any and all information regarding my loan, including payment history and balance information to (your name, address, phone). Here is the necessary information:

Borrower Name _____
Property Address _____
City, State, Zip _____

    Thank you for your prompt assistance and attention in this matter.

Sincerely,

(borrower signature)
(borrower name)

Figure 14.5   Borrower Release Form (Private Lender)

Calculating Equity

I don't know about you, but I think that this is a lot of work. You've met with the homeowner, pried into their financial privacy, did county records research, haggled with multiple lenders, and examined the home for condition and repair issues. You may even have gone out for repair estimates from contractors as well. All of this research and negotiation has one purpose . . . to arrive at the number reflecting the equity or profit potential in the home if you continue with this deal.

    Remember—you are not actually negotiating to buy their property, you're negotiating for their equity.

(date)

(lender name)
(address)
(city, state, zip)

RE: Property Address: _____;
      Borrower Name: _____

Dear (name),
      Please send the following information regarding my loan via fax to (your name) at (fax number), or by e-mail to (e-mail address) as soon as possible.

Original Loan Amount: $_____ Current Principal Balance: $_____

Principal/Interest Payment: $_____ Interest Rate: _____%

Taxes/Insurance Payment: $_____ Amortization Period: _____ Yrs.

Total Monthly Payment: $_____

Prepayment Penalty?   ☐ Yes ☐ No

Date of Original Loan: _____ Payment Due Date: _____

Current Escrow Balance (If Any) $_____

Total Amount Currently in Arrears: $_____

This Is True and Accurate as of: _____(date)

Signed: _____
Phone:_____

      Thank you for your prompt assistance and attention in this matter.

Sincerely,

(borrower signature)
(borrower name)

 FIGURE 14.6 Estoppel Form (Private Lender)

You have also gone out and gathered comparable information on sold properties, as well as detailed listing information on properties for sale right now.

Now we're tallying the results. What is your plan for the property? For example:

- If a flip, what do we expect to clear after repairs and rehab?
- If we're keeping it as a rental, what is our return expected to be?
- Do we have a buyer ready, perhaps through assignment?
- What are all of our acquisition costs, including satisfaction of liens, closing, and repair/rehab?
- What do we think the owner and lender will accept for a purchase offer?
- Will that number work for our purposes and profit goals?

It's all pluses and minuses. Add up the costs of acquisition and rehab and subtract from what we're getting in a flip, and if the number is positive enough, then going ahead may be the decision. After all, we've got a lot of time and effort involved already.

If we're not flipping, but keeping the property for a rental, we will want to look at the equity we expect to have from day one at closing, and the expected appreciation near and long term. We've done an analysis of the rental market, and we have determined our cash flow. We have studied how tax advantages will help our return on investment as well. If these numbers look good, we can go ahead and get our rental property ready for a tenant.

Robert Helms is a good friend, international real estate syndicator, and host of the syndicated radio talk show "The Real Estate Guys." One of his best tips for new investors is to remember that this is a numbers game. The numbers either work—or they don't. As Robert puts it, "If they don't work, there are a lot of other deals waiting for me!"

If the plan you have for the property isn't supported by the numbers at this point, cut your losses and end the process.

If there is a high risk of the lender not working with your purchase offer, cut your losses and move on. It is nice to help an upside-down homeowner out of a predicament, but you are not a charity. You should move on to a profitable opportunity.

CHAPTER 15

Doing Your Homework

If you're anything like me, you hated homework. There was always something much better to do. I could never understand the logic . . . I just got home from school all day, and now I should do more schoolwork at home? Unfortunately, that argument didn't work and I'm glad I learned the benefits of homework because now I get to do it all day long.

To establish an edge in the pre-foreclosure market, you have to be faster, more skilled, and more discerning than the next investor. In this chapter, we uncover the value of doing your homework—but this time you get paid for it!

Starting with Basic Research

It may take a little time and sometimes a minimal investment, but you can find a lot of information on a property with just a little due diligence. In the public record, you may find what you need quickly to help you determine what kind of an offer to put in on a property. You can find valuable data such as:

- Sellers who are getting a divorce, which could mean they are more motivated to sell
- The number of times a home has been put on the market
- How long the seller has owned the home
- How much is owed
- Whether the home is already in foreclosure
- Deeds
- Encumbrances

- If the seller has filed for bankruptcy
- If the seller is involved in litigation

Many counties maintain records online—to find out, call and ask the county Registrar or Assessor's office what the web site address is. Then search for property tax records and ownership filings, where you can find out:

- Name of the owner(s)
- Tax ID number or parcel number
- Amount of taxes and whether the taxes are paid
- Lienholders of record
- Mortgages and deeds
- Recorded assessments or miscellaneous notices

Other web sites offer consumer information for free. Many web sites allow you to search for property by area, and some give data on unlisted homes not for sale. These include:

- Realtor.com
- Zillow.com
- Trulia.com
- Google Base
- Vast.com
- Oodle.com
- Edgeio.com
- eBay.com

Be careful because some of the information on these sites may be outdated, inaccurate, or the estimates a bit off. Always verify information with at least two different sources.

Due Diligence Checklist

When doing property research, I like to use a checklist to make sure I don't forget anything. Figure 15.1 is the checklist I use, which you can download from my web site. As I search each database, I check it off the list, and record the findings

Due Diligence Checklist

☐ Ownership Search—Current and Prior Owners for Last 10 Years

☐ Legal Records Search—Court Filings for Owners and/or Property
  ○ Federal Court
  ○ District Court
  ○ Bankruptcy Court

☐ Property Records Search—
  ○ Register of Deeds Office
  ○ Equalization and Mapping
  ○ Online Aerial Photograph
  ○ Flood Zone Mapping

☐ Tax records Search—Owner and Property Tax Filings
  ○ Tax Assessor's Office
  ○ State Tax Liens
  ○ Federal Tax Liens

☐ Title Search—Owner of Record and Liens
  ○ Abstract or Commitment Done
  ○ Liens of Record

☐ Building Records Search—Code Violations, Building Records
  ○ County/City Building Dept.
  ○ Zoning/Code Violations

☐ Comparable Sales Search—Realtor/MLS/Online

☐ Demographic Data Search—
  ○ Real Estate Board / Convention & Visitors Bureau /
    Dept. of Labor & Statistics
  ○ Crime Statistics
  ○ Bankruptcy Court

☐ Insurance Claim Search—C.L.U.E.'s History

☐ Online Search—Property; Owners

 FIGURE 15.1 Due Diligence Checklist

in the Foreclosure Tracking Worksheet (see Figure 11.1) and my Homeowner and Property Worksheets (see Figures 14.1 and 14.2).

Ownership Search

You can find the owner through the office of the tax assessor for the city or county where the property is located.

Make sure you track down *all* of the owners of record. I go back and research at least 10 years' worth of data.

You will also need to make sure to find out if the owners are married because dower and homestead rights are different in different states—which are also handled differently than community property states. You don't want to get a deal nailed down, only to find out that an estranged spouse also needs to sign off—and they're nowhere to be found.

There are many web sites dedicated to helping you find and track down people and property information. Some may charge a nominal fee, so do your homework first and see what they have to offer. These sites include:

www.peoplefinder.com

www.ussearch.com

www.personinfo.com

www.privateeye.com

Owners can also abandon properties for several reasons, including financial issues, death or divorce, or when the property becomes uninhabitable due to dilapidation.

Many cities are struggling with the growing problem of vacant and abandoned homes. This is a side effect of the housing market downturn and rise in foreclosures. For the educated investor, this is prime time to make a move into the market.

Foreclosures have gotten so bad that the city of Syracuse, New York, started selling vacant homes for $1 each to nonprofit groups and is considering extending the offer to private companies. Lengthy foreclosure processes and complicated chains of ownership can contribute to the idle time for the vacant properties. You must be able to recognize these opportunities and be decisive. There are tons of properties in stages of pre-foreclosure; they aren't going to knock on your door—you must find them!

Everything you need to know is on the other end of a question. Talk to neighbors and find out who owns an abandoned property. Visit with local agents, let people know you are a buyer, and see what information they can provide you. Leave them a business card with a working number to contact you. You can also find the property owner's mailing address at the local tax assessor's office. Do a search online at www.netronline.com, you can find tons of properties in your area.

Legal Records Search

There are several types of legal public records searches:

- *Court records:* Go to your county courthouse to find records of divorces, court cases, judgments, bankruptcy, and criminal cases. Check the federal, district, and even the small claims court on the owners and cross reference by property address.

- *Real estate records:* These allow you to find out who owns property and if there are any legal problems. You also may be able to find out the history of the property. If you're looking at a new piece of property, you may find this search useful in locating issues with the title.

- *Lien filings:* With this public records search, you'll be able to find out if the title is clear. You'll find previous judgments, tax claims, or legal claims. Conducting this search can save you a lot of time in the end. It also may reveal whether the property owner has had any previous financial problems.

- *Business entity filings:* Here you'll find information about a company including location, ownership, and date of establishment.

- *Death records:* Search death records to learn about family and personal histories. This is used a lot in cases of identity theft, where someone fraudulently assumes the identity of the deceased.

Property Records Search

Some of this can seem like drudgery, but believe me, when you're putting your money into a home as an investment, you don't want to cut corners. Visit the local recorder's or register of deeds office to find real property legal documents, marriage applications and certificates, surveys, condominium and plat maps, Torrens documents, real estate excise tax affidavits, and other general documents. By state law, most real estate transactions must be recorded, including deeds, mortgage documents, liens, and notices. The nice part is that, thanks to technology, a lot of this is now online in many areas.

You may have to physically visit your county offices for information on the tract and to obtain mapping and aerial overlays. There are many web sites that also offer property records access, most notably www.netronline.com. Find access to deeds, vital records, tax data, and GIS maps from state and local governments.

Tax Records Search

The Internet has made it possible for individuals and businesses to conduct a tax records search to find public tax records, business tax records, and tax listings online. It used to take a lot more time and effort to physically search through paper records. Today, you can access this information easily in most cases, and it may prevent a trip to the courthouse.

Title Search

A title search is performed to determine:

- The seller's saleable interest in the property
- The presence of property liens that must be paid before the sale can be completed (including taxes, mortgages, mechanical liens, assessments)

It also should find any easements or recorded legal rights to the property or portions of the property. Usually, the property buyer will purchase title insurance, which protects the buyer from any title problems that may arise after sale. If the owner of a property wishes to mortgage it, the bank will require him to insure his transaction.

Never purchase a property without purchasing title insurance—ever! The risks are too great, and I've seen some people lose everything without it.

There are two main types of title searches:

1. *Full coverage search:* This type of search is usually done when putting together a title report for a sale transaction or transaction that includes a construction loan. With this, you'll find information about easements, covenants, agreements, ordinances, liens, and conditions and restrictions. It will find liens against the owner, liens against the buyer, and any bankruptcy proceedings against the owner of the property.

2. *Limited coverage search:* Typically, this is done for refinance situations and ownership equity loans. It can search for property liens, liens against the owner and other parties on the title, and bankruptcy proceedings against the property owner.

Building Records Search

Logic tells us that building permits are given to those who want to build something, but we can learn a lot more than that. Very few owners who allow their homes to fall into disrepair have applied for building permits (for add-ons and the like). If an owner is adding on to his house, you can make a general assumption that he probably has taken decent care of the home. This is just another indicator to put in the back of your mind when searching permits. Take a trip down to the county building department and you'll find technical information on the property, including additions and any zoning or code violations.

Comparable Sales Search

Comparable sales or comps are recent sales of similar properties in the nearby neighborhood or in a similar neighborhood with similar prices. They are comparable to the house you are buying or selling.

The comparable sales method is the best way to determine market value for one- to four-unit properties. If you're a seller, your listing agent will help you determine your sales price by showing you some recent comps. If you're a buyer and preparing an offer, your selling agent will probably show you some comparable sales so you can come up with your offer price.

Whether you are a buyer or seller, you'll have to make adjustments based on the property and any recent changes in the market. What you want to pay for the house doesn't exist in a vacuum. You must take inventory of what has sold in the area under similar conditions.

An appraiser's main role is to justify a market value or purchase price, not to establish one.

Typically, buyers will have to get an appraisal because the lender wants to be sure that the property is satisfactory equitable collateral for the loan. Generally, appraisals of one- to four-unit homes use the comparable sales method to justify a purchase price or market value.

It can be quite easy to find comparable sales. For example, if the home is in a housing tract where most of the homes were built by the same builder, it is pretty simple to get comparable sale information. As time goes by and individuals modify their homes, it can get a little more complicated. More adjustments need to be made when Mr. Jones adds a three-car garage, three baths, and a pool next door to a two bedroom, two bath home.

Occasionally, comparable sales are impossible to find. This can happen in newly built-up areas where the sales tract has just been completed.

Demographic Data Search

There are many web sites available that allow you to find average income, ages, and market data, including home values. By using a zip code or phone number, you can learn:

- Labor statistics
- Public schools
- Population
- Number of homes for sale and average price
- Ages
- Climate

Crime Statistic Search

Visit the local police department to learn the general crime statistics in your city and neighborhood. There also are numerous web sites dedicated to crime statistics, allowing you to compare the statistics of different cities including violent and nonviolent crimes. In our area, the city police department actually has a web site that reports crimes in almost real-time.

Flood Zone Search

Don't forget to check with your county records department to make sure the home you are considering is not in a flood plain area. You can check the federal maps at www.msc.fema.gov.

Insurance Claim Search

Research the property's claim history to determine if there have been damages and repairs to the property. This is vital because if someone needs homeowner's insurance, the insurance company needs to be able to determine the risk of loss. With the advent of computers, insurers can quickly assess the risk of loss by searching the applicant's claim history right on the Web.

There are two major property claim databases, C.L.U.E. (Comprehensive Loss Underwriting Exchange) and A-PLUS (Automated Property Loss Underwriting System). Most people refer to the reports generated by either system as C.L.U.E. reports. These databases allow insurers to check the claim history of both the homeowners and the property.

Property Liens

There are two types of liens that can be placed against a parcel or real estate:

1. *Statutory liens* are involuntary liens created by the operation of law. Statutory liens, such as tax liens, do not require the consent of any party or court order to be enforceable.

2. *Equitable liens* represent the right to have a demand satisfied out of a particular fund or specific property without having possession of the fund or property.

When you are researching the property, you will need to check very carefully for liens against the parcel. There are 16 particular forms of liens that fall within these two categories. Here's a list of the kinds of liens you're looking for:

1. Mortgage
2. Property taxes
3. Mechanics
4. Homeowners association or condo association
5. Judgments
6. Federal tax
7. Federal debts
8. State inheritance tax
9. Code enforcement
10. Corporate franchise tax
11. Bail bonds
12. Municipal

13. Welfare

14. Public defender

15. Marital support

16. Child support

Verifying Liens

Ultimately, it is the job of the title company to verify liens. You will be able to help out immensely by tracking down verifications, payoffs, and lien waivers. For purposes of verification, the title-closing officer will check with the local:

- County Recorder
- County Clerk
- Circuit and District Court
- Federal Court
- Utility Department (sewer and water code enforcement)
- County Treasurer
- Building Department
- Homeowners Association
- Any other lienholders of record (companies, lenders, or private individuals)

Using Title Companies

The title company you work with also works in tandem with real estate professionals to transfer the property to you. The title company will search public records for terms of ownership to determine if previous owners have "enhanced or diminished the total and free use of the land." They will find if there are any liens on the property that have to be cleared before purchase. The records search also will turn up outstanding mortgages, judgments, liens, taxes, easements, and right of ways. In other words, title companies do their research—so do yours as well!

The title company will provide a report to you, your Realtor, attorney, and lender. Your team will then determine what needs to be cleared up before you assume ownership. Once that is done, a closing will take place and the title company will produce a document that conveys ownership and records that with the county court.

Your title company has the responsibility of collecting and disbursing all of the funds necessary to complete the sale and transfer of real estate. They hold the moneybag.

At the completion of your transaction, your owner's title policy protects you against a financial loss. A mortgage title insurance policy will be issued to your lender so that the lender also has the protection necessary to protect their interest in the property.

Your title company is involved from the signing of the agreement of sale through the completion of the acquisition. For a fee paid at closing, they protect you for the entire term of ownership (and your heirs should you die) while owning the property.

CHAPTER 16

How to Conduct a Complete Property Inspection

NEWS FLASH: seeing is not believing!

It's imperative that you take time to conduct a thorough property inspection because what you see is not what you necessarily get. Instead of relying on the word of a motivated seller, you'll want to inspect every inch of the property with your own eyes.

In this chapter, I show you how to properly conduct a complete personal property inspection, what to look for on the inside and the outside, and I provide you with numerous checklists to make this a simple, pain-free process.

Before You Arrive

Make sure you leave plenty of time before your scheduled appointment to drive through the neighborhood and take a look around. You won't necessarily be particularly familiar with the neighborhood, so it's important that you learn as much as possible. Some urban areas may look relatively tame during the daytime, but can change radically when the sun goes down.

Look carefully at the condition of other properties in the neighborhood and pay particular attention to the surroundings. If you come across fresh police department crime scene chalk outlines on the ground, take the hint! The neighborhood might be inappropriate for an investment.

Another reason to pay attention to the neighborhood is so you can form a rough estimate in your mind as to how much the property you'll be inspecting could be worth. It also gives you some context on which to judge the property, especially if there is a considerable difference in the overall condition of the house you will be looking at.

Arriving at the Property

It's important that you not intimidate the owner of the property by your appearance. While you want to give every impression of being a successful real estate investor, you don't want your appearance to distract them or intimidate them. Don't show up wearing a tuxedo and riding in a 60-foot stretch limousine.

By the same token, you also don't want to appear to be destitute, so if your vehicle is well-worn, you might want to consider borrowing something more appropriate from a friend or a relative. Leave the 1978 LTD at home, please. Business casual dress is appropriate for these situations because it lets people know in a mild sort of way that you are successful. Conservative is better than wild and flashy. Remember, visual impressions are important and people will remember what they see first. People don't know what you know; they just know what they see.

The Walk-through

I like to do the walk-through first—then if I don't like the property, I can cut the visit somewhat short and not have to dig into their paperwork. When walking through the property, ensure that the owner accompanies you. As is frequently the case when someone is selling something, many sellers will attempt to mask or otherwise conceal major defects, such as painting over stains caused by a leaky roof or by covering a gaping hole in the wall with a picture of dogs playing poker. They may cough loudly every time you walk over a spot the creaks at 50 decibels.

☞ Make sure that you have a flashlight, tape measure, and gloves when inspecting the property.

While you walk, listen attentively to the owner for clues that could come in handy later, and complete a property dossier at the same time. This gives you the opportunity to make special note of damages as well as features that you could potentially forget long after you have left.

Digital cameras have gotten very inexpensive, so there's no excuse not to point and shoot to your heart's content. A good memory card costs between $20 and $30, so take multiple shots of each room from different angles. If you see any damage, be sure to get close-ups. Those shots can help you decide later on if you're interested in completing the property purchase.

Get a digital camera that has built-in rechargeable batteries, and plugs directly into your computer without special software or connections. I use a combination Sanyo C40 camera/video camera so I can also take video if needed.

Exterior Inspection

Use the Inspection Checklist in Figure 16.1 to ensure that you don't miss any critical areas.

Pay special attention to the structural integrity of the house. Make sure it isn't about to fall off of the foundation and that the foundation is not sinking. In addition, look for loose or missing roof shingles or tiles, as well as a sagging roof. It's critical that you be aware of any serious structural defects because some repairs are extremely costly. A new roof could set you back between $5,000 and $10,000 depending on where you live.

If it's a wood frame house, look for evidence of termite infestation. You know you have a problem with termites if they swarm all over you and try to carry you off to their nest, but in most cases they're not that bad, so you'll have to look for clues that they are there. A good visual clue that a property has had problems with termites is wood that is soft and spongy in the center, and will easily fall apart or break. Look carefully along the outside joists and sill plate in the basement or foundation.

Interior Inspection

When you go inside, use the Inspection Checklist in Figure 16.2 to make note of the condition of everything on the inside of the house. If you see anything unusual or that could potentially be a problem, write it down. I know it goes without saying, but making note of potential problems can be beneficial to you later on. I can't tell you how many times I've made a mental note and had the thought blow away within moments of thinking it. You can't remember it all, and a written record is an efficient way of jogging your memory.

Water stains are more than unsightly. They are also visible evidence of a leaky roof or a broken pipe. In addition, untreated water damage can cause rotting and, if it remains a moist environment, can facilitate the growth of mold.

There are numerous interior structural defects that can negatively affect the price you might be willing to pay for a property. For instance, look for evidence of water leakage around windows and doors. Individually, a door or window may not cost much, but if you have to replace multiple windows, it can set you back

Property Address: _____

Pre-inspection Items:

Homeowner:	
Contact Info:	
House Style:	Condo Townhouse Detached Semi-Detached Multi Unit Single Family Co-Op Other
Occupancy Type:	Owner Rental Vacant
Age of Home:	
Square Footage:	
Lot Size:	
Property Taxes:	
Heat Type:	Gas Oil Propane Elect.
Air Conditioning:	Central Window None
Sanitary System:	Sewer Septic tank
Water Source:	Well Municipal
# Bed / # of Bath:	
Style / Stories:	
Finished Basement:	Yes No
Parking:	Garage Carport On Street None
Fireplace(s):	Gas Wood None
Pool:	In ground Above Ground
Deck:	Yes No
Fence:	Yes No
Notes:	

The Neighborhood

Neighborhood Style:	Brick Frame Mix
Are there many boardups:	Yes No
Neighborhood Makeup:	Adult Family
Neighborhood Listing 1:	
Address:	
Listing Price:	
Neighborhood Listing 2:	
Address:	
Listing Price	
Neighborhood Listing 3:	
Address:	
Listing Price:	

Public Transportation:		Yes	No
Traffic Volume:	Busy	Moderate	Light
Condition of Street:	Good	Fair	Poor
Near Airport?		Yes	No
Near Train Tracks?		Yes	No
Near Factories?		Yes	No
First Impression:	Good	Fair	Poor
Positive Features:			
Negative Features:			
Other Notes:			

Curb Appeal

Type of Construction:	Brick Wood Other	Vinyl Pebbledash	
Exterior Colors:			
Exterior Paint Condition:	Good	Fair	Poor
Driveway:		Yes	No
Condition of Driveway:	Good	Fair	Poor
Garage:		Yes	No
Condition of Garage:	Good	Fair	Poor
Condition of Yard:	Good	Fair	Poor
Any Large Trees:		Yes	No
Landscaping:		Yes	No
Roof Condition:	Good	Fair	Poor
Number of Windows:			
Type of Windows:			
Outside Lighting:			
Direction Facing:			
Front Door Condition:	Good	Fair	Poor
Notes:			

FIGURE 16.1 Exterior Property Inspection Checklist

Property Address: _____

Homeowner:

Contact Info:

Inside the Home

Smell	Clean	Musty	
	Air Freshener		
Cleanliness:	Good	Fair	Poor
Kitchen Impression:	Good	Fair	Poor
Floor Type:			
Floor Condition:	Good	Fair	Poor
Cabinetry:	Good	Fair	Poor
Countertops:	Good	Fair	Poor
Appliances (if included)	Good	Fair	Poor
Sink Hardware:	Good	Fair	Poor
Lighting Fixtures:	Good	Fair	Poor
Ceiling Condition:	Good	Fair	Poor

Kitchen Notes:

Bathroom Impression:	Good	Fair	Poor
Floor Type:			
Floor Condition:	Good	Fair	Poor
Cabinetry:	Good	Fair	Poor
Sink Hardware:	Good	Fair	Poor
Tub/Shower Hardware:	Good	Fair	Poor
Lighting fixtures:	Good	Fair	Poor
Ceiling Condition:	Good	Fair	Poor

Bathroom Notes:

Bedrooms

Bedroom 1

Condition:	Good	Fair	Poor
Size:			
Closet Size:			
Number of Windows:			
Number of Outlets:			
Floor Type:			
Floor Condition:	Good	Fair	Poor

Bedroom 1 Notes:

Bedroom 2

Condition:	Good	Fair	Poor
Size:			
Closet Size:			
Number of Windows:			
Number of Outlets:			
Floor Type:			
Floor Condition:	Good	Fair	Poor

Bedroom 2 Notes:

Bedroom 3

Condition:	Good	Fair	Poor
Size:			
Closet size:			
Number of Windows:			
Number of Outlets:			
Floor Type:			
Floor Condition:	Good	Fair	Poor

Bedroom 3 Notes:

Important Things to Check

Inside:

Doors & Windows:	Good	Fair	Poor
Pipes (Plumbing):	Good	Fair	Poor
Mold or Water Damage:		Yes	No
Laundry Hookup:		Yes	No
Signs of Insects or Mice:		Yes	No
Smoke Detectors:		Yes	No
Standing Water:		Yes	No
Overall Floor Plan/Access	Good	Fair	Poor
Crawl Space	Good	Fair	Poor
Insulation	Good	Fair	Poor
Furnace	Good	Fair	Poor
Water Heater	Good	Fair	Poor
Living Room / Family Rm	Good	Fair	Poor

Overall Impression of Home:

FIGURE 16.2   Interior Property Inspection Checklist

thousands of dollars. Every dollar you have to spend on repairs or renovations is a dollar you cannot deposit into your bank account.

Environmental Inspection

You'll want to be extremely vigilant to the possibility of environmental issues (see Figure 16.3). While not prevalent throughout the entire country, large sections of the Northeast and some parts of the South have homes that are heated by heating oil. If the property you are looking at has one of these oil tanks, inspect it carefully to ensure that the tank does not leak. Be careful to look for bad seals and leaky valves. In addition, look for evidence of past leakage on the ground.

Other parts of the country, most notably the Midwest, rely heavily on liquid petroleum tanks for cooking, heating, and hot water. When you inspect these tanks, you'll need to lift the metal lid to inspect the valve system underneath. These are generally located at the center of the tank on the top. If they leak, you'll be able to

Environmental Property Checklist

Date of Inspection_____

Property Address:_____

> ☐ Immediate Vicinity and Adjoining Properties—History & Visual
>
> ☐ Maps of Property
> - o Aerial Photographs
> - o County Mapping and Overlays
> - o Google/Online Mapping Search
> - o Flood Zone Mapping
>
> ☐ Exterior of Subject Property
> - o Above Ground Heating or Fuel Oil Tanks
> - o Below Ground Oil or Gas Storage Tanks
> - o Online Aerial Photograph
> - o Flood Zone Mapping
>
> ☐ Interior of Subject Property
> - o Lead-based Paint
> - o Mold or Fungus
> - o Standing Water or Damp Spots
> - o Asbestos
> - o Old Ceiling Tiles or Pipe Wrapping
> - o UFFI Insulation
> - o Radon Gas Emissions

 FIGURE 16.3 Enviornmental Property Inspection Checklist

smell the gas. If you're conducting your inspection during warm weather, be extra careful when you lift the lid on the tank. Bees like to build nests inside these lids.

Another environmental hazard could be tanks owned by neighbors. They could be any of the above types of tanks or even sewage tanks. A leaky sewage tank can present an additional environmental challenge because they're extremely large and it is costly to remove the tank in order to repair or replace it. In addition, any leakage into the ground would result in contaminated soil that would need to be replaced to avoid running afoul of EPA rules and regulations.

Lead-based paint is rarely an issue anymore, but if the house was built prior to the early to mid-1970s, there's a possibility that the home could still have some remaining lead-based paint. Watch for flaking, peeling, or chalky dust.

Asbestos was used in numerous ways for many years. Insulation around pipes, in ceiling tiles, and in siding are just a few of the applications in which this cancer-causing building material was used. It is expensive to replace.

Any evidence of mold on the interior of the house will need to be addressed. Mold indicates that there was or is a leak in the roof or in a pipe. Left uncorrected, mold growth can spiral out of control and make a home uninhabitable. In addition to being costly to remove, it can also cause severe illness.

Using a Professional

Regardless of the level of investing experience you have, it's imperative that you call in professional assistance to inspect the property prior to purchase. Your inspection, while thorough, isn't as effective or all-encompassing as the inspection performed by a professional property inspector. Make any agreement to purchase the property contingent on the property successfully passing an inspection. It's the best couple of hundred bucks you'll ever spend.

If you're not familiar with the area or do not already have a professional property inspector with whom you are familiar, you can ask neighbors if they can recommend a good certified inspector. In addition, your local REIA is also a good resource to tap into for advice (www.NationalREIA.com). Other investors will be happy to recommend a good inspector to you as well. If all else fails, refer to your local telephone directory or go to the resource of last resort: the Internet.

Next, let's nail down the real value of this property!

CHAPTER 17

Accurately Estimating the Current Market Value

When purchasing a property, it is imperative that you accurately and quickly determine how much the property is worth. If you fail to do this, you run the risk of dramatically overpaying for a property or offending the homeowner when making an offer. If you offend the homeowner, you might never get the chance to purchase the property. However, if you overpay for a property, you might as well decide to walk away from real estate investing altogether, convinced it's not for you.

In this chapter, I show you how to evaluate the real value of property in today's volatile real estate market.

What's It Worth?

A property's value varies depending on the situation. John and Jane Citizen may be purchasing a property in which to live. If that is their intention, they would be willing to pay retail value for the property, which is normally within 10 percent of its assessed valuation.

However, you're a real estate investor. As an investor, you need to locate property below market prices. Depending on whether you want to buy and hold or assign your contract to another investor, you might want to purchase property between 40 and 60 percent of market value (or less).

As an investor, there are six values you are concerned with, and all yield six different numbers:

1. Retail value
2. Wholesale value

3. Tax value

4. Loan value

5. Appraised value

6. Replacement value

Retail value is what the owner wants, while wholesale value is what it's worth to you. The tax value is used by the assessor, and the loan value is used by the lender. Appraised value is provided to support the loan for the lender, while replacement value indicates what it would cost to rebuild after a fire.

While we are most interested in the wholesale value, for acquisition, the other number we want to get to is known as the equity value—after all, that's what we're really buying here.

Equity Value

Quite simply, equity is the part of a home's value that is owned by the property owner. Let me give you an example. Pretend for a moment that your own personal residence is worth $217,000. If you owe the bank $95,000, your equity is $122,000. In other words, equity is the value of a home minus any outstanding loans. In this example:

Retail value:	$217,000
Loan balance:	$ 95,000
Equity:	$122,000

How much are we willing to pay for that equity? You will see in Chapter 18 that the maximum I want to purchase that equity for will be $61,000. You add that to the loan balance (plus any other payoff costs), and the total equitable value to me is $156,000:

Equity at 50 percent:	$ 61,000
Loan balance:	$ 95,000
My max bid:	$156,000

But does that make it a good deal—or even a doable deal? Not sure yet because we have to look at the other values involved.

Appraisal Versus Assessment

The value of a property can fluctuate if you are looking at its appraisal value or assessment value. A property's appraisal value is the best guess of a real estate professional that has received specialized training in determining the value of residential or commercial property. Assessment value is a numeric figure given a property by a taxing authority. For instance, the city or county tax office will give a property value for figuring property taxes, which in many cases is less than the value that a property appraiser would come up with.

Appraisal value is simply the appraiser's point of view of what a particular property is worth. As an opinion, this figure is subject to debate and interpretation. A property is worth only what someone else might be willing to pay for it, so if one appraiser thinks that a property is worth $200,000 and someone is willing to pay $250,000, that property was worth $250,000—at least to the person paying for it.

A well-trained property appraiser generally uses one of three methods for establishing the value of a property: comparable sales, replacement cost, or income valuation. Let's look at each one:

- *Comparable sales:* This is a method of establishing the value of a property based on what other properties in a given neighborhood or area have recently sold for. The appraiser will compare similar properties with similar features in similar neighborhoods, and perform some calculations to account for physical differences in each property. Some of the differences that are considered are square footage of the home, number of bedrooms, amenities, whether the home has a garage, and the size of the yard. These are all given values, and added or subtracted from the subject property.

- *Replacement cost:* This method of establishing the value of the property is based on how much it would cost to rebuild that same property in that same location in today's dollars. When the appraiser uses this method, he or she must take into consideration the cost of building materials, labor, and other variables. When replacement cost is used to establish the value of the property, the appraiser must take into consideration depreciation as well to account for current condition.

- *Income valuation:* When an appraiser uses income valuation in determining the value of a property, he or she is basing the value exclusively on how much income that property can produce. Income valuation is rarely used when determining the value of single-family homes, but rather for multi-family and commercial properties. The appraiser bases this figure on the net income the property can produce—times 10. Net income is a total income of the property minus expenses. For example, if a property has a gross annual income of $400,000 and total expenses of $350,000 (including debt service), the net income of the property would be $50,000. If you multiply $50,000 times 10, the income valuation method places the value of the property at approximately $500,000. This is a generalization because the multiplier can change based on market conditions, property types, and location, but you get the idea. An investor is only concerned about the returns—if I plunk down $500,000, will I get a return of 10 percent on my money for the risk? Yes or no.

Defining and Estimating the Current Market Value

There are four steps to figuring out the real value of a property you're considering. Here's the process:

1. *Obtain the tax assessed value.* In order to obtain the assessed value of a property, you go to the county courthouse or city hall, depending on the location of your property. The tax assessment office can provide you with the tax figures. These figures are also increasingly available online, so if you have access to the Internet, you may be able to determine the assessed tax value of a property from the comfort of your living room.

2. *Search for comparable sales.* Locating comparable sales used to be a difficult, time-consuming process. That's now changing as more and more information is available online and through a variety of information brokers, such as Zillow.com. This free resource can give you comparable sales in most metropolitan areas of the country; however, if you are in a smaller or a rural area, chances are you'll have to find another way of locating your comparable sales figures.

   Remember—these numbers found on Zillow and others may be off by quite a bit, so don't rely on them solely!

   If you have a good relationship with a realtor (which you should by now), there's a chance that you might be able to get comparable sales numbers from them. If all else fails, you might have to venture into the dark halls of your local courthouse and search for it the old-fashioned way: by hand.

3. *Analyze and make adjustments for subject property.* Once you have comparable sales figures, you need to closely examine the similarities and differences between your comparable properties and your subject property. For instance, if your subject property doesn't have a garage and your comparable properties do, then you will have to make an adjustment in value for that difference.

CURRENT PROPERTY VALUATION WORKSHEET

Property Address: _____

Tax & Appraisal & Replacement Value

Taxed Assessed Value (as of Year_____): $_____
AV x Gross Multiplier
Appraised Value *(if Known)*: $_____

Comparable #1: _____Sale Date_____

$_____ +/− $_____ Adjusted Value $_____

Comparable #2: _____Sale Date_____

$_____ +/− $_____ Adjusted Value $_____

Comparable #3: _____Sale Date_____

$_____ +/− $_____ Adjusted Value $_____

Average Comparable Value: $_____

Square Footage_____ Replacement Cost Value: $_____

Value & Offer Reconciliation

Estimated Retail/Street Value from Above: $_____

Less 15–20% Profit Margin
(Minimum Depending on Market):   −_____

Estimated Repair & Clean-up Costs: −_____

Estimated Marketing Costs: −_____

Cost to Extinguish Liens (Senior and Junior):   −_____

Cost for Property Search, Misc.
Acquisition, and Closing Costs: −_____

Holding Costs (3 Month Minimum):   −_____

Maximum Acquisition Cost (for Equity):   = $_____

Total of Liens + Equity Acquisition =
Maximum Offer Price: $_____

FIGURE 17.1 Current Property Valuation Worksheet

4. *Calculate replacement costs.* Calculating the replacement cost of your subject property can be done one of two ways: either by estimating a replacement cost on a square footage basis or by using the cost of all of the raw materials necessary to rebuild your property in the exact condition that it is in. This is somewhat difficult because it's necessary to look at the overall quality of construction, the materials used, and so on. Different properties are put together with different levels of care. For instance, a custom-built home has a higher cost of materials because the quality of the materials is much better than it would be for a cookie-cutter, assembly style construction.

To make it a little easier, use the worksheet in Figure 17.1 to walk you through how to determine the current market value of a property.

Now that we've got a better handle on what the "true" value is of the property, both to the public (retail) and to us (wholesale and equity), let's move on to the next step and see if the numbers are going to work. Now it's time to analyze our costs—and more importantly, our profits!

CHAPTER 18

Analyzing Your Costs and Profits

Figuring out how much you're going to spend fixing up an investment property can be tricky. How do you calculate fix-up costs, closing costs, and profits? Because we are in the business of making money, we have to balance all of this very carefully. In this chapter, I discuss the issues involved with fixing what needs to be fixed without eliminating your profit.

Estimating Repairs and Renovations

An analysis of necessary repairs and renovations is crucial to figuring out costs and profits. Minor repairs can usually be done by you or your local "Honey-Do list" company . . . but when it comes to major repairs, it makes more sense to use professionals who specialize in what you need done. Here are a few things to keep in mind:

- It seems like obvious advice, but before you do anything, make sure you are clear on exactly what you want to do. Put your ideas down on paper. If you plan to redo the entire house over a period of time, put together an overall list of your renovation projects in order of their importance. Changing plans in the middle of the project will cost money and cause headaches for you as well as the person doing the job.

- There's a reason why contractors put their signs in the lawns of the homes they're working on. Don't be talked into having work done just because the rest of the neighborhood is doing it or because the price is a "bargain." If the deal sounds too good to be true, you know the rest.

- Renovations don't automatically add to the value of your home. You must renovate that which brings immediate value. If it's a major project, get the advice of a professional before the job is started. An architect or engineer can provide expert guidance on design by recommending the most efficient and inexpensive way to achieve your goals.

- Unless you're a qualified do-it-yourselfer, hire a capable contractor recommended by friends and neighbors. You may also be able to get the names of reliable home renovators from your local building-supply store.

- Start by contacting a few companies. Have three or four companies visit the home in person and provide a written estimate. Local firms sometimes have better prices, and dealing with an out-of-town company may be inconvenient if issues arise. If repairs are needed and the company's equipment is far away, you may have trouble enforcing the warranty. Keep it simple and use the professionals who are in your area.

- Don't discount references. Most people don't think you're going to ask for references, so ask. Then be sure to check them. I've found out some crazy things while talking to references. Also, make sure the people they gave you as a reference had similar work done. A guy that fixed a drywall hole really well might not know how to install a water heater.

- If someone has recommended a contractor, find out whether the firm has changed owners. If it has, you may want to call recent references. Follow up on references both from the recent past and further back in time. Sometimes, problems like leaky roofs don't surface for a while.

- Expect to be asked some questions. The company should know your requirements in terms of the quality of materials. If they just say, "Yeah, we'll do it" without asking questions, RUN!

- Keep down payments to a minimum and never, never pay the full amount of the contract before the work is completed. You want to make sure that they finish the job.

- Don't let the contractor talk you into making a large down payment "to pay for materials." That is a material lie! Respectable firms should have enough credit or money in the bank to buy the materials they need.

- You may want to consider arranging your own financing rather than agreeing to payments with a contractor. You not only save on interest charges, but you also control payments to the contractor in case of trouble. If you are getting financing, shop for credit carefully.

- Never sign a blank contract. When you are ready to sign a contract, make sure all the prices are broken down and that the materials and work specifications are clear. Always get a written contract before the work begins and make sure it includes the name and address of the contractor and their insurance information.

- Make sure you ask about the warranty, and that it is clearly spelled out in writing. Warranties take on a life all their own, right after you pay for them.

- There are several organizations that may have information on whether the contractor you're considering is reputable and reliable. These include local building inspectors, chambers of commerce, and Better Business Bureaus.

(i) Since you don't own the property yet, schedule all estimates on one day so that it minimizes inconveniences to the owners. You do not want to be having a different contractor there every day for bids—that will cause added stress to both of you!

You can find more valuable information on this topic in Chapters 16 and 27.

Estimating Holding Costs

Working with just the purchase price and the market selling price is simply not enough to make an informed decision on whether a property will be a sound investment. You must know both the holding and closing costs.

Holding Costs

When real estate investors purchase property, their main goal is to sell the property for a profit. But the investor also must consider the money needed to pay out before the home is sold. Known as carrying costs, holding costs include the purchase price and deduct operating income to come to an estimated figure.

You must carefully consider holding costs when thinking about an investment. Without calculating this cost, an uninformed investor could be faced with a disastrous situation. It doesn't matter how much you can make on selling a home if you can't keep it up until it's sold.

Pay close attention to estimated carrying costs before investing in a property. It's not just the payment. Carrying costs include operating expenses, mortgage payments, utilities, and the marketing costs of the property.

For example, let's say you've got the following expenses (all figures are monthly):

Mortgage payment (PI)	$1,745
Property taxes	$ 417
Insurance	$ 187
Utilities (electric, gas, water, sewer)	$ 150
Advertising	$ 300
Total	$2,799 per month

On a $250,000 property, you are spending just over 1% of the property value per month. In just four months, that will be $11,196 out of your pocket. That is why you must plan in advance to reduce the holding costs as much as possible.

Be ready to execute your repair and renovation plan the day you close. Have contractors lined up and stick to a tight schedule. Time costs money!

Before purchasing an investment property, analyze the carrying costs over a six-month period by starting with the sale price and then deducting associated costs such as:

- Purchase closing costs
- Clean up and decoration of the property
- Mortgage repayments
- Taxes
- Insurance
- Resale broker commissions
- Resale closing cost

Take the purchase price, plus the carrying costs, and the total of the two should be deducted from the resale price of the property in order to get an estimation of the profit margin.

First and foremost, real estate investors need to know what to expect from holding costs when looking for an investment property. While these costs are important to factor, the savvy investor will always be able to creatively come up with solutions to decrease costs, or find ways to make extra income from the property to make it more profitable—and do it fast!

Assessing the Homeowner's Options

It is vital that you gather a solid understanding of how desperate a situation is. Has the homeowner tried everything? Have they tried refinancing, savings, family, friends, loans, selling other assets? Make sure when you enter a situation that you are the last resort. Last resorts are usually taken when there is nothing else next in line to do. You want to be early to the deal, but late as to the homeowner's options. Once they are out of choices, you need to calculate what you're willing to pay for their equity.

What Do You Pay?

As I've stated, it's always helpful to find out why the seller is selling; however, you might not be able to obtain that information because the listing agent may refuse to tell you, or the seller will play games. But you can gather information without relying on the listing agent's cooperation. Here are some things to consider as you try to figure out the seller's true motives. Their motives can give you a good idea on exactly how to negotiate, and where to start your pricing. When trying to figure out what to pay also get the following information:

- Determine the market.
- Find out how much the seller paid.
- Determine the seller's mortgage balance.
- Examine comparable sales.
- Analyze list-price to sales-price ratios.
- Check square-footage cost estimates.
- Ask for the home's history and the number of days it has been on the market.

Negotiating a deal with a young single mother one time, I finally hit on the true motivation behind the sale—she wanted to get enough money to fly back home to Brazil to be with her family. Once I knew that, I used my frequent flyer miles to get her and her son one-way tickets—and I had a deal. Of course the flights weren't scheduled until *after* closing!

Here are some scenarios that will affect your offer:

- *Vacant properties:* Vacant properties have tons of risk associated with them, and should be discounted right from the word go, given the empty rooms, broken windows, and the absence of "personality." Buyers can assume the owner has secured an additional mortgage on another property, or at least found another home. This means they need to unload their house quickly. Vacant properties are often abused by squatters, vandalism, drug use, rodents, deferred maintenance, overgrown landscape, pipe erosion, prostitution, on and on. All of this equals a lower price. In these situations, my offer will reflect that the owner will get nothing for their equity.

- *Occupied properties:* Occupied homes can also be an indicator of lower prices. If one spouse has taken a new job and the remaining family member must stay in the home until it is sold, it creates motivation to move the household. Although an occupied home may seem stable, the truth may very well be the opposite. A beautiful home can cover up a multitude of stress. On these properties, I start my offer at about 30 to 35 percent of equity, but never more than 50 percent—there's just not enough profit in the deal otherwise.

- *Trashed properties:* In these cases, you can pretty much assume the seller is very motivated. The seller either has to invest in extensive repairs or sell the house "as is." Trashed homes are probably not appreciating in value. It may just be "cosmetic" problems, but I recommend a low offer. Then stick to your guns with little flexibility. Remember, in a bad market when homes aren't selling you have the ultimate advantage.

I am trying to buy homes at 50 percent or less of the owner's equity, by any means necessary. The worse the situation, the slower the market, the more time the house has been up for sale, the worse it looks, the deeper I discount the property.

CHAPTER 19

Negotiating with Property Owners

Half the battle of successful real estate investing is getting a property owner to nibble at your offer. Understanding the rules of negotiation is your opportunity to seal the deal and bring home the prize. How you respond at this point will determine whether you go home triumphant—or left imagining what might have been.

In this chapter, I walk you through the rules of real estate negotiation and lay out a simple—yet attainable—road map for building a robust real estate portfolio.

Six Rules of Negotiation

If the concept of banging your head against a brick wall appeals to you, skip this chapter. However, if reaping the rewards of your efforts is more palatable, let me walk you through six golden negotiation tips that will have a dramatic impact on your results and put you well on the path to being in the top income tax bracket for the rest of your life. The six rules of negotiation that you need to learn are:

1. *Stay professional and nonconfrontational.* When you're in the middle of intensive negotiations, human nature is to get emotional and take things personally. The key to winning at the negotiation game is to maintain your cool at all times, stick to substance, and be obviously patient.

2. *Don't believe everything you hear.* Motivated sellers will occasionally embellish or even tell a bold-faced lie. It's highly unlikely that their nose will grow, but be prepared with a camera in the event that it does!

3. *Place emotional items in the deal that you wouldn't mind negotiating away.* Don't be afraid to offer emotional treats that don't mean much to you and won't cost much money. Motivated sellers are frequently motivated by things that you and I might laugh at, but due to their dire financial circumstances

they might find these items compelling enough to say yes. Try to get to the root of the seller's issues. Once after negotiating for six hours, it dawned on me that the seller kept saying, "I need a vacation, I wish I could get away." I had received a coupon from one of the finest vacation spots only two hours away. A weekend that would normally cost $800 would only cost me $200. I offered to send the seller there, *after* the deal was done, and immediately things got easier.

4. *Stay conversational.* Talking to your prospect and not at them is always a winner. Keep in mind that you are trying to purchase the property, but never forget that you're dealing with a human being with real thoughts, fears, and emotions.

5. *Negotiate face-to-face with the owner.* Don't negotiate with attorneys or other intermediaries.

6. *Present your offer to all owners, not one at a time.* If all owners aren't present at the same time, don't engage in negotiation. Make sure all principals are in the room. It's a dangerous tactic to get roped into letting one of the owners give your proposal to the other owner without the benefit of your full and complete explanation. If you miss somebody, something will get lost in the translation.

Before You Start

You have to wake up with yourself every day and occasionally look in the mirror. As tempting as it might be to tell what you perceive to be a little white lie or to embellish certain details, resist the temptation at all costs. It can only hurt you. It's not honest and not ethical. Maintain a high standard in negotiations and in life. Honesty isn't just a moral position; it's the best business strategy.

Image is everything when you're negotiating with a distressed property owner. While you don't want to go completely over the top by over dressing for the occasion, you also don't want to show up in blue jeans and a T-shirt. Look the part of a successful, professional real estate investor. Simple, clean, and groomed speaks volumes in your favor!

It's important that you realize most distressed property owners don't want to have to sell the property to you. In many cases, they love their home and they would like to be able to continue living there. However, sometimes their circumstances make that difficult—or impossible.

For them to feel comfortable in a negotiating environment, they're going to have to enjoy negotiating with you. If you're pleasant, engaging, and attentive, they will be more likely to enjoy the interaction with you. If they enjoy interacting with you, they'll be more willing to listen to you, to hear what you have to say, and to do what you want to do. You must strike a tender balance between understanding and being personal. Don't get personal; simply be understanding while pushing the deal forward.

It's imperative that you allow the property owner to maintain his or her dignity. If you talk down to them, raise your voice, or belittle them, your deal is dead. They'll tune you out, shut you down, and they will become increasingly unwilling to listen to your points.

While it's not necessary for you to pretend that you work for the Department of Homeland Security, you do need to verify the identity of the party or parties with whom you are negotiating. I can't tell you how many times imposters had taken a real estate investor for a ride by pretending to be someone that they weren't. It only takes a second to verify that you're speaking with the right people. Trust but verify! I loved it when Reagan used that line.

One of the most important aspects of negotiation is that you follow the KISS (Keep it simple stupid!) method. A wise man developed this technique and as a result successfully purchased billions of dollars worth of residential real estate with nothing but a handshake and goodwill.

The more problems you can solve, the better off you're going to be. Motivated sellers need cash. The simple truth is that they are selling their home because they can no longer afford to keep it. If you can appeal to some of the emotional triggers that will drive them toward making a decision, they'll be more likely to listen to you.

Although the owners of a home that you're trying to buy are experiencing severe financial distress, they won't be motivated by just anything you throw at them. However, they will be more likely to be swayed by financial considerations. They may very well need financial assistance in order to move out of the property and get on with their lives.

If you can provide them with tools that will help solve real problems that they are currently experiencing, you're likely to get ahead. Here are a few financial incentives you can throw their way that won't cost you much, but could make the difference between a deal and a "Thanks for stopping by":

- Cash (Only when the deal is "done," and *never* before the close!)
- Moving expenses
- Rent and security deposit
- Moving van

Regardless of the level of their financial needs, never pay for anything until they've signed on the dotted line and have moved out of the house. If you give up cash without requiring them to leave, there's a possibility that they may not want to.

Striking a Deal

As tempting as it might be, don't negotiate with anyone other than the owner. I really don't have a problem with the seller having a personal representative there, but when they have multiple spokespeople, everything I say is met with sarcasm.

As I have previously indicated, the owner is motivated to sell because they're experiencing severe financial problems. Be certain to stress the fact that accepting your offer will not require them to spend any cash. If they're already hurting financially, it doesn't make sense that they would be interested in incurring any additional financial pain.

A major problem novice real estate investors have is they begin talking and don't know when to stop. Pay attention to what is being said and listen to the owner of the property because they will typically choreograph exactly what they want, need, and expect. Listen carefully, and when the time is right, be willing to shut up.

You may think you're at a crossroad in the negotiations because you've given all you can afford to give based on the numbers. Silence is awkward, uncomfortable, and human nature almost always compels us to open our mouth and say something—anything—to fill the time until someone breaks the silence. If you want to win at a negotiation game, you have to be willing to be quiet and put your prospects on the defensive. If they believe that you are about to walk away from the table, they'll be more likely to seriously consider what you've been saying, as well as what the implications are of not giving you what you want.

They may very well decide not to give you what you want. That's actually okay, because if that's the case, you'll be no worse off than you were when you came in. You didn't own their property when you arrived and if you walk out the door without it you won't have less money than you did when you walked in the door. In addition, you'll be a little richer for the experience.

This is a sample script that can be used during your negotiations with the homeowner.

HOMEOWNER: Hello.

YOU: Hello Mr./Mrs. _____, Thank you for meeting with me today. I would like to jump right in and let you know my thoughts on how best to push this transaction forward, but first could you please talk to me about some of the things you feel need to happen to push this deal through today?

HOMEOWNER: [While the homeowner is speaking, you are listening intently, forward-leaning body position and occasionally taking notes; eye-contact is crucial]

YOU: I hear you loud and clear and I think we are going to be able to meet your needs today. I think my solution meets all of your concerns and that this transaction will allow you and your family to move forward in a positive manner toward bigger and better things. This is a difficult situation for you, but I can tell you from experience, things will get better and hopefully today will be the start of that new direction.

YOU: [This is where you change your body position to lean back in a slightly more relaxed stance as you lay out the details of your offer.]

I'd like to make two additional points:

1. Only provide debt relief to the owners of vacant properties. No cash. You don't want to have to provide relocation expenses if they're already out of the property they are planning on selling.

2. I am willing to provide debt relief as well as relocation expenses if the owner is still living in the property. It's an excellent means of getting them to vacate the property quickly and get them to cooperate.

Don't forget, you don't get what you deserve; you get what you ask for! Anything you want added in the deal must be verbalized and written into the agreement!

Negotiating Uphill

You're likely to experience any number of objections from the owners of the property. Keep in mind, objections are normal and an expected part of all negotiations. It will be an uphill battle, but by addressing some of the core financial, emotional, and psychological needs of the owner, you're more likely to be able to meet those needs. The owner of the property might object to not receiving more cash out of the deal. Are they just being greedy or is there an actual reason that they need more money? That's the sort of question you need to identify when you're negotiating. A simple no tells you nothing. If you find out why, you increase the likelihood of turning that no into a yes by addressing the core need. The core need may be satisfied without cash so keep pressing for details.

There are certain situations that don't lend themselves to a positive negotiating outcome. For instance, if you're negotiating with a couple that is divorcing, that situation can be painful and difficult. Not only do they have many memories together in the home, but they are contemplating dissolving their marriage while walking away from four walls that have heard some special conversations. Times like this are extremely emotional, so be vigilant and aware that it can get very difficult very quickly. Stay calm and be patient.

There is one negotiating situation that I adamantly refuse to participate in. Take it from me, any time you're dealing with what I call "flakes," you're better off walking away immediately. What do I mean by flakes? I'm referring to drug addicts, alcoholics, and the like. While I don't place the mentally impaired in the flake category, I will not negotiate with them for obvious reasons.

Years ago, I was negotiating with a man who was trying to sell me his home. He was behind in his mortgage payment and the bank was about to foreclose. After talking with the bank and learning more about his situation, I discovered that he had the money to bring his mortgage current, but instead he opted to buy drugs with the money.

Because of his actions, he was willing to give up his home and force his family to move. All for drugs. He was out of his right mind and unable to make a proper decision.

Never negotiate with people who are incapable of being held responsible for their own actions. If you buy a property from someone like that, a judge could very easily reverse the decision. It's not worth it.

I've given you plenty of information with which to form the basis for a successful property negotiation. Take this information and put it into play. In very short order, you will be building a powerful, thick real estate investing portfolio.

Money is waiting for you, go get it! But first, let's get our share out of the lender's pocket.

CHAPTER 20

Negotiating with Lenders and Lienholders

A deal is finally within your grasp. You can feel it! It took a lot of work to get to this point, so don't lose sight of your goal at the eleventh hour. Lender and lienholder negotiations can be some of your most challenging, invigorating, and rewarding experiences. Maintaining your composure and being able to navigate through this sea of uncertainty is critical to closing the deal.

In this chapter, I demonstrate all of the important tactics you need to understand in order to keep a lucrative deal from slipping through your fingers, and your wallet!

Understanding State Lien Laws

Every state has different lien laws. Understanding yours and how they work will make or break your deal. Take the time to read through the legal mumbo-jumbo and get to the least common denominator. Not only will you feel smarter, but you'll be able to answer just about any question someone might choose to pose about liens. There are numerous resources available in bookstores, public libraries, and through a variety of government agencies explaining your state's lien laws.

Liens are *always* negotiable. The only ones I have had a hard time with are state and federal tax liens and property tax liens. Everything else can be brought down—after all, they will be worthless once the foreclosure goes through.

i I have even had success with IRS liens. It never hurts to ask—the worst that will happen is they say no.

Senior Versus Junior Lienholders

There are two categories of lienholders: senior and junior. Senior lienholders are your primary lienholders, sometimes known as first position lienholders. Junior lienholders would be represented by second and third mortgage holders.

When a mortgage loan has gone into default, trustees are required to send a notice of default to all lienholders. Various state laws require that all subordinate lienholders be notified of the impending foreclosure action. However, all lienholders are not created equally. Some are not contacted at all.

If the work was completed within the last 90 days, the lien may not have made it through the system yet. If a contractor is unlicensed, the lien can be nullified. Unlicensed contractors are not permitted to file legitimate liens.

Whenever the senior lienholder opts to initiate foreclosure proceedings against a property owner, all junior lienholders are listed as defendants on the ensuing legal action.

Types of Liens

There are two basic types of liens that can be filed on the public record in a real estate transaction: judgment and consensual. A judgment lien is the kind that is filed in the event that a property owner loses a lawsuit. For instance, if you owe a medical bill that you don't pay for some reason and you are sued, a judgment lien could be sought and approved by a judge. This type of lien will not be released until it has been satisfied. Many times these liens can be forgotten and stay on record for years only to resurface when the home is about to be sold.

The second type of lien, a consensual lien, is one that is filed with the full knowledge and permission of the property owner. A good example of this type of lien would be a mortgage filing. Yes, your mortgage is actually a lien! This type of lien stays on the public record until the mortgage has been paid in full.

Common Types of Subordinate Liens

In the event of foreclosure, the primary lienholder (who is the one usually filing the action) gets paid first, followed by the junior lienholders (if any). While anyone with a legitimate claim can file a lien, the six most common examples after the primary are as follows:

1. *Junior lien holders* (second and third position lienholders): These lienholders are typically represented by mortgage lenders.

2. *Judgment liens:* In the event that a property owner is sued and is unsuccessful in defending against the lawsuit, a judgment lien can be entered in favor of the prevailing party.

3. *Mechanic's or builder's liens:* These liens are filed in response to your failure to pay a bill for some kind of a service. For example, if you were to have your car worked on or you had some kind of remodeling work performed that you failed to pay for, the mechanic or the contractor (if licensed) would be permitted to file a mechanic's or builder's lien against your property. You don't want to have a licensed handyman file a lien on your house!

   i   Usually a lien of this type has to be filed within six months of the work being completed, sometimes less. If not, they have no claim. Check your state guidelines.

4. *State and federal welfare, medical, and child support liens:* In the event that a property owner is receiving any kind of welfare benefits and receives an intentional or accidental overpayment, or for any reason is found to have received benefits to which they are not entitled, they would be required to repay those funds. In addition, unpaid medical bills or child support can also result in a lien being filed.

5. *Local, state, and federal tax liens:* If a property owner has an unpaid tax bill at the local, state, or federal level, the appropriate government agency is authorized to file a tax lien in order to recoup the money owed.

6. *Utility liens:* In the event of an unpaid utility bill, such as electric, gas, or water, the corresponding utility company would be permitted to file a lien to enforce payment of the bill. Utility liens follow the property, which means that until the bill has been satisfied, the utility would have the right to deny service to the current owner.

Verifying Liens

Before moving forward with a property purchase, you should verify the existence of all judgment liens. This is actually a simple process, which just requires a visit to the county courthouse or a telephone call. In addition, this information is sometimes available online.

In the event that an unlicensed contractor has a lien on the property, you can petition the court to have that lien removed. There is not a huge financial cost involved, but this is a step that must be taken. File a notice with the court, and send a warning letter to the contractor. That will usually make them back down. I actually had an $8,000 lien removed once because a brick contractor was not licensed to do the work.

In order for title of a property to pass, all legitimate liens must be satisfied. It doesn't matter if the amount of the lien is inconsequential or massive.

Removing a Federal Lien

In order to have a federal tax lien legally removed, the taxpayer will be required to sign an IRS Form 8821, which is a power of attorney assignment form, and gives you the right to obtain their tax information and settle or dispute the lien. Trust me, the homeowner won't do it himself.

Bankruptcy cases can be researched at the county courthouse, in newspapers, and sometimes online. Go to www.13DataCenter.com, which is run by the U.S. Department of Justice and contains bankruptcy records.

Fraudulent Liens

Although most states have statutes against fraudulent liens being filed, the practice does occur. There had been any number of high-profile cases of judges having their personal property attached by members of militia groups and other misinformed or vengeance minded taxpayers.

In the event that this does happen, and you discover it in the process of doing your due diligence prior to purchasing a property, you can notify the offending party by certified mail that you are going to require them to remove the fraudulent lien or face slander of title charges.

Contesting a Lien

In order to prepare the property for purchase, you can contest the validity of a lien in court. The lienholder will be notified that the validity of the lien is being challenged. They're given an opportunity to explain the lien and to prove its legitimacy. If they're unable to provide evidence that it is a legitimate lien or if the lienholder fails to respond to the notice, the lien will be released.

Finding Nonexistent Lienholders

People disappear! Occasionally, you'll discover that a lien has been filed against the property by someone whom you are unable to track down or by a seemingly nonexistent person or entity. In these situations, you'll be required to make a diligent effort to locate the party responsible for filing the lien. If you're still unable to locate them, you can file a quiet title action and, after the appropriate waiting period with no response, the lien can be removed.

Due to the number of subprime mortgage loan defaults, a number of prominent institutional bank lenders and mortgage companies have ceased to exist. If the lender was acquired by another lending institution, you would have to deal with them. However, the lenders are so overwhelmed with bad loans on their books that they're frequently unable to respond to a quiet title action in time to prevent the lien from being released. *Question*

Discounting Liens

Do you like to save money? If so, you'll enjoy this money-saving strategy. You can approach almost any lienholder and attempt to get a discount in exchange for payment of the lien. Every creditor is different, but frequently if you approach a lienholder and explain to them that you are considering purchasing the property, they'll be willing to discount the amount owed—sometimes by as much as 90 percent. While this strategy doesn't always work, it's certainly worth the effort. In challenging economic times this strategy is in your favor, so use it!

I'd again like to point out two groups who will adamantly oppose any attempt to discount monies owed to them: State and federal governments. Because they are government agencies, they're unable to accept less than is owed under any circumstances.

Lienholder Worksheets

You can use the handy lienholder worksheet in Figure 20.1 in order to calculate the value and position of each lien and what you would like to offer to make the deal work. Each of the lienholders will want to make sure everyone is being treated fairly though, so don't play favorites!

Contacting Lienholders

Keep in mind that the foreclosure clock is always ticking, so time is on your side. Subordinate lienholders are understandably resistant to the idea of offering or accepting a discount in exchange for releasing a lien, but they really have very few choices available to them. Imagine that you are playing a basketball game and

Lienholder Worksheet

Lienholder: _____

Contact Name: _____

E-mail Address: _____

Phone Number: _____ Fax Number: _____

Address: _____

_____

E-mail Address: _____

Type of Lien: _____ Lien Amount: $ _____

Date Recorded: _____ Libor/Page: _____

Principal Bal Left: $_____ Total Payoff: $ _____

Payoff x _____% (30/40/50%)   = Payoff Offer: $ _____

Counter offer: $ _____

Comments:

Amount Approved $_____ Confirmation Letter_____ Satisfaction_____

FIGURE 20.1   Lienholder Worksheet

(date)

(lienholder name)
(address)
(city, state, zip)

Dear (name),

It has come to my attention that you have a lien in the amount of $(amount) recorded against the property located at (property address) currently owed by (seller name).

As you are probably aware by now, a foreclosure action has been filed by (senior lender), and the public auction date is scheduled for (date). As you also know, if (seller name) is unable to bring his payments current by that date, which is highly unlikely at this point, then your lien will be extinguished and you will receive nothing.

Presently, I am negotiating with (seller name) to possibly purchase the property prior to the foreclosure auction. The only way I can get the numbers to work, and prevent the foreclosure from wiping out the amount you are owed, is to have all the subordinate lienholders discount their positions by 60 percent.

I am willing to offer you $(amount) to purchase your lien as total settlement, in exchange for a signed satisfaction of lien. If this is agreeable, I can send you a cashier's check along with the form via overnight delivery.

I know this is difficult, but I believe that something is better than nothing, and want to help prevent your lien position from becoming totally worthless.

If this offer is acceptable, or if you have any questions, please feel free to call me at (your phone). Thank you for your consideration, and I look forward to working with you in getting this resolved.

Sincerely,

(your name)

 FIGURE 20.2 Sample Letter to Subordinate Lienholders

you're winning by one point. You have possession of the ball and the clock is winding down. All you have to do is run the clock out and you win. If the primary lienholder forecloses on the owner of the property, all junior lienholders will be wiped out. That means they'll get nothing. As a result of this, they are in the unenviable position of accepting a little bit of something or walking away with nothing.

This is very, very important for you to understand as you enter into negotiations. You must know who has what to lose and who is motivated the least. A clear understanding of this will shape everything you say and do.

Because you would like to complete the purchase, you really do want the lienholder to give you a discount. However, if they reject your original offer, you have two winning choices available to you: you can either make a counteroffer or offer them a short sale. *Question*

You won't know whether they'll accept your counteroffer or offer of a short sale until or unless you try. You will be surprised at what answers a simple question can bring. The key is knowing what questions to ask.

If you like, you could give the lienholder a strict time limit in which to accept your offer, and you could stand in front of their office holding a sign counting down the minutes until they lose everything. Probably not the best strategy, but I'm just trying to remind you that in this case you truly do have the upper hand. Chances are very high at this point that they will realize how few options they have. Given a choice between receiving nothing and receiving very little, most creditors at this point would be ecstatic to see anything.

Figure 20.2 on the previous page is a letter I use to contact lienholders to start the negotiating process. It is amazing how well it works!

If they say no, then make a counteroffer! Ask them what they *will* accept to settle this, all the time reminding them that they are about to get nothing if the foreclosure proceeds.

A little prodding will usually do the trick. Next, we need to negotiate with any attorneys and trustees involved to get them to sign off on our deal. Let's look at that process.

CHAPTER 21

Negotiating with Attorneys and Trustees

At this point, it's time to get this deal done. A lot of work has gone into locating the property and negotiating with the property owner. If the deal falls apart at this point, the real loser will be the homeowner.

Although you will lose a potentially lucrative real estate investment, the property owner stands to lose the few remaining crumbs of his or her dignity, not to mention his or her credit rating. This is where you have to really dig in and ask yourself, "How bad do I want it?"

In this chapter, I show you how to negotiate with attorneys and trustees. As a part of your resources, it wouldn't be a bad idea to become friends with an attorney or trustee who can mentor your thinking. Attorneys think differently, as there's always a but or a hedge in every statement. Use this understanding of style to help your negotiation tactics.

Loan Loss Mitigation

Depending on the financial institution, the actual office may have a different name, but the end result is the same. The loss mitigation office is charged with minimizing mortgage loan losses. Don't go through the regular customer service number, as they are trained to say no to settling the claim.

Right now, thanks to the mortgage meltdown that started in 2008, housing and credit markets are in turmoil, so they have an extremely difficult job. The loan loss mitigation department has to try to get as close to full value as they can without losing money. Unfortunately for the bank, the odds of this happening are not good.

In order to increase your chances of successfully negotiating a sale or short sale, you have to get in front of the right person. There are a number of strategies for doing this. You can play guessing games, which I don't recommend, or you can pick up the telephone and make a call.

There is an art to asking questions. Before making the call to fish for information, place yourself on the other side and think, "What would I want to hear that would cause me to help somebody?" People answer phones all day, giving script answers, and putting other calls on hold. Be nice; you'd be surprised how rarely they hear "Good Morning."

Courtesy almost always helps. Try it! Thank the person for the information before they give it. I have found this helps a lot. The person almost feels obligated to validate your trust in them by helping you get to the right person.

If the loan you're calling about is a Federal Housing Administration (FHA) loan, there's a special set of circumstances and rules that come into play. A normal conforming loan can be had for whatever you can convince the bank to agree to—and right now the chance has never been better of getting great terms. But, as I said, an FHA loan is an especially challenging situation today.

So what happens if you try to do a short sale on an FHA loan? First of all, you've got to get your numbers right. If you try to get the loan mitigation department to accept a short payoff of less than 82 percent of full market value, you're out of luck. It simply won't happen because the federal rules are set in stone. For a copy of the procedures and forms, go to the special download on my web site at www.ChipCummings.com/CashingIn.

Negotiating with Lenders

Lenders have a team of professionals, including legal attack dogs. These professionals get paid to foreclose on houses, and they do tons of them. These attorneys are not paid to negotiate with the homeowner, work things out, hold hands, or counsel them. They get paid to foreclose, that's it. They have absolutely no incentive or time for anything else. Understand this and act accordingly!

There is still powerful motivation for you to try to get the lender to accept a short sale. There is something in it for you and the seller will get to walk away from their home without having to face the indignity of being foreclosed upon. However, the lender isn't in the business of losing money. Neither are you!

The lender had one single goal in mind: to try to force the homeowner into a corner where he will be left with no choice but to reinstate the loan. If that can't be done, the lender is willing to foreclose and push the homeowner out into the street as quickly as possible to minimize their losses.

(i) Lenders can be very shortsighted. I went back and forth with a lender, starting at $93,000, only have them counter at $169,000 (almost the full value of the loan). I countered back at $96,000, and they come back at $165,000. The deal didn't come together, and three weeks later they had the property listed on the market for $89,000!

When the Numbers Don't Work

Sometimes despite your best efforts, the deal you're working begins looking like a dog. All you can do is negotiate to the best of your ability and hope the lender will see the light. Fortunately, the one thing you have going for you right now is that the current housing situation has lenders running scared and more willing than ever to make a deal.

Every time a homeowner falls into foreclosure, the lender is required to place between $600,000 to $800,000 aside to cover potential loan losses. It doesn't take ~~Question~~ long for the lender to grow weary of setting these funds aside and having them tied up indefinitely.

Your best bet is to be professional, honest, and show integrity. Although the lender doesn't have much incentive to go along with a short sale, they have even less incentive not to.

The question that needs to be answered is this: Is the lender willing to foreclose and incur huge carrying costs just to make a point and teach a homeowner a lesson? I really don't think so. They aren't teachers, they are businesspeople.

The numbers won't always work out in your favor, so all you can do is hope for the best and negotiate to the utmost of your ability. Even when you think a deal is dead there is always an off-chance that the lender will change his mind when he realizes he's better off with part of the pie than none at all.

Russell Gray, a real estate investor and co-host of the syndicated radio show "The Real Estate Guys," indicates that the one thing that most novice investors do wrong is continue to pound on the numbers. "If they don't work, or you're talking to the wrong person, move on. The attorney will do what the lender tells them to do, so stay focused!"

Keep your head high, stay professional, and continue talking with the lender for as long as possible. By doing so, you increase the opportunity for a successful short sale and you keep hope alive for a homeowner desperately in need of a solution to his or her foreclosure turmoil.

CHAPTER 22

Negotiating and Securing Short Sale Transactions

Once a homeowner is "upside-down" in their home mortgage, there is an opportunity for you to prosper while helping them out of a tough situation. Everybody wins!

Temporary market fluctuations, life situations, and just weird stuff can force homeowners to sell their properties through a short sale to avoid foreclosure. Most investors, and even homeowners, walk away from these situations, but this is when your work in locating these properties and your knowledge of the process can bring you big rewards that are well worth your efforts.

Short sales have become a buzzword in the real estate community, but few people know how to negotiate one, let alone how to profit from one.

(i) Here's a simple rule for you as an investor: If the owner has less than 15 percent equity in the property, we look at short sale opportunities. More than 15 percent, we are buying the equity. *Question*

In this chapter, let's focus on the short sale transaction, find out who's involved, and how to get deals done.

What Does "Upside-Down" Mean?

The basic American dream of owning a home is still alive and strong, albeit a little sickly lately. We all want the very best we can afford and to improve our lifestyle over time. Many homeowners have purchased a home that really was at their affordability limit, or even beyond it. They were able to do this using creative lending products that may not have been in their best interest.

Adjustable rate mortgages (ARMs), made larger homes affordable to borrowers when they first purchased by providing low interest rates. Then, at some point, those low rates were preset to adjust upward. The buyers assumed they would continue in their jobs, with pay increases, prosperity, and trips to Disney. Then, when the ARM interest rate went up more than they thought it would, all hell broke loose. Couple that with the fact that their home did not appreciate in value as they expected, possibly even losing value, and a lot of people now owe more on their mortgage than the home is worth in the current market.

With the upward spiraling home valuations of the late 1990s and the early 2000s, many homeowners took out second or even third mortgages to remove equity from their homes to make improvements or to finance other purchases. Now they find that their total loan balances far exceed the current appraised value of their homes. When you can't sell it for enough to cover the amounts owed on the home, you are "upside-down." In other words, your head is under financial water! Recent statistics indicate that at the end of 2008, one in every five properties with a mortgage was upside-down!

Understanding a Short Sale and a Short Pay

When a lender releases a homeowner from their mortgage at anything less than the full amount owed, they are accepting an amount "short" of the agreed-on pay-off. The costs to foreclose on a home can be quite high, with estimates starting at $50,000 in costs on average for the lender. It's not hard to see that the lender might be willing to accept something short of the entire mortgage balance in order to get out of the situation. In a short sale, the homeowner is basically paying a small percentage on each dollar owed.

If the lender proceeds to a foreclosure, it is a legal action, and the time necessary to carry it to completion can be months to more than a year. When the foreclosure sale is over, if the amount received doesn't cover the mortgage, fees, and costs, the lender can file a *deficiency judgment* against the borrower for the difference.

The problem with deficiency judgments is that they are a legal claim on the money, with no indication that they'll actually *receive* it. Further collection actions must be taken, and those can cost the lender even more money. Another drawback is that the lender usually has reserve requirements for nonperforming loans. They must maintain liquid funds to cover these shortfalls. These funds cannot be reinvested or used to generate income. As you can imagine, this isn't a fun position for the lender.

As a result, you can see why a lender might agree to a sale to a qualified buyer for an amount short of the mortgage owed by the homeowner. But, some buyers and homeowners are confused by the terms *short sale* and *short pay*. The difference is simply who gets the home in the short purchase. Let's spell out the differences even further:

- _Short pay:_ In a short pay transaction, the lender allows the homeowner to buy the home for an amount less than they owe. Why would the lender do this? It certainly isn't charity on their part, and the motive is purely financial. One common reason for a short pay transaction is tax liens or other claims on the property that take precedence over the first mortgage. If the lender forecloses on the home, those liens remain and must be paid. A buyer will not be enticed to take them on. In this case, it could net the lender the same amount of money or more by allowing the homeowner to short pay and deal with the liens on their own.

- _Short sale:_ In a short sale, there is a third-party buyer who is willing to purchase the property at an amount that will not satisfy the balance of the loan. The lender may be willing to allow this because the cost and time involved to foreclose on the home would cost them more than the shortfall, or they aren't certain to receive more in a foreclosure sale or auction. They will also avoid the requirement for holding reserves during the foreclosure process. A successful short sale requires that all parties involved see that it is in their best interests, in other words—everybody wins.

The Four Parties Involved

There are actually four parties involved in a short sale transaction. They are:

1. _Property owner:_ Though their credit score is usually impacted the same in a short sale as in a foreclosure, new Fannie Mae rules make the time frame shorter for buying another home if the borrower used a short sale than if they went through a foreclosure. As an investor, this gives you some extra ammunition to motivate the seller into a transaction. They need to look past the current situation and start to think about how to rebuild their financial lives (although it may be hard).

2. _Investor who owns the loan:_ Loans are bought and sold in packages in the financial markets. The investors who own these loans could be pension funds as well as banks. Banks and financial institutions are regulated, and those reserves issues come into play when they have loans that aren't performing. Pension funds and private groups who purchase mortgages also have incentives to get bad loans off the books. They will also have to agree to the short sale.

3. _Servicer who is servicing the loan:_ This is the business or entity who is handling the collection and disbursal of mortgage payments, as well as funds escrowed to pay taxes. Whether they were paid up-front, by ongoing transaction fees, or both, the loan servicer is not interested in continuing to try to collect payments

from a borrower unable to make them. They will be the main party you deal with, but cannot individually sign off on a short sale.

4. *Purchaser buying the property:* This could be you, an investor looking for a great deal on a home purchased below true value. Or maybe it's a home in which you want to live. Either way, buying a home through a short sale can result in instant equity if you understand the process and work through it properly.

Who to Talk to

One of the first questions is: Who do you talk to? Homeowners will not have a clue where to start (or may not even know a short sale is possible), and most real estate agents don't have the expertise or they wait too late. You need to get started early. Consider these questions:

- *Who processes short sale requests?* The servicer (not necessarily the same party as the end lender) is who you need to contact about the possibility of a short sale. They will coordinate the decision as to whether they (including the end investor) want to allow it, and how much of a shortfall they are willing to take.

- *Why don't lenders want to do it?* It's a last resort. Just as the homeowner has made a promise to pay his or her mortgage, the lender has made promises to investors as to their likely return on the funds they invested in mortgages. Settling for an amount short of the expected return is damaging to their credibility with investors, causing formal and informal negative effects on their ability to gather future funds for new mortgages. You've got to show them why a short sale is the best option.

- *Can the borrower pass a hardship test?* The borrower must prove to the lender that they are truly in a hardship situation that makes it impossible to follow through on their mortgage payment commitments. Because the lender is going to take a negative hit for a short sale, they want to be certain that there's no other alternative.

- *Who makes the final decision?* The money for this loan came from an investor. This investor put up the funds with an expectation of a certain return, and he will make the decision as to whether the short sale is in his best interest or not.

- *Who do I contact first?* Start with the loss mitigation department where the borrower is making their payments. Do *not* talk to the customer service folks—you will get nowhere fast. Ask them to send you a short sale request package, and get a contact name, phone number, and e-mail address.

Key Factors for Approval

Obviously, a short sale is a tough decision for the lender, and they will take a very thorough look at the borrower's financial situation. They want to be certain that the borrower is truly in a position that is highly likely to result in a foreclosure if a short sale is not completed. They want to make sure the borrower is officially broke with no possibility of a quick recovery. Will a short sale result in a better financial outcome for the lender than a foreclosure? That's where their primary consideration lies. These are the 10 factors that will decide whether a lender will approve a short sale:

1. Financial condition of the lender, and number of nonperforming loans
2. Loss mitigation policy of lender
3. Loss mitigation authority of the lender servicing the loan
4. Loss mitigation policy of the government agency insuring the loan (if any)
5. Borrowers overall financial condition
6. Current value of the property
7. Cost to put the property back on the market and resell
8. Property's repaired market value
9. Cost of securing and maintaining the property while being resold
10. Cost of marketing and selling the property

Some of these you can control, others you can't. As you will see, your presentation package will focus on the ones you can.

Private Mortgage Insurance Factor

Another possible lifeline for you is Private Mortgage Insurance (PMI)—,which is an insurance policy that covers the lender in case of a default by the borrower. Industry practice has been to require PMI for borrowers with less than a 20 percent equity position at the time the loan is originated. A premium is paid, and the insurer is usually guaranteeing the lender a payment of up to 20 percent of the loan value if the borrower defaults on the loan to cover its losses. This type of insurance makes it possible to have lower interest rates because it lowers the risk to the lender.

Obviously, if PMI is in place for a loan, this will influence whether the lender will accept a short sale, as well as the amount for which they will ultimately settle to try and break even on the loan. The PMI company will also have to sign off on the sale.

Three options exist for the insurer in this situation:

1. Advance the funds to the borrower to cure the default and reinstate the loan.

2. Purchase the loan from the lender and do a loan modification.

3. Approve the short sale and reimburse the lender for any losses up to the coverage amount.

Recently, there have been more and more PMI companies stepping up to the plate and either giving the borrower cash to stay in the home, or approving a short sale to limit their losses. Knowing that there is PMI coverage gives you an advantage in negotiating a short sale, so use it! The coverage amount is that much less than the lender can settle for and still break even on the loan and costs in avoiding foreclosure. In other words, they're covered for some of the loss! I love these types of situations since the bank is insured for that loss, and most homeowners don't even realize the advantage this gives them in negotiating the short sale.

Steps in a Short Sale Transaction

Before you undertake the process of short sale negotiations with a lender, it is critical you understand the steps in the process, who is responsible for what, and what documentation will be needed to get the lender's acceptance. These 11 steps will be necessary to get a successful short sale approved and to the closing table:

1. *Situation analysis*: After evaluating the value and condition of the property and the outstanding balance on the lien(s), it is determined that the property is upside-down, and a sale would not pay off the lender.

2. *Get permission:* You will need to obtain a signed borrower authorization form (see Figure 14.3) to make contact with the lender. They won't speak to you without it.

3. *Contact lender:* Contact the loss mitigation department or person listed on the letters from the lender to the homeowner. Try to make initial contact while the borrower is right there—it's easier in case the lender wants to receive verbal authorization as well.

4. *Write hardship letter:* The borrower will have to write a detailed letter regarding his or her situation. Must include compelling reasons for lender to do a short sale, and that the alternative is foreclosure or bankruptcy.

5. *Get repair estimates:* Get three estimates from licensed contractors as to the costs to bring the property up to marketable condition.

6. *Supporting documentation:* Put together supporting documents to prove the hardship and paint the picture for the lender. These include financial statements, paycheck stubs, bank statements, tax returns, credit reports, medical bills, divorce decree, and so on.

7. *Purchase agreement:* Next step is to agree with the homeowner as to the purchase price and payoff amounts to the lender. The borrower should net zero, or the lender will not go along with the short sale.

8. *Submit package:* Submit the short sale package to the lender demonstrating that this is the best solution for them. (See list for what to include.)

9. *Lender evaluation:* Lender will get a broker price opinion, which is similar to a drive-by appraisal to support value and situation.

10. *Negotiate with lender:* You may go back and forth a couple of times. Develop rapport with the loss mitigation specialist, but they will need to get approval from the servicer of the loan as well.

11. *Close the deal:* Lender will issue an approval letter to accept a short payoff, which will only be valid for up to 30 days. Close the deal quickly.

Short Sale Package Checklist

If you locate a seller who has begun the process on their own, they may have gathered some or all of the items necessary for the short sale process. They may be working with a realtor who has guided them as well. If not, then you, as a buyer, will need to shepherd them through the gathering of information and production of documents for the submission of a short sale package to the lender. What should be included?

The presentation of the package is one of the key factors in getting your short sale approved. The following are items that should be included in the package to a lender (in order):

1. Cover letter of proposal from investor (see Figure 22.1)
2. Completed lender's short sale application package
3. Borrower hardship letter
4. Borrower supporting documentation:
   a. Credit report
   b. Financial statement
   c. Paycheck stubs

(date)
(lienholder name)
(address)
(city, state, zip)

RE: Mortgage Loan #_____;

Borrower Name: _____

Property Address: _____

Dear (name),

Enclosed you will find a complete "short sale" package for the loan and borrower listed above. After careful consideration and calculations, I would propose a purchase price of the property for $(amount). This offer is based upon the following:

1. The borrower is insolvent, and currently has insufficient assets or resources to bring this loan current. Public auction of the lien is imminent, resulting in increased costs and deteriorating property conditions.

2. Research of comparable properties in the area, the current "as-is" value is estimated to be between $(value1) and $(value2). I have enclosed a list of comparable sales for your reference.

3. Estimates from several licensed contractors (attached) indicate that the repair costs to bring the property back up to marketable resale condition are approximately $(repairs1) to $(repairs2).

4. There is an increased supply of homes on the market at the present time, resulting in a longer than normal sales cycle, and

5. Property values in the neighborhood and surrounding areas have decreased substantially over the past 12–18 months.

As you review the package, you will note that it is structured so that borrower will not be receiving any cash at closing. I have thoroughly reviewed the borrowers' situation, have had several inspections completed, and believe that this is the best situation for you, resulting in the least financial loss possible.

I have liquid funds available for this transaction, and upon your acceptance, am in a position to close within 24–48 hours.

Thank you for your consideration, and please feel free to contact me at (number), or by e-mail (e-mail) if you have any questions. I look forward to your response.

Sincerely,

(your name)

FIGURE 22.1   Sample Short Sale Letter to Lender

    d. Bank statements

    e. Tax returns

    f. Unemployment compensation verification

    g. Medical bills and/or reports

    h. Divorce decree

    i. Any other documentation to support the hardship letter

5. Purchase agreement

6. Short sale transaction worksheet (see Figure 22.2)

7. HUD-1 closing statement

8. List of required repairs

9. Contractor estimates

10. List of other properties for sale or that have sold in the area

11. Pictures of the property—inside and out!

One of the most important items in the short sale presentation package is the basic short sale letter to the lender. It is a cover letter stating the insolvency of the borrower, and listing all the items that are included in the package. It comes from you—the investor/purchaser.

We want to show the lender that the buyer is no longer able to make the payments, and that foreclosure is the last and only option. Market data should be included and mentioned in this letter as verification that the market value of the property has dropped. This shows the lender that they stand to lose in a foreclosure action because they can't sell the property for what is owed on it.

Basically, as shown in our example letter in Figure 22.1, we want to give the lender a summary of the facts and situation, and list the supporting documents included.

Your job is to document the borrower's and the property's situation to convince the lender this is their best alternative. Chances are, the lender has never been to the property, and are only looking at numbers on a screen along with hundreds of other cases. You have to make an impression.

Establishing value is another key. Real estate and foreclosure expert Terri Murphy suggests you get a broker price opinion (known as a BPO) and submit it with the package to help establish independent value. Murphy's suggestion is to use the broker price opinion and the Short Sale Worksheet to clearly show how far the homeowner is upside down in the home.

A broker price opinion will be ordered by the lender, but it shows you are committed to the deal if you get one up front.

"I've seen a huge increase in the demand for broker price opinions, with about 20 percent tied specifically to short sales" indicates Giff Cummings, a 20-year veteran real estate agent in California with Creative Real Estate Services. "I've done over a hundred in the last several months. Most of these evaluations are drive-bys, but several are interior ones as well—and I've seen some real messes. Food and garbage everywhere, torn up floors, you name it."

That's the kind of stuff that doesn't show up on the lender's computer! Pictures are worth a thousand words, and they will help sell your case. Take lots of pictures and include shots of the inside and outside to support your cost estimates for bringing the property back to market condition. That doesn't mean that's what you would spend, but it is what the lender might spend!

Another key element to be included in the package is a sample HUD-1 Settlement Statement. This standard closing document itemizes the costs and disbursements that will happen at closing. It lays out the details for cash in and out to make the deal happen, with the most important item to the lender being their net proceeds on the deal. You can download a HUD-1 form from www.hud.gov/offices/adm/hudclips/forms/files/1.doc.

Why Short Sales Can Fail

- *Property owners can balk.* Whether they just get cold feet, or they begin to resent the discounted price you will be paying for their home, sellers can balk at any time during the process. It could just be the thought that they can find a way out before foreclosure. Pressure mixed with embarrassment can cause weird things to happen.

- *The credit score falls after a short sale.* Most experts agree that the borrower's credit score will take roughly the same negative hit from a short sale that it will from a foreclosure. The negative effect is likely to be of shorter duration with a short sale as compared to a foreclosure. Changes in Fannie Mae rules provide an advantage to short sellers in a faster track to a new home loan.

- *Short sales have tax consequences.* The Mortgage Forgiveness Debt Relief Act of 2007 effectively takes away the tax consequences of the amount of debt forgiven in a short sale of a principal residence. This is a plus that should be mentioned early on to the homeowner in enticing them to move on a short sale.

- *The timing of the sale is important.* Of course, we want to work with the lender to make sure that we don't get deeply into the short sale process, only to find a foreclosure filing in the mail. A buyer who has a tight time line, as in the case of a 1031 Exchange, will not want to entertain purchase through a short sale.

Short sales can take months, and there are pitfalls and delays in every step of the process.

"The number one thing people need when completing a short sale is patience," indicates RE/MAX real estate broker and foreclosure specialist Mark Barager "It's not what people are used to. We just had one that took seven months to close because the first bank got bought out by another bank half way through, and then we had to start over."

Yes, sometimes patience can be the real key to getting to the closing table! But it doesn't always have to be a drawn-out drama. Nate Martinez, a top realtor with Re/Max Professionals in Phoenix, shows why being prepared can save time: "I just completed a short sale deal in 45 days from start to finish—and the borrower wasn't even delinquent yet! While this isn't typical, the key for approval was in the package and showing the lender that this borrower was done with making payments!"

Robert Helms adds, "one of the problems is that lenders have procedures in place for foreclosures, but there are no written rules for dealing with short sales."

You need to help them write the rules.

Determining the Short Sale Offer

A property can be valued in a variety of ways. You might get an appraiser to do a full appraisal, using the approved methods and producing a comprehensive valuation report. However, it is rarely done this way in a short sale situation. The lender is usually relying on one or both of an AVM automated valuation module (AVM) or a broker price opinion (BPO). The computerized AVM takes data from comparable sales in the area to estimate value.

The BPO can be either a drive-by or a more thorough inspection of the property. A lot of drive-by BPOs are conducted by real estate brokers for lenders. Obviously, we can't be sure of the interior condition of the home, or even know if the nonvisible rear side of the home is not grossly damaged or missing.

In our short sale package delivered to the lender, we want to be sure to present a full and detailed value estimate that includes the condition of the home, and the estimated cost of any repairs that will be necessary to bring the property up to a condition that will enable it to sell in the marketplace.

To help you with this, use the short sale worksheet in Figure 22.2 to use multiple resources in calculating the value of the home and the amount you can offer for the purchase. It's a balance between the needs of the lender and your expectation of the value needed to make it a good investment.

Short Sale Transaction Worksheet

Lienholder: _____

Contact Name: _____

E-mail Address: _____

Phone Number: _____ Fax Number: _____

Address: _____

E-mail Address: _____

Type of Lien: $_____   Lien Amount: $_____

Property Value: $_____   Owner Equity: $_____

Principal Bal Left: $_____   Total Payoff: $_____

Foreclosure Costs - _____

PMI Insurance ☐ Yes ☐ No   Repair Costs - _____

Purchase Price: $_____   Closing Costs - _____
                X 80%
Lender Base Price: = $_____   Holding Costs - _____

Lender's Net: = $_____

Comments: BPO or Value: $_____

Profits - _____

Holding Costs - _____

Repair/Closing Costs - _____

Short Sale Max Bid = $_____

(Lower of Base, Net, or Max / 90%) **Short Sale Actual Bid =** $_____

Short Sale Offer $_____ Date_____ Counter $_____

FIGURE 22.2   Short Sale Transaction Worksheet

Tackling FHA Short Sales

The FHA Loss Mitigation Program attempts to encourage lenders to engage in loss mitigation procedures to minimize the negative effects of mortgage problems on the FHA, as well as home and mortgage markets. Tools and incentives are given to lenders to help homeowners avoid foreclosure, with a short sale as one of the options.

The HUD National Servicing Center was formed to help FHA homeowners and lenders find creative solutions to avoiding foreclosure. You will find help at their web site in the form of information, suggestions, and current incentives available to homeowners and lenders in avoiding foreclosure actions.

The FHA makes frequent changes, and you should check their web site for current information. Generally, these items are required to qualify for short sale on an FHA loan:

- Reason for default letter signed and dated by all borrowers
- Utility bill or verification of occupancy (is the property vacant, if so for how long and why?)
- Authorization/acknowledgment
- Negotiation agreement
- The HUD 90038 Homeowner's Counseling Certificate
- The HUD 90036 Application to participate signed and dated by all parties to the loan. (In addition, the form must be completely filled out with all questions answered.)
- The HUD 92068F Request for Financial Information completed, signed, and dated by all parties to the loan

Richard Guerra, long time HUD specialist on short sales from HUD's Atlanta office, shares that "the guidelines haven't changed since 1994, where effective February 1, 2000 the minimum net sales proceeds were established at 82 percent, and the appraised value must be at least 63 percent of the outstanding mortgage. It's pretty straight forward."

I'd have to agree, and this gives us the exact parameters of how to structure the deal.

Navigating VA Short Sales

Like the FHA, the Veterans Administration (VA), has a program to aid homeowners and lenders in the avoidance of the foreclosure of a VA home loan. It is called the

Compromise Sale, and is outlined at their web site at www.vba.va.gov/ro/houston/lgy/compsale.html.

You can also get information and help at any of the VA regional loan centers. The goal is to avoid foreclosure, and the VA really works with the lender and homeowner to negotiate a sale. Remember, as an investor, VA deals are easy to assume as well.

CHAPTER 23

Nailing Down the Purchase Agreement

I've talked a lot about the "process" of a short sale and a foreclosure. This is because it truly is a process, and the successful closing of a deal is dependent on your knowledge of the process and on you following it carefully and completely.

Once you've identified a property as a desirable candidate, you need to prepare a purchase agreement. This agreement is a binding contract between you and the seller, and you want to be sure that it is written in a way that protects you and your investment of time and money. Here are some tips:

Agreements Not to Use

- *Agreement prepared by seller's attorney:* Attorneys are advocates for their clients. Any purchase agreement prepared by the seller's attorney will likely be written very much in their favor. Not yours! This usually isn't a major concern because the seller doesn't have enough money to pay for an attorney anyway. They will rely on you instead.

- *Real estate agent agreements:* There are a couple of excellent reasons for not using purchase agreements that the real estate agents use. First, most are copyrighted by the Realtor Associations, and it isn't legal for you to use them. More important, they are carefully drafted to be balanced and to protect both the buyer and seller. Plus, they are designed to provide protection for realtors as well. We aren't seeking balance; we are seeking an agreement that mostly benefits you and me, the buyers.

- *Office supply store contracts:* This one is a big no-no. Very few generic purchase agreements are specifically written to be legal in your state of residence. Even if they say they are, the cheap price means that it is unlikely they are up to date with current law. Remember, this is a transaction that could be under very close scrutiny, and you don't want to screw this part up.

What to Use

- *Your own contract:* Hire your own attorney to prepare your purchase agreement. You can have the attorney prepare a template agreement that you can use in future purchases without having to pay a high fee for creating one for each deal. That way you can just fill in the names, property address, price, and terms. But it is important to use an attorney to protect yourself and to comply with your state's laws.

Key Mandatory Elements of the Purchase Agreement

Even if you use an attorney, you should understand the necessary elements of a valid purchase agreement. Use my list of 16 key elements to guide you. Whether a short sale or a normal purchase process, the time and money involved in getting to the closing table is such that you want to have a complete understanding of the purchase agreement. This will help you to avoid deals that crash and burn due to misunderstandings that could have been avoided. In 25 years, I have only had one deal not close right at the closing table. This was early on, and it happened because I forgot to include a clause in the purchase agreement. A very expensive lesson.

Above all else, a real estate purchase agreement must outline all of the necessary steps each party must take through the process, who is responsible for what, and which costs are paid by the buyer and which ones are paid by the seller.

Time lines and delivery deadlines are also critical items in the purchase agreement. When a document must be delivered by a certain date, it should be very clear as to the date and time, as well as any requirement for response or objections to the document. Inspection deadlines must be met, or you may risk losing your rights for objections, corrections, or your earnest money.

Make sure that you construct the agreement so that you can assign or sell the agreement to another investor if necessary.

Four Mandatory Contingency Clauses

1. *Property title:* You don't want to close on a property only to find out that it is a smaller lot size than you thought, or worse, that you bought the wrong property. A clear legal description is critical, and you'll want to verify it with a survey if necessary to determine property lines. I think I'll say that again—determine property lines. This one determination can help you avoid tons of stress. Does the seller own the property they're selling? Yes, you want to be sure because there could be an ex-spouse out there who can cause problems later if he or she asserts rights.

I had a property deal one time where the sellers had an incorrect property description, which resulted in six inches of their garage being on the neighbor's property. The resulting lawsuit went back over seven previous owners, and ended up costing nearly $20,000 for those six inches! Not the best use of time or money.

2. *Status of existing liens:* Verifying if liens exist against the property is something you want to do early in the process. How would you like to be a co-owner with the IRS? There may be contractors out there with repair liens. The fact that they exist may not kill your deal, but the money to take care of them must be handled in the contract. You can't handle it if you don't know it exists.

3. *How and when does the seller vacate the property?* The how of this is more of a "how quickly can I get you out" clause. Do not close on a property with the seller still in it! I have made few exceptions over the years when I leased back the property to the seller, but this is rare because they couldn't afford it the first time.

   You also need to sort out the "what do they take and what do they leave" mess. They will try to take anything of value unless you specify that it stays. Real estate expert Terri Murphy tells a story of sellers that actually dug up the shrubs and trees and took them away the night before closing! Your purchase agreement must be clear as to when they are out, and what stays and what goes so that you don't arrive to find all of those great custom light fixtures leaving in a moving van. Agreeing on a date and a time for the property to be completely empty of the belongings of the seller is very important.

4. *Property condition until you take possession:* An important contingency is that the seller maintains hazard insurance through the closing date. It should also be clear that the property will be changing hands in the same condition as on the day the deal was sealed. The seller must safeguard the property from damage until it's officially yours. Don't let them cancel the insurance early. If the lender finds out, they will force insurance on you that can cost thousands of dollars extra. Worse yet, if the property burns down or gets damaged, the deal goes bust and everyone loses!

Constructing the Agreement

Use a Real Estate Attorney

Yes, I'm saying it again. Don't be "penny wise and pound foolish" in saving money by not using an attorney. Your attorney knows the current law, and they will draft a purchase agreement that favors your interests. If the seller strikes out items or counteroffers with changes, your attorney can review them to be sure your interests are still covered. Pay for the first one, then use it as a "template" to save money on future deals.

Find a Real Estate Attorney

Not all states are the same, but many will have different specializations or board certifications for attorneys. There will be attorneys who are certified in the practice of real estate law. This is who you should seek out, not the best divorce lawyer in town. (Though you may need one later if you lose a bundle on a real estate investment!) The Yellow Pages list attorneys by specialty. You might also contact a real estate investment club or mortgage broker for recommendations, or check my recommended online resources in the back of the book.

Agreements Must Be Witnessed

Though not required in all states, many require that agreements be witnessed by a third party, or notarized. This makes it possible to prove later that the two parties were present and did actually agree on the terms set forth.

California has some of the most protective real estate and contract laws. Figure 23.1 shows an example of forms required in California.

Your state may be similar or very different in their forms and contract requirements. Become very familiar with them because your money is at stake. To get you into the mindset of interpreting purchase agreements, look at Figure 23.2.

Seller Disclosures

Not all states require that the seller deliver a disclosure of property condition. Most do though, and some require that the disclosures from the seller be much more detailed, with information concerning:

- Liens known to exist by the seller.
- Current local development that might impact ownership later.
- Known proposed changes to ordinances or homeowner association rules.
- Environmental hazards on or near the property.

There could very well be others. Even if your state does not require disclosures, you can write the requirement into your purchase agreement, and have the seller answer questions provided by your real estate attorney about these items and any known defects in the property. Figure 23.3 is a sample of a seller disclosure statement.

NOTICE REQUIRED BY CALIFORNIA LAW

Until your right to cancel this contract has ended,_____ or anyone working for _____ CANNOT ask you to sign or have you sign any deed or any other document.

The contract required by this section shall survive delivery of any instrument of conveyance of the residence in foreclosure, and shall have no effect on persons other than the parties to the contract.

You may cancel this contract for the sale of your house without any penalty or obligation at any time before: _____.
(Date and time of day)

See the attached notice of cancellation form for an explanation of this right.

NOTICE OF CANCELLATION

_____
(Enter date contract signed)

You may cancel this contract for the sale of your house, without any penalty or obligation, at any time before _____.
(Enter date and time of day)

To cancel this transaction, personally deliver a signed and dated copy of this cancellation notice, or send a telegram to _____,
(Name of purchaser)

at _____ NOT LATER THAN _____.
(Street address of purchaser's place of business)   *(Enter date and time of day)*

I hereby cancel this transaction _____.
(Date)

_____
(Seller's signature)

ACKNOWLEDGMENT OF RECEIPT OF NOTICE

I hereby acknowledge that I received two copies of the required "Notice of Cancellation" document as required by California law.

_____
(Seller's signature)

 FIGURE 23.1   **Notice of Cancellation**

REAL ESTATE PURCHASE AGREEMENT

This agreement is made this _____ day of _____, 20__ between _____
_____, known hereinafter as the "Buyer," and _____
_____, known hereinafter as the "Seller."

Seller agrees to convey, transfer, assign, sell, and deliver to Buyer all of Seller's rights, title, and interest in and to the following real property commonly known as _____, and further legally described as:

_____

_____

1. Seller agrees to sell to Buyer, and Buyer agrees to purchase from Seller under the following terms:

Total Purchase Price: $_____

Earnest Money Deposit: - $_____ *to be held in escrow by:*
_____

Balance Due: = $_____

Mortgage(s) to be assumed/subject to: - $_____ *as further described as:*

_____

_____

_____

Payments in arrears *(including interest & fees)* - $_____

Balance to be paid via Cashier's Check: = $_____

2. Balance is subject to adjustment based upon actual payoff balances of liens, verification of unpaid payments, accrued interest, legal fees, taxes, assessments, judgments, and any other outstanding costs. Seller agrees to assign any escrow balance maintained by lender without further consideration.

3. Seller will execute a Warranty Deed to convey title to the property at closing, of which Buyer must approve of marketability and title status prior to closing.

4. Buyer must approve of status of all existing liens on property prior to closing, and Seller warrants that no undisclosed or unrecorded liens exist beyond those listed above.

5. Should any portion of the property be damaged or destroyed by fire, theft, or other casualty before closing, Buyer shall have the right to terminate this Agreement and will be entitled to an immediate refund of the earnest money deposit.

6. This Agreement is subject to and contingent upon Buyer conducting a property inspection by an inspector/contractor(s) of their choosing. Seller agrees to make the property available for said inspection(s) upon reasonable notice.

 FIGURE 23.2   Sample Real Estate Purchase Agreement

7. Seller agrees to completely vacate the property prior to closing, and leave the property in roughly the same physical condition, including maintaining all fixtures and attachments, which includes but is not limited to plumbing, electrical, heating and cooling, structural attachments, landscaping, insulation, siding, windows, doors, and any other attachments to the property, which are all included in the purchase price.

8. Additional provisions:_____

   _____

9. Buyer may assign any or all rights and interest in this agreement to a third party at any time prior to closing. Closing shall take place on _____
   _____, 20___ at _____am/pm at the following location:
   _____

   _____
   Seller and Buyer hereby further agree to appoint _____ to act as Escrow Agent for the purpose of holding any deposits, and closing this transaction in accordance with the terms herein.

10. All provisions of this Agreement shall extend to and become binding upon any heirs, executors, successors and/or assigns of the Seller and Buyer. Seller acknowledges that they are acting of their own freewill, act and deed in accepting this agreement.

IN WITNESS HEREOF, Seller and Buyer accept this offer, and agree to sell and purchase the property described herein under the terms and conditions specified.

_____   _____
Witness   Purchaser

_____   _____
Witness   Purchaser

Dated: _____

_____   _____
Witness   Seller

_____   _____
Witness   Seller

Dated: _____

FIGURE 23.2 (*Continued*)

SELLER'S RESIDENTIAL REAL ESTATE SALES DISCLOSURE

State Form 46234 (R4 / 1-07)

Date (*month, day, year*)

Seller states that the information contained in this Disclosure is correct to the best of Seller's CURRENT ACTUAL KNOWLEDGE as of the above date. The prospective buyer and the owner may wish to obtain professional advice or inspections of the property and provide for appropriate provisions in a contract between them concerning any advice, inspections, defects, or warranties obtained on the property. The representations in this form are the representations of the owner and are not the representations of the agent, if any. This information is for disclosure only and is not intended to be a part of any contract between the buyer and the owner. Indiana law (IC 32-21-5) generally requires sellers of 1-4 unit residential property to complete this form regarding the known physical condition of the property. An owner must complete and sign the disclosure form and submit the form to a prospective buyer before an offer is accepted for the sale of the real estate.

Property address (*number and street, city, state, and ZIP code*)

1. The following are in the conditions indicated:

A. APPLIANCES	None/Not Included	Defective	Not Defective	Do Not Know
Built-in Vacuum System				
Clothes Dryer				
Clothes Washer				
Dishwasher				
Disposal				
Freezer				
Gas Grill				
Hood				
Microwave Oven				
Oven				
Range				
Refrigerator				
Room Air Conditioner(s)				
Trash Compactor				
TV Antenna / Dish				
Other:				

B. ELECTRICAL SYSTEM	None/Not Included	Defective	Not Defective	Do Not Know
Air Purifier				
Burglar Alarm				
Ceiling Fan(s)				
Garage Door Opener / Controls				
Inside Telephone Wiring and Blocks / Jacks				
Intercom				
Light Fixtures				
Sauna				
Smoke / Fire Alarm(s)				
Switches and Outlets				
Vent Fan(s)				
60 / 100 / 200 Amp Service (*Circle one*)				

NOTE: "Defect" means a condition that would have a significant adverse effect on the value of the property, that would significantly impair the health or safety of future occupants of the property, or that if not repaired, removed or replaced would significantly shorten or adversely affect the expected normal life of the premises.

C. WATER & SEWER SYSTEM	None/Not Included	Defective	Not Defective	Do Not Know
Cistern				
Septic Field / Bed				
Hot Tub				
Plumbing				
Aerator System				
Sump Pump				
Irrigation Systems				
Water Heater / Electric				
Water Heater / Gas				
Water Heater / Solar				
Water Purifier				
Water Softener				
Well				
Septic & Holding Tank/Septic Mound				
Geothermal and Heat Pump				
Other Sewer System (*Explain*)				

	Yes	No	Do Not Know
Are the improvements connected to a public water system?			
Are the improvements connected to a public sewer system?			
Are there any additions that may require improvements to the sewage disposal system?			
If yes, have the improvements been completed on the sewage disposal system?			
Are the improvements connected to a private/community water system?			
Are the improvements connected to a private/community sewer system?			

D. HEATING & COOLING SYSTEM	None/Not Included	Defective	Not Defective	Do Not Know
Attic Fan				
Central Air Conditioning				
Hot Water Heat				
Furnace Heat / Gas				
Furnace Heat / Electric				
Solar House-Heating				
Woodburning Stove				
Fireplace				
Fireplace Insert				
Air Cleaner				
Humidifier				
Propane Tank				
Other Heating Source				

The information contained in this Disclosure has been furnished by the Seller, who certifies to the truth thereof, based on the Seller's CURRENT ACTUAL KNOWLEDGE. A disclosure form is not a warranty by the owner or the owner's agent, if any, and the disclosure form may not be used as a substitute for any inspections or warranties that the prospective buyer or owner may later obtain. At or before settlement, the owner is required to disclose any material change in the physical condition of the property or certify to the purchaser at settlement that the condition of the property is substantially the same as it was when the disclosure form was provided. Seller and Purchaser hereby acknowledge receipt of this Disclosure by signing below.

Signature of Seller:	Date (*mm/dd/yy*):	Signature of Buyer:	Date (*mm/dd/yy*):
Signature of Seller:	Date (*mm/dd/yy*):	Signature of Buyer:	Date (*mm/dd/yy*):

The Seller hereby certifies that the condition of the property is substantially the same as it was when the Seller's Disclosure form was originally provided to the Buyer.

Signature of Seller:	Date (*mm/dd/yy*):	Signature of Buyer:	Date (*mm/dd/yy*):

FIGURE 23.3   Seller Disclosure Statement

Property address (*number and street, city, state, and ZIP code*)

2. ROOF	YES	NO	DO NOT KNOW
Age, if known: _____ Years.			
Does the roof leak?			
Is there present damage to the roof?			
Is there more than one roof on the house? If so, how many layers? _____			

3. HAZARDOUS CONDITIONS	YES	NO	DO NOT KNOW
Have there been or are there any hazardous conditions on the property, such as methane gas, lead paint, radon gas in house or well, radioactive material, landfill, mineshaft, expansive soil, toxic materials, mold, other biological contaminants, asbestos insulation, or PCB's? Explain:			

E. ADDITIONAL COMMENTS AND/OR EXPLANATIONS: (*Use additional pages, if necessary*)

4. OTHER DISCLOSURES	YES	NO	DO NOT KNOW
Do improvements have aluminum wiring?			
Are there any foundation problems with the improvements?			
Are there any encroachments?			
Are there any violations of zoning, building codes, or restrictive covenants?			
Is the present use a non-conforming use? Explain:			
Is the access to your property via a private road?			
Is the access to your property via a public road?			
Is the access to your property via an easement?			
Have you received any notices by any governmental or quasi-governmental agencies affecting this property?			
Are there any structural problems with the building?			
Have any substantial additions or alterations been made without a required building permit?			
Are there moisture and/or water problems in the basement, crawl space area, or any other area?			
Is there any damage due to wind, flood, termites or rodents?			
Have any improvements been treated for wood destroying insects?			
Are the furnace/woodstove/chimney/flue all in working order?			
Is the property in a flood plain?			
Do you currently pay flood insurance?			
Does the property contain underground storage tank(s)?			
Is the homeowner a licensed real estate salesperson or broker?			
Is there any threatened or existing litigation regarding the property?			
Is the property subject to convenants, conditions and/or restrictions of a homeowner's association?			
Is the property located within one (1) mile of an airport?			

The information contained in this Disclosure has been furnished by the Seller, who certifies to the truth thereof, based on the Seller's CURRENT ACTUAL KNOWLEDGE. A disclosure form is not a warranty by the owner or the owner's agent, if any, and the disclosure form may not be used as a substitute for any inspections or warranties that the prospective buyer or owner may later obtain. At or before settlement, the owner is required to disclose any material change in the physical condition of the property or certify to the purchaser at settlement that the condition of the property is substantially the same as it was when the disclosure form was provided. Seller and Purchaser hereby acknowledge receipt of this Disclosure by signing below:

Signature of Seller:	Date (*mm/dd/yy*):	Signature of Buyer:	Date (*mm/dd/yy*):
Signature of Seller:	Date (*mm/dd/yy*):	Signature of Buyer:	Date (*mm/dd/yy*):

The Seller hereby certifies that the condition of the property is substantially the same as it was when the Seller's Disclosure form was originally provided to the Buyer.

Signature of Seller:	Date (*mm/dd/yy*):	Signature of Buyer:	Date (*mm/dd/yy*):

FIGURE 23.3 (*Continued*)

VOLUNTARY ACTION DISCLOSURE

I,_____ the owner(s) of the property located at:_____
_____ have voluntarily entered into a Purchase
Agreement with _____.

There have been no "side deals" or separate agreements outside of what has
been agreed upon in the Purchase Agreement, and I (we) have entered into the
terms and conditions of said agreement without duress, and of my (our) own free
will and accord.

_____   _____
(Date)   *(Seller's signature)*

                                 _____
                                  (Seller's signature)

Figure 23.4   Voluntary Action Disclosure

Disclosure of Voluntary Action

It's an unfortunate fact of life that there are scam artists out there in every area of
buying and selling. Real estate is no exception, and particularly in the area of short
sales and foreclosure of homes. This disclosure is for the seller to state that they
are agreeing to this sale without any pressure on your part as a buyer. You want
their voluntary statement that it is an arms-length transaction, and you have no
power to force the sale and have not done so. Figure 23.4 is an example of a voluntary action disclosure:

Presenting the Offer

Have all the parties present when you present the offer! If the seller tells
you he is using an attorney, then you probably want the attorney there as well. If a
real estate agent or broker is involved, they need to be there also. The best way to

be sure of a clear understanding of everyone's intent is to get them all together for the offer.

(i) You always have the right to be there when an offer is presented. If an agent is representing the seller, make sure to demand that you be included in the presentation so you can make your case.

If everyone will agree to it, and without hiding it from anyone (illegal in many states), you will go the extra mile toward avoiding misunderstandings by recording the offer presentation. I use a simple digital recorder. Video and/or audio is fine.

When presenting the offer on a short sale transaction, remind the seller that the process will not result in any cash in their pockets. The lender will not allow it, and you want to be sure that they understand this fact and acknowledge it. Also stress that the transaction will not cost them any money—remember to structure your offer that way.

- *Go through the offer line by line, and answer objections right up front.* I read the purchase agreement aloud, line by line, and consult with the seller at each clause to get their agreement or any objections to it. This is much better than getting a document the next day with 50 objections that could have been handled easily at the presentation.

(i) A series of yes's will lead to acceptance. If you go for shortcuts, a silent no will kill the deal.

- *Set a tight time frame for acceptance.* We're not trying to rush the homeowner into a poor decision. However, we have other homes that might be as good an investment, so we don't want to waste too much time while they think it over. I give them no more than 48 hours. This puts subtle pressure on the seller to consult their relatives, friends, or attorney quickly and to consider their options. I also don't want to give them a lot of time to shop my offer with other potential buyers. Remember, we are in the business of making money.

- *Getting the seller to say yes and sign.* You don't have to play the used car salesman to be a good negotiator and help the seller to make the deal. Just be polite but firm in helping the seller to meet the response deadline, perhaps suggesting a follow-up meeting to seal the deal just before the offer expires. That always works to filter out any indecision.

CHAPTER 24

Protect Your New Assets, Immediately

Congratulations! You've done the research, prepared a comprehensive and purchase agreement, negotiated successfully with the homeowner, and you have a signature. It's a great accomplishment, but unfortunately, it doesn't mean anything if we can't get to closing. Even if you want to buy it, and the seller wants to sell it, you still have to do a few things to get ready before the transaction is final. You need to confirm payoffs with lienholders, and if it is part of the deal—negotiate and work with the lender's representatives to finalize the short sale. So, what do you do to safeguard your future property during the final stages of the process? Well, let's start with what *not* to do!

Three Things You Never Do!

1. *Access without permission:* You don't own it yet, so treat this home as if it belonged to a stranger and you needed to borrow their phone to call in a flat tire. Your signed purchase agreement gives you no more rights than that. If you need to inspect the property, or in any other way to access it, always set up an appointment, and get permission on a case-by-case basis.

2. *Give the owner any cash prior to closing:* Lenders can act really odd sometimes. They are very likely about to take a loss on this property, and this doesn't put them in a good mood to begin with. They can sometimes change certain conditions, terms, or timing without warning. In addition, the homeowners could change their minds (I know you have an agreement, but it still happens), or one of them could end up in jail (yes, I had that happen once too). The point is, that anything can and usually does happen before the closing. Do not give the homeowner any cash until you seal the deal at the table.

3. *Start working on the property or place anything on/in the property:* We're back to . . . it isn't yours yet. Do not place anything on the property, nor should you make any repairs or changes to the property. If it doesn't close, you end up wasting the time and money and the homeowner won't reimburse you.

    I had a client once who, against my advice, spent the weekend painting the exterior of a house to satisfy one of the conditions to close. Well, it didn't close and the homeowner ended up with a freshly painted home without having to spend a dime! Don't do it!

Three Things You Need to Do Now!

Okay, now that you know what *not* to do—what *should* you do to protect your deal?

*   *Schedule a closing as fast as you can:* Once the seller has signed on the bottom line, pressure to move fast is not only okay, it's the rule. With everyone anxious to get it done, you do not want to drag this out any more than you have to. This is where your "title company partner" on your dream team comes in handy. They need to get everything in order on the double. Set them in action—fast.

*   *Get insurance on it right away:* Even though your purchase agreement states that the homeowner will maintain insurance through closing, you want to protect yourself. Contact the homeowners insurer and try to get the policy extended in your name, or at least put them on notice that it will be transferring ownership. If you can't get a guarantee from the insurer to inform you of any temporary claim or notification of loss, a couple of courtesy phone calls will have to do. Many insurers will not permit you to have a policy for a property you do not own yet, but you can try to be added as a co-insured party. But, the best defense is the offense of buying a policy to protect your investment. Again, that's where your team players can pitch in.

*   *Hire a lookout:* You need to know what's going on around your new investment. Find a nosy neighbor and pay them to keep you informed of the activities in and around the home. If the seller is moving things out early, you want to know. If there are contractors or truckloads of material coming or going, you need to know. It is nice to be nice, and trusting people is a virtue. However, this is an investment in misfortune. And the misfortune of the homeowner can lead them to do things that they wouldn't ordinarily even think about doing. Don't close on a home to find out that all of the plumbing fixtures and appliances have been removed. Worse things have happened.

Drive by the property at least once per day, and at different times to check activity. That's your best insurance.

Avoiding New Surprises

- *Tax and mechanic's liens:* One of the first things you need to have done, or do yourself, is an updated title search on the property (remember Chapter 15). If the senior lienholder is a regular financial institution that escrowed for taxes and insurance, the taxes are probably up to date. If not, check to make sure that there are no new tax liens or old tax bills about to be sold (called tax certificates). If so, you will want to purchase those, or you will be paying additional interest and costs just to clear the taxes.

  You also want to know if there are any mechanic liens for work done, such as improvements when the owner thought they were going to be able to sell "normally." Many a homeowner has listed his home for sale with high expectations, paying contractors to come in and do everything from repairs to landscaping. Then the reality of the situation sets in, and he finds that he can't sell for a price that will cover his mortgage . . . he is upside-down in his home, and the contractors never get paid (along with most of his other bills!).

  Go to the courthouse yourself, hire a title research attorney, or use your title company team member. But, whatever you do, have a thorough search done for liens, but also ask about any claims that may be out there or that may come up in the future.

- *Divorce Proceedings:* Marital problems can also throw a monkey wrench into things. Divorce is a terrible experience for a husband and the wife, but it can be almost as terrible for you, the buyer. A judge can say, "Mrs. Jones, you can live in the home and your husband must relinquish his claim or buy you out." That judge can't extinguish the note held by the lender, but the lender will want you to get a sign-off from the spouse. You can see where this is going. Not fun.

  Don't find yourself the proud new owner of your rental property, only to meet the ex-spouse who claims they have ownership rights and were not a party to the transaction. What about the seller who bought the home and then later married? The ex-spouse may have rights under community property laws. Just because the occupant is the only name on the title, don't assume they are the only owner. A thorough search at the courthouse for any records pertaining not only to the home but also the owner(s) is a must.

One time we had a property that closed with a couple, but a sharp closing agent smelled a rat. Upon some investigation, it was learned that the man had brought in his secretary to act as his wife to sign off on the home! Oops—busted.

Additional Security

One of the rules many successful real estate investors have employed over time is not investing outside their areas. Not only do they normally have a much greater awareness of market trends because they live there, they are also much better able to monitor their investments.

Driving by the property frequently up until closing can alert you to a problem before it becomes a nightmare. If the grass starts to get very deep, you might want to see if your seller is still living there.

Call the homeowner now and then, just to check on her well-being . . . or at least that's the stated reason. You really want to see if she is still there (and if her phone works), and you may want to find an excuse to stop by to drop something off or to check something one of your "repair contractors" wants to know about. It is all about watching your investment while it is not in your control before closing. A tricky balance, but one that is necessary.

What if the home is vacant? Maybe the sellers had to move for a better job, or they had an opportunity to get a good rental deal if they moved early. Either way, you now have a future asset without anyone living there to safeguard it. First, take photos of the property on the date you made the offer and when it was accepted. This documents the condition when you cut the deal.

Even a lender can understand their obligation to turn over the product you bought, can't they? Well, they may understand it, but they'll make you prove there is a problem. The lender is looking after the lender, so you need to look after you. Document the home you purchased with as many photos as necessary, using a digital camera that dates the photos. Send them to someone via e-mail to document the date they were taken.

Have a neighbor help you out, even if you have to pay for his help. Give him your number to call if he sees weird activity around the home. Perhaps he will even work with you to let your approved contractors into the home when you authorize it ahead of time. The goal is to keep as many eyes on your investment as possible until you close and have full control.

CHAPTER 25

Closing the Deal

A s you near the day of closing, it's easy to get a comfortable feeling. After all, you've gone through an amazing process. You've had to negotiate not only with a distressed seller, but also an unenthusiastic lender. Inspections have been done, repair estimates gathered, title researched, and much more. But, don't rest just yet. Stuff can still happen. In this chapter, I talk about how to avoid eleventh hour screw-ups, and get the deal closed.

Before You Close

Before you actually close or take title to the property, there are some things you need to prepare for. Let's start with the documents:

- *Check documents for mistakes*. Did you know there are errors on documents in a great many deals? Real estate agents can tell you of many instances where there have been problems, delays, and extra cost to correct errors in legal descriptions. You'll want to compare your deed with the legal description of the property you're purchasing. A small error now could be a large cost later. Just because it looks official doesn't mean the information is correct.

I once had a transaction where the seller sold me an extra 20 acres of the neighbors' yard by mistake! A simple typo in the legal description was missed by more than 10 people until just after the closing. Fortunately, it was a simple fix, but even the pros make mistakes. Check it carefully!

Another area where errors are overlooked frequently is in the title insurance exceptions and requirements. Early in the process; you'll receive a title insurance commitment, or a binder for title insurance. This document binds the title insurer to issue your title insurance policy. However, it will have certain "exceptions" to coverage, meaning things not covered, as well as some requirements for documents to make the binder . . . well, binding!

Things excepted from coverage are those things that already exist in the property records, thus the title insurer can do nothing about them. You are accepting the property subject to these existing conditions and can't make a claim for coverage later. These include easements, any claims or liens that can't be removed, as well as the history of transactions in the past. You really need to be careful that you know all the exceptions.

Don't rely on a real estate agent to read your title documents or check them for accuracy, because few will. They deliver them and consider their responsibilities resolved at that point in most cases. You need to read and understand all of the documents, the past deeds, restrictions, and covenants, as well as the easements involved. If you have a question, get it answered by the title company, an attorney, or both. You do not want these types of problems later. By the way, people act frustrated when you let on that you want to read everything through. Ignore that. This is your money; protect it. If they want to save time, have them provide you with a complete set of documents the day before.

- *Review the HUD-1 for accuracy.* You would think computers would have done away with math errors on things like the highly computerized HUD-1 property settlement statement. Wrong! We've all heard it, and "garbage in means garbage out" is very much the case here. A real estate sale transaction is a complex process, and mistakes are made, usually by the hourly employee punching in the numbers in the software.

  There are a lot of line items on the HUD-1, and you shouldn't take the accuracy of any of them for granted. Do you understand pro-ration of items like rents, taxes, and insurance? Depending on the date and the amount of the taxes or insurance policy premiums, an error here could mean serious money. Do you know the difference between a banker's year and a calendar year? Bankers use 360 days, or 12 months of 30 days each. The difference could be minimal, but why leave even one dollar on the table?

  Be especially watchful of the lender slipping in some charges at the last minute. You should have a hard number for the satisfaction of the lien and all costs, so there shouldn't be surprises at the closing table. Get these items lined out in writing earlier in the process, and have them calculated for the projected closing date. If the date changes, have a new itemization prepared for the new date.

Watch for "junk" charges. I had a title company add an e-mail fee of $35 to a transaction once! I asked them what it was for, and they said to e-mail the documents to the lender. I told them that I would be willing to drive them over for free or else I would start charging them for my phone calls. Needless to say, the charge was removed within about 60 seconds.

- *Do a walk-through inspection preclosing.* Depending on the state laws and your purchase agreement terms, you should demand and schedule a preclosing walk-through of the property the day of, or at least the day before closing. This walk-through gives you the opportunity to make sure that everything is as it should be. If all of the light fixtures and appliances are gone, you will want to start a new negotiation. Your "big stick" is that you will not close until you get everything you paid for. Don't be afraid to wield it!

    If there are damages that have appeared between the purchase agreement acceptance date and the walk-through, you will want to stop the closing process and negotiate compensation for them. Use your original photos, comparing them to the as-is photos taken during the walk-through. You can see why that boring photo of a bare living room wall is important now that the studs are showing!

    By the way, hopefully you won't find your seller still living there, or his furnishings all around the house. As I said before, closing on a home with the seller still in it is a bit like buying a submarine with a screen door . . . not gonna be a good fit! What you want to find during your walk-through inspection is an empty home without damage that you didn't agree to in the first place. Figure 25.1 is an example walk-through inspection checklist.

    Another pro-ration item to include is the utility bills. You'll want to get meter readings for the closing date to make sure that the seller is paying for their use of utilities until you take over the property (if they're still on). Document the readings and get them to the title company and/or the utility company as appropriate to get the billing paid by the right party.

    Right up through the day of closing, make sure that the insurance company is covering the home. Get an insurance binder document from your company, or an extension of the owner's policy in your name guaranteeing coverage on a certain date and time. If you're borrowing money, the lender will want to confirm this, and the title closing agent will not complete the transaction without it. If you're paying cash, as in most short sale situations, this is your problem to follow up on. Don't own the property for even one un-insured minute. A lot can happen.

FINAL WALK-THROUGH CHECKLIST

Property Address: _____

Date of Walk-through: _____ Time: _____

Accompanied by: _____

Are there any posted notices on the property:	☐ Code Violations ☐ Condemnation Notices ☐ Other _____ ☐ None
Are there any signs of environmental hazards on the property?	☐ Yes ☐ No Comments:_____
Are there signs of infestations:	☐ Termites ☐ Rodents ☐ Carpenter Ants ☐ Other_____
Is there visible standing water?	☐ Yes ☐ No
Any additional exterior damages?	☐ Yes ☐ No Comments_____
Any additional interior damages?	☐ Yes ☐ No Comments_____
Items removed from property:	_____ _____

FIGURE 25.1   Final Walk-through Inspection Checklist

Closing Time

- *When and where:* They can't finish without you, but you should be sure that you know where to be and when for the closing. If your attorney or real estate agent is coming, make sure to coordinate. It's embarrassing and time consuming to show up at the wrong title company branch office because they moved the closing closer to the seller or to accommodate their attorney. I try to schedule and coordinate the closing at my preferred title branch whenever possible (which is about 90 percent of the time).

- *Use an attorney or title company:* The actual closing should be in the office of your attorney or at a title company. If you've followed the safe transaction practices up to this point, then you've hired one or both of these entities to protect your interests and to make sure that your purchase is appropriately researched, documented, and recorded.

- *The role of the title company and escrow agent:* Just what does the escrow agent or title company do? What is their responsibility? First, the title company or escrow agent safeguards and accounts for all funds. If you placed earnest money up for deposit, they will place it in an escrow account and apply it appropriately at closing.

    Generally, the escrow or title company produces documents, gathers information, does title and ownership research, and coordinates the issue of title insurance. They satisfy lender requirements for documentation, answer your title questions, research county records right up to closing, and generally assure that your purchase is lien-free unless there are liens you're accepting in the deal.

After the closing is complete, and all documents are signed, notarized, and properly recorded in county records, the title company or escrow agent will release funds. In a short sale, there usually aren't any for the seller, but the pay-off money for the mortgage will be released to the lender. Either they or you should then be sure to order the release of lien from the lender if it isn't part of the closing documentation already. Figure 25.2 is a copy of a closing checklist to help you keep things on track.

Make sure to get a complete copy of the signed closing documents, including copies of all disbursement checks. You want to make sure your bases are covered in case of a discrepancy or a check getting misrouted.

- *What Is RESPA?* The Real Estate Settlement Procedures Act (RESPA) is the regulation that governs the way closings are handled and monies disbursed

CLOSING CHECKLIST

Property Address: _____

Review of Title Insurance:	☐ Accurate ☐ Discrepancy_____
Legal Description Matches on All Documents:	☐ Accurate ☐ Discrepancy_____
Zoning Designation:	☐ Accurate ☐ Discrepancy_____
Property Tax Payment Status:	☐ Accurate ☐ Discrepancy_____
Review of Survey:	☐ Accurate ☐ Discrepancy_____
Check Government Agencies for:	☐ Building Code Violations ☐ Fire Code Violations ☐ Health Code Violations ☐ Safety Code Violations ☐ Environmental Hazard Citations
Review Pest Inspections:	☐ No visible Infestations ☐ Non active Infestation ☐ Active Infestation
Hazard Insurance Policy:	☐ Accurate ☐ Discrepancy_____
Review Deed:	☐ Accurate ☐ Discrepancy_____
Review Note:	☐ Accurate ☐ Discrepancy_____
Review Mortgage:	☐ Accurate ☐ Discrepancy_____
Review Assumption Documents:	☐ Accurate ☐ Discrepancy_____
Review Closing Statement:	☐ Accurate ☐ Discrepancy_____
Review Tax & Interest Prorations:	☐ Accurate ☐ Discrepancy_____
Does Property Have a Certificate of Occupancy:	☐ Yes ☐ No

 FIGURE 25.2 Closing Checklist

in transactions involving government guaranteed loans, meaning just about all transactions. Even if you're not getting a loan, it's highly likely that the one being paid off in the short sale makes the transaction subject to RESPA rules and procedures. Familiarize yourself with the rules.

The RESPA is changing (new rules were released in November 2008 which take effect in January 2010), trying to further protect the borrower from predatory lending practices or kickback arrangements between service vendors. There are already strict rules about "cooperative businesses," or things like a title company referring buyers to certain lenders with whom they might have a relationship that results in compensation. Those rules are going to be tightening even more.

What you should remember is that RESPA likely governs the way in which your transaction will be settled, and the title company and lender are subject to strict rules of conduct, disclosure, and billing practices.

The RESPA procedures do not apply to commercial transactions, even though you may use a similar settlement statement. Make sure everything is documented completely—especially all the disbursements.

After the Closing

As I mentioned before, one of the tasks normally handled by the escrow agent or the title company is dispersing funds to lien holders and recording deeds. If you aren't using these services, you must be sure that you get this done, whether on your own or with the help of an attorney. Even with the title company having responsibility, follow up to keep the process moving. You want that lien release from the lender, particularly in a short sale situation, as well as copies of all lien waivers or payoff statements. You also want to have a notarized and sealed copy of your recorded deed from the county clerk. This will take awhile to receive, but keep a copy until you receive the original.

Well, it's a joyous day! You've done everything right. The deal is closed, the vendors are paid, the lender has its money, and the seller has vacated, leaving you a home in reasonable condition. You have the keys in your pocket . . . but who else has keys?

Go directly to the home, do not pass "Go," do not collect $200, just go and immediately change the locks and secure the property.

The old locks could have been there for years. The previous residents may have given keys to repair persons, their teenager's friends, or any number of other people. You need to safeguard your new investment, and new locks are a small investment for peace of mind.

i   If they're in good shape, save the old locksets and reuse them for your next property.

CASHING OUT!

Nothing we have covered so far means anything—unless you make a profit! You did buy this book to learn how to create wealth, didn't you? In Part III we take a closer look at what to do with the property once you own it!

Whether you decide to quickly flip it to another investor, fix it up and sell it, or play for the long term and rent it out for monthly cash flow—now it's time to put it all together . . .

CHAPTER 26

Flipping Out—Quick Profits through Wholesaling

How quickly you turn a profit on your investment will vary from investor to investor. There is a great deal of appeal in rolling a property in the door and out again at a profit. Called *flipping* by many, this process depends first on getting a good buy at a below-market price. If you start in the hole, there is little chance of a flip profit when you add in the costs of a sale.

This chapter is all about the quick liquidation of your recently purchased property.

Selling Your Position

Let's start by looking at who might be your customer for the property. There are a number of customer types who might see a value in the purchase of your property even after your mark-up. Let's take a look at them individually for motivation and potential:

- *Junior lien holder:* Junior liens, such as home improvement or second mortgages, were involved in the short sale negotiations, so you know what, if any, compensation they received. Since the property was headed for foreclosure, they may have accepted little or nothing. There is at least some motivation on the part of a junior lienholder for buying the property.

  They lost some or all of their investment. If it was a large loan amount, they could seize the opportunity to recoup some or all of it by purchasing the property and improving it or renting it out while waiting for appreciation. If you are aware of a lienholder who had to forgive a significant loan, approach them with a package showing how they can improve and resell the property, making a profit. Remember, you can never be told yes unless you ask.

The key here is to come with market studies, comparable sales, and a detailed estimate for repairs or improvements from contractors. Have your stuff together! The more complete your proposal, and the more detailed the numbers, the better chance you have of convincing them of the value of the transaction.

- *The previous owner:* This isn't a viable option in most cases, since he didn't have the money to pay for it in the first place. However, if the owner managed to clear multiple junior liens and no longer has those payments, or the entire reason for the foreclosure was temporary circumstances, then he may be able to arrange private financing to buy the home back. It is unlikely that he can get a regular mortgage, but it could be a spouse who wasn't on the previous loan and still has good credit, or relatives who could buy it for her. After all, she will be able to get her home back with much lower payments after all the junior debt is gone. It is worth a try.

(*i*) As a general rule, I don't like to get previous owners involved in a buyback. It can be risky from a liability standpoint, not to mention the problems you've already waded through!

- *Other investors with different goals:* Your goal is to wholesale flip your property, and there are many investors out there searching for a home that will yield a profit if repaired or remodeled. If you can present a proposal that includes detailed repair or improvement cost estimates, as well as a market analysis with an after repair value (ARV) that would yield them a profit, you have created a wholesale opportunity.

I know an investor in Detroit who recently purchased a foreclosure for $8,000, did some fast repairs and sold it to another investor for $15,000. That investor turned around and sold it within a few months for $43,000 and everyone made out pretty well. That is, except for the lender who had to take the loss in the first place. Just a year earlier, the home was appraised for $93,000!

The other type of investor prospect is one searching for a long-term rental property. Their goal is to manage multiple properties, realizing the cash flow from rentals as well as the appreciation over time—and tax advantages. If there are repairs or improvements necessary, provide those estimates to the prospect. However, you'll want to add a few more items into your marketing package for this type of investor.

This type of investor will also want to know the rental income potential of the property. They usually do their own research; however, you want to present them with a sale package that has the work done for them so all they need to do is check it for accuracy. You need to get comparable property rental rates for the area, as well as occupancy rates. If there is little competition, or occupancy rates are high, this is a plus for your proposal. Include a return on investment analysis with their cost to purchase and rehab compared with the expected rental income.

This type of investor is also usually less risk-tolerant, so you'll want to prepare a very detailed analysis of the potential for rental of the home, including a pro forma showing cash flow expectations for the next few years. Disclaimers are in order because you're not guaranteeing anything, but you do want to present a realistic picture of the home's potential as a long-term rental property investment.

- *The builder or remodel contractor:* Another excellent potential buyer can be the building or remodel contractor. They can do the work wholesale and their profit is the mark up of the time and materials in the project. You save them the search and development cost for land, and you provide a home in an established neighborhood and market that is ready for improvement and fast resale. Remember, the best business deals are the ones that present what the other party was already looking for.

In this case, you do not need to get repair or improvement estimates, but you do need to put together a detailed list of defects of which you are aware. You want to give the contractor a set of basic data that will help him to decide if the home is a potential profitable rehab. Again, a disclaimer of your actual knowledge of all problems is important, but providing what you do know builds trust and could make the difference.

Assigning Your Interest

In most states, unless a purchase agreement specifically excludes it, you can assign your rights in a property or contract to another person. You've gone to all the trouble, effort, and expense to get this property, so why would you want to sign away your rights? In most cases, assigning your rights will not relieve you of responsibility for the property or mortgage, but you could structure a short-term contract until the new investor completed repairs or refinanced the property. I've created some nice short-term interest income for 3- to 12-month periods this way.

Aggregators

There are real estate aggregators who locate multiple properties and aggregate them into bulk purchases for large investor buyers. You could be the aggregator, or you could work with one. You would, in effect, be locating properties that fit their profile for their investors. You do the work to make the foreclosure sale happen, and then resell the property to the aggregator or assign your rights during the process.

This can be the ultimate in flipping because you can structure it so you never really even take possession of the property. You work through the process with the seller, get the deal to closing, assigning your rights immediately to the aggregator. A sweet deal any day of the week! I have a friend in Indianapolis who puts 20 to 30 properties together at a time this way.

If you are into the fun of doing deals, this could be your strategy of choice. After all, you're negotiating all over the place. You negotiate a purchase agreement with the upside-down homeowner. Then you work through the short sale or foreclosure process with the lender. All the while, you're working with buyers for the property you don't even own yet! You really can sell something you don't own . . . you just can't close on it until you do.

This can be fun, especially if you like waking up to new situations and problems every day. The downside is the failure and uncertainty sometimes of the whole foreclosure and short sale process—especially if you've already found a buyer for the property. It's a bit like having a truck waiting for your entire crop of corn, and the field burns. And, if you plowed it with a mule, the work was similar to the dealings with the lender in the process!

CHAPTER 27

Fixing Up Your New Investment

If you've purchased the home with the goal of fixing it up, the rules are the same whether you're going to rent it out long term or resell it for a profit. Do it right!

I am a big proponent of the "Clean, Repair, Replace" philosophy. Clean it first. If that doesn't work, repair it; and then only as a last resort—replace it. Even on major items, if you are going to resell the property quickly, less expensive air conditioning, heating, plumbing, and other equipment and fixtures should be used. It may not all be a quality issue because it might just mean shorter warranties, both equipment and labor. At any rate, the upfront costs will take precedence over considerations about length of life and extended warranties. Let's go a little deeper.

Eight-Step Repair Plan

Here is my basic eight-step plan for repairing and renovating a property. Obviously, the faster you can get the property to market, the faster you can get to your profits. So let's dig in.

Step 1—Analysis of the Work to Be Done

Take any inspection reports, whether from the previous owner or those done during the purchase, and begin your task list from those. Do your own walk-through and write up everything you see that isn't on the list already. Then walk through the property again. Missing items here will cause delays and possibly cost overruns later. Take your time and do it right. The next budget step will be thrown into chaos if you miss a lot in this step.

We discuss some things to start with next.

Clean Up the Property

Get a trash dumpster if necessary, and clean up the exterior first. Get rid of all trash, cut the lawn, cut back the shrubs, and give it some curb appeal. Chances are that the property has been neglected a bit, and neighbors will be watching to see what's going on. Make them feel good about you right away.

The interior will probably have a lot of trash as well—be prepared. Get several heavy-duty trash bags, and start filling with everything in sight.

Next, power wash the exterior completely. You can rent a power washer if necessary to get everything clean—the siding, concrete, windows, soffits, garage, doors, even the neighbor's dog if it's within reach. It takes a minimum of 3500 PSI pressure to remove years of dirt, and also expose what additional items need repairs.

Don't use a power washer with too much pressure because you can damage wood and other porous surfaces easily—which will just add to your repair costs! I use one that has variable pressure tip attachments, and make sure it's gas powered, not electric.

Eliminate Odors

The last thing you want a prospective buyer or tenant to say is that the house has an unpleasant odor. Use some heavy-duty cleaner with a lemon or orange scent to give the property a fresh smell. Go to an industrial supply store and get the commercial strength cleaner. It will be worth it.

Repair and Replace Checklist

Go back through your inspection checklist and make a list of items you can repair right away. I like to put new higher wattage bulbs in all the light fixtures, and invest in simple things that will have an immediate effect like inexpensive light and plumbing fixtures.

Carpet Cleaning and Replacement

I replaced the carpet in almost every property I have ever owned. This is one item that will pay for itself immediately. But don't do it until the end. I tear the carpet out, then repair and renovate with the floors bare, paint everything, and then have the new carpet put in. Do not use expensive carpet. I like remnants that are low-pile and neutral earth-tones. I do use a slightly better pad than normal, direct from Lowe's because it will make the carpet last longer and feels better to prospects walking through the house.

If you do happen to get a property with relatively new carpet, have it professionally steam cleaned. I use Stanley Steemer; they are nationwide, consistent, and reasonably priced. But I doubt you'll find many properties that have carpet worth saving.

Security

I also mentioned in a previous chapter that you must replace the door locks first thing. Do not wait, do it right away. I have had parties in my house—and I wasn't invited.

Also check the window locks, garage door opener (if electric, change or reset the access code), basement windows, and exterior lighting. I also install a motion detector floodlight in the front drive area.

Color Schemes

Keep everything neutral. Nobody wants blue walls, gold countertops, and orange shag carpeting. No matter what you like, or how cheap the sale was at the discount store, these types of items become a distraction. I once bought a property that had been owned by a world-champion balloonist. Everything in the house was done in bright primary colors—I had to wear sunglasses just to get past the front door. Don't get creative, leave that for the next owner.

As you think about the finished product, just keep in mind—beige, off-white, and lightly tinted yellow or off-white. Not that you can't use any color, just don't overdo it. You might think it's cool, but you're not going to live there.

i For best effect, kitchens should be off-white with a slight tint of yellow. Use bright white, flat latex paint for the ceilings.

How about things you do not want to repair? This could depend on your holding period. If your plan is long term, you might repair items just to avoid maintenance issues in the future. If you're selling after repairs, you might not fix things that are visually and operationally acceptable. One example of a repair you probably wouldn't make would be the inspector's recommendation to install sediment filters in the water supply. This is common with well water, and not a dangerous or bad situation, just a recommendation. If you plan on selling soon, this is a repair that would not add to value, but would subtract from profit. So leave it alone. But at the same time, if the water has a sulfur smell, that could turn off prospects. Remember—clean, repair, replace.

i The best way to keep on track and not forget anything along the way is to use my Renovation Planner Worksheet (see Figure 27.1). This can also be downloaded from my site at www.ChipCummings.com/CashingIn.

Property Address: _____

Project	Room	Start Date	Completion Date	Material Costs	Labor Costs	Total Costs

TOTAL MATERIAL COSTS _____

TOTAL LABOR COSTS _____ +

**20% OVERAGE FOR
UNEXPECTED EXPENSES** _____ +

GRAND TOTAL _____ =

 **FIGURE 27.1   Renovation Planning Worksheet**

Step 2—Build a Budget for the Project

This isn't a cost estimate step. It is a planning process based on your available funds. If you've had this renovation plan since the beginning, then you likely have already planned on a certain expenditure for bringing the property to a saleable condition. At any rate, arrive at an amount that you intend to spend on the project.

The biggest rookie mistake I see is regarding repairs. Here's a huge "Chip Tip" for you: don't over-improve the property. Look for repairs that don't add value and skip them. If an improvement will not increase the selling price, then it probably should be dropped from your list. Let the next owner do it. There are hundreds of resources, contractor cost estimate books, and web sites to help you in comparing cost-to-value of improvements.

If your goal is immediate resale, then you want to minimize the time between your purchase closing and the sale of the property. Every day you hold the property carries a cost in taxes, insurance, and utilities. If you are doing an extensive remodel, there will be additional insurance or costs associated with the project. Getting it all done as quickly as possible will cut holding costs, every dollar going back to profit.

Here is where I believe you should spend your time and dollars first:

- Painting
- Carpeting
- Kitchen
- Bathrooms
- Electrical fixtures, including outlets and switches
- Plumbing fixtures—faucets

As you can see, these are all visual items. These will have the greatest impact on your prospect, and the best return for your dollar.

A daily repair cost worksheet (see Figure 27.2) will help you budget and track the project. It keeps a running total of all your expenditures.

Step 3—Cost Estimates

Always remember that estimates are exactly that . . . estimates. When you're calling in repair and building contractors to give you estimates, always give yourself a little padding on the top to cover their errors (or yours) in defining the scope of the work. The more details you tell them, the better the estimates will be. Call on more than one contractor, and get a written estimate for each phase of the project.

Property Address: _____

DATE	ROOM	PROJECT	MATERIALS COST	LABOR COSTS	MISC. COSTS	TOTAL COST

Figure 27.2 Repairs—Daily Tracking Worksheet

Unless there is a huge difference, take the higher one to use as an estimate for this step in your plan.

(i)   I do not necessarily use the lowest bid for work. I want it done inexpensively, but I want it done right and on time.

There is repair estimate software available for free at many of the major lumber and home improvement centers. Check at their Contractors' Desk. There are also many online repair estimate resources and software programs. One that works with Excel can be found at: www.ozgrid.com/Services/excel-repair-cost-estimator.htm. I have listed several more in the resource section at the end of the book.

Contractor web sites have approximate costs for major renovations and improvements. In most localities, there is a contractor or two, or an architect, with more localized estimates for repairs or renovations, usually on their web site. For repairs for major appliances or heating, air conditioning, and plumbing, there are many flat rate contractors out there who can give you pretty firm quotes for work over the phone.

Don't be afraid to also check out the major home improvement stores for estimates. They have contractors on reserve for subcontracting work out to their customers and can quickly get you a competitive bid.

(i)   You can save money by negotiating a contract where you provide all the materials and they provide the labor. This will allow you to shop for the best value on fixtures, or find discounts on model overruns.

Step 4–Laborers, Contractors, and Vendors

If you're doing this only once, you may not be concerned with some of the aspects of your dealings with contractors. But you're probably planning on repeating this process again in the future. For that reason, you want to maintain good relationships with laborers, contractors, and vendors. Try not to over use their bidding services without giving them a job now and then. If you don't do this, you may find it difficult to get an estimate in the future. Make sure that they are licensed, bonded, and insured, or you could end up blowing all your profits in corrective actions—without any recourse.

Should you hire handyman types or contractors? There is nothing negative about a handyman business. Generally, these are single person or family operations, and you need to get references and check insurance and licenses, as well as whether they have the equipment and resources for your project. The larger the project, the more likely it is that you should work with more established and larger contractors. It could make the difference in on-time completion and reducing holding costs. I don't even consider using a general contractor unless there are major renovations being done involving at least seven subcontractors. Then I will need help.

Regarding estimates, try to get everything you can as a hard bid, rather than an estimate. This is more likely if the job is simple in nature, or if your specifications are clearly defined. Whether an estimate or a hard bid, get them in writing, with clear descriptions of what they will accomplish for payment. "Install countertops" is not good enough. What material, and how will they be trimmed up with the cabinets, and so on? Some other considerations include:

- *Use a contract.* If it's not in writing, expect things to change, usually to your detriment. You may not need an attorney for this. There are contracts available online and in office supply stores for contracting. If the contractor has his own, read it carefully, and feel free to make changes or additions to cover your concerns.

- *Lien laws in your state.* This is an area of concern for you, especially if you are dealing with a general contractor who is hiring subs. Check the lien laws in your state to see what power the contractor or mechanic has in placing liens against your property. Have clear payment clauses in your contract and require lien releases from all subs involved before they get final payment. You don't want to finish the project and place the home up for sale, only to find a lien recorded at the courthouse.

(i)   In most cases, charges for work done in a licensed profession by an unlicensed contractor cannot be placed as a lien against the property.

Insurance

Require proof of liability and worker's compensation insurance from all contractors on the job. You can find a lien against the home in the future due to a claim of on-the-job injury by one of their employees. Keep a file of these insurance certificates with your file of lien releases.

I have found that many headaches can be avoided by simply listening to your gut. If the contractor is spitting snuff on your living room floor, you probably should pass on him. Common sense can go a long way.

Ask all contractors for a copy of their license. If there's ever a problem, you will need the information that's on it for filing a complaint or claim.

Step 5—Supervision

Don't assume that hiring a general contractor will take you off the hook for supervision of the project. You become the supervisor of the supervisor. If you are acting as your own general contractor, and you're hiring multiple subcontractors, your job gets a lot more complicated. There is a lot of coordination required among the building trades in a remodel project. Would you like to guess at the problems and extra costs if you let the drywall contractor close in the walls before the electrician or plumber finishes his work? Take my word for it, it isn't cheap.

The important considerations in this step involve your knowledge and abilities. If you aren't sure that you have the knowledge and the time to supervise and coordinate contractors, hire someone who is suited for the job. Trust me; you'll save money in the end.

Step 6—Work Schedule

Whether you're doing one contract with the general, or multiple agreements with subcontractors, each document should set out a definite completion date and schedule for phases of the work. One contractor can be dependent on the work of another. You need to be sure that all of those involved at least know your drop-dead date for completion. There should be contractual penalties for delays that are the fault of the contractor. The more critical your time line needs, the greater the penalties. Financial penalties work like a charm. You'd be surprised how efficient workers can be when they know late equals a smaller check.

Your best strategy is to peg payments to performance or job completion milestones. An example would be breaking down the payments to a contractor as they are tied to observable completion items. These can be items on a punch list. If you pay the general a progress payment based on the completion of all wiring, and then another one when the walls are completed, you have definite and easily observed checks related to money.

(i) To keep really good contractors happy, and me at the top of their list, every once in a while I will pay them a separate bonus for doing a good job and getting work done ahead of schedule. I've passed out $50 bills directly to workers as a tip. It pays in the long run to keep your best contractors in a good mood!

As the job moves forward, a logically arranged punch list will keep everyone on track, with deadlines and payments keyed to the items on the list. Again, money is the greatest of motivators.

Step 7—Quality Control

Are you capable of determining the quality of a contractor's work? Most of us can do an okay job in this area. However, if you're in doubt as to whether a certain job is satisfactory, or if an item of equipment is properly installed, pay for another expert to come in and tell you. Make at least one inspection daily of the project because you can't look inside a wall that's been closed in over the wiring and plumbing.

Get your contractors and subs used to the fact that you will release payments only after you have personally walked the job and checked the quality of the phase or item for which they want payment. This sets the tone for the job, and they know that you will not let money move unless the work is done right. Use a punch list on a final walk-through with a contractor to compile items that need to be completed before final payment is released.

i Make sure to ask for copies of all building permits that were applied for by the contractor, as well as any final inspection reports from the building inspector.

Step 8—Completion Date

One of the most important items in your original contracts is the completion date and the amount of money to be withheld from each contractor until you've signed off on the satisfactory completion of their job. A typical number is 10 percent. If a contractor is hired for a job at $1,000, then progress payments can be made through the job, but $100 would be held back until your satisfaction that the job is completed satisfactorily. This is usually done by holding back 10 percent of each project phase or draw. So, a total job of $25,000, even if there have been multiple draws against the work, would see $2,500 remaining when the contractor asks for final completion payment.

Once the job is complete and satisfactory, pay the contractors right away. Your reputation is everything, and word will spread like wildfire throughout the contractor community if you screw around with their money.

When all of the work is completed, and no contractors will be on the site again, hire a professional cleaning company to come in and get the place sale-ready. This is one of the most important expenditures you'll make. None of the work in the walls or attic will be visible to the potential buyer, but the first impression when they walk in shouldn't be the crushed coke cans the workers left behind.

When releasing final payment to any contractor, request a signed lien waiver from them. You will need it for the title company if you sell the property within six months. If dealing with a general contractor, demand one from all subs and get a signed sworn statement that details all the costs and payments.

CHAPTER 28

Renting Your New Property

Making steady monthly money from real estate over the long term helps to round out a solid investing plan. This means keeping your new property and renting it out. The benefits are many, but there can also be the hassles. If you stick in there, the rewards can be enormous. There are a great many real estate investors living a life of luxury in early retirement from building up an inventory of rental properties over time. Let's talk about how to get it done, and get it done right!

Becoming a Landlord

There are undoubtedly headaches that come with being a landlord. Take a look at why those headaches are small in comparison to the benefits of owning and managing rental properties:

- *Positive regular cash flow:* If you own properties outright, or if you can structure a mortgage that is lower than your rent and direct expense payments, your ongoing rental payments generate a regular positive cash that flows into your investment account. That's a good start!

- *Depreciation tax deduction:* Consult your accountant, but generally you will be able to write off depreciation of the rental home. Current tax law allows a 27.5-year depreciation of a residential rental property. If you paid $200,000, this would be $7,273 per year as a depreciation deduction. That much of your rental cash flow would then be free of federal income tax. Again, consult with a tax professional about your specific situation.

- *Mortgage interest deduction:* If you purchased with a mortgage, or took out equity later with one, the interest would also be deductible. If you still have positive rental cash flow, this would have the effect of adding to it.

- *Inflation is your friend:* While investors in stocks and bonds are fretting over inflation rates eating away at their returns, you will likely be raising rents to go with the flow. You will also likely be realizing an appreciation in value because inflation usually causes home prices to rise as well.

- *Long-term appreciation in value:* Home prices increased over the past 30 years. As a landlord, you will be taking in the rent, with your tenants paying for the property while you realize the gains.

- *Long-term capital gains versus short-term:* Check with your accountant, but long-term capital gains when you sell after an extended holding period have always been significantly lower than the short-term capital gains rate if you flip the property.

Now you're excited about getting a tenant into the property and going to the bank each month with your rental payments. You'll have plenty of opportunities to deal with tenant attitudes and complaints. Don't compound your problems with renters who were previous owners and who still consider it "their home." That is a recipe for disaster. They could feel that you took advantage of their situation, and this can only get worse over time. Make a clean break from the previous owners.

💣 You just might be tempted to rent back to the previous owners, especially if they approach you with this inquiry during the short sale or purchase process. Let me whisper something in your ear: don't do it.

I had a property I purchased and held for several years, only to have the previous owners come back and buy it on a two-year lease option. They still thought it was "their" house, except when it came to the repairs. They ended up moving out, so at least I got to keep the option money—but it wasn't worth the hassle.

What to Do First

The excitement of the purchase or short sale process, and the business of the remodel and repair projects didn't leave you any time to consider the next and long-term step of becoming a landlord. You probably have some very funny memories, many from *Saturday Night Live* skits! Get all that out of your mind and just ask yourself:

- Am I suited to work with tenants?
- Is my personality conducive to landlord-tenant relations?

- Do I have the time to devote to managing properties?
- More importantly, can I manage people?

You must really be honest with yourself here. You may need a property management company.

Getting Your Questions Answered

These are all good questions, and there are going to be others you'll have over time. Experience is the best teacher, but you can get help. You might want to join a national association such as the National Real Estate Investors Association (www .NationalREIA.com).

Or, check out a local rental property owner association (RPOA). There are hundreds, just search online for RPOA or rental property association for information. There you can regularly talk with other landlords, sharing information and research, and of course—horror stories.

State Legal Requirements and Landlord Tenant Relations

Some of your responsibilities will be obvious in the lease agreements you use. These should come from your attorney or another trusted source for up-to-date legal information in your state. For the detail of your obligations and those of your tenants, you'll want to get a copy of your state's landlord tenant laws and requirements. Many states have them online.

Don't risk your profitability or your property by getting involved in lawsuits with tenants because you didn't understand the rules for your relationships. The first and foremost consideration is the Fair Housing Act. If you get on the wrong side of this law, a simple complaint from a tenant can bring a great deal of grief.

Listen closely—the government takes this law very seriously, and the fines are huge. This act governs not only how you deal with tenants and applicants for tenancy, it controls wording in advertisements as well. You might be surprised at the seemingly innocent items you might place into an ad about children or retired persons that will put you on the wrong side of this law.

If you interview a white couple as a tenant, then a minority couple walks in, make sure you are asking the same questions, and for the same information! I have had "testers" walk into properties before—you never know.

Don't assume that just owning the home and placing a "For Rent" ad is all you must do to start your business. There may be local ordinances that require you to get a business license, special codes or inspections for rental properties, and more. Go to your local government offices and get all the details, licenses, and register as required. Fines later are almost always much more expensive than the proper licenses and registration done right at the beginning.

Finding Tenants

Let's talk about marketing for tenants first. You don't need to know the rest of this until you have a paying renter. Don't sit in a vacuum and make rental and marketing decisions. Go out and drive around. Look for rental signs and special banners like "One month free with one year lease," and so on. You need to call your competition like a tenant, and determine what similar properties are renting for. Use the classifieds to compare rental homes just like you did in researching comparable sales in your purchase process.

Be objective and rate your property against the competition. You want to get the best rent you can, but pricing too high will just keep the property empty longer. Too low, and you might get the wrong tenant. It doesn't matter what you think your property is worth, what matters is what someone will pay. As an example, if you are holding out for another $100 per month for $1,000, when $900 would get it rented, you would lose the excess in less than 45 days of "no occupancy."

If the "one month free" tactic seems to be working for others, then increase your rent to allow you to do it. If you add $900 to the annual total, it would increase your monthly rent by $75. Then just give them their last month, or a middle month free. Your end result is the same.

Run ads in the classifieds section of your newspaper. Also post your listing on Craig's List and similar sites. If college students are a possible market, then place cards on authorized bulletin boards and at college hangouts. Contact the college housing office and register your property.

💣 I have owned and managed lots of student housing—make sure to increase the rent to plan for not receiving it during the summer break. Also invest in a lot of paneling—drywall breaks too easy.

Put ads on supermarket boards in the area. You aren't just looking for someone who's looking to rent. You're looking for someone who is already renting. They may be getting close to the end of their lease and could be looking for a change.

Once you have some response to your advertising, you'll get applicants. Be prepared with a very thorough and complete rental application. The biggest mistake that most landlords make is to ask for too little information. If you upset an applicant by asking for financial, credit, reference, and contact information, then you probably don't need that person for a tenant. Go with your gut, the gut always warns you.

It is a lot cheaper to maintain an empty apartment than to evict a bad tenant. Proceed cautiously!

Tap a local landlord organization or an online resource to find a very thorough rental application. Be careful about the questions from the Fair Housing Act perspective. Wherever you get the form, verify that it complies with Fair Housing standards. You can't get too much information. A cell phone number is better than a home phone because people move around, but keep their cell number for years. Get their relatives' cell numbers and addresses, drivers' license number, and written permission to get rental references.

As far as credit checks go, your lease application should include written permission to check their credit history. You can find companies that will do this for you, and some will even do background checks as well, such as AccurateCredit .com. There are many good people out there with poor credit, so you may want to cut them some slack. Ask them to explain any derogatory marks on the credit. However, you need to know what the case is, and it could influence the amount you ask for a security deposit.

Many states restrict the amount you can collect for a security deposit, and how it has to be used and returned. Find out what the rules are!

Now, let's look at what we need in our lease agreement to make it a valid contract and to cover all aspects of our landlord-tenant relationship:

- *A lease is a legal contract.* Make sure that your prospective tenant is of legal age and competent to enter into a contract.

- *Have an adequate description of the property.* An address might be sufficient, but be sure that you have described the property in such a way that it can't be confused with another. If an exterior storage unit is included, then have it in the agreement.

- *Define the time frame of the lease.* Start with the date and exact time that the lease starts and state a date and time for the end of the lease and when the unit should be vacated.

- *Outline security deposits and rent payment terms.* The lease agreement needs to be very specific as to who will hold deposits, whether they earn interest, what they're held for, and how they will be handled at the end of the lease or in case of default.

Make sure to spell out the late fees. I prefer to include an early payment discount to tenants instead. Many will take advantage of it, and it's actually the same amount. It's all in the marketing!

- *Explain sublets or assignments.* If you don't tell them they can't, they may do it. You don't want to address this as an "after the fact" situation. Make sure the people living in your property are the people you rented to.

- *Outline use and occupancy limitations.* Be clear as to who and how many can live there, how many cars can park, and if they can have a home-based business or not.

- *Specify your rights of entry and inspection.* Many states give specific notice rights to tenants. Make sure that you follow the law and be clear about how and when you might gain access.

- *Be clear about renewal terms.* Can the tenant renew the lease, and what will the new rent amount be? If they go into a month-to-month tenancy, what rights change?

Don't sign a lease for longer than one year, unless it is for a commercial use tenant. Too many things can happen, and you don't want to be locked in for too long. If they like it, they'll renew.

What about deposits? Again, read your laws, and consult an attorney and an accountant. If you can hold the last month's rent, then you might want to do so. It could cost you some tenants if they don't have that much cash, but you could also allow them to pay an extra amount each month for a while to build it up.

If you can hold a damage deposit, be clear as to how it will be handled when they move out. The best approach is a thorough inspection checklist when they move in and another one when they vacate. I always do a walk-through with tenants when they get the keys. Be clear as to how you will hold back money and how long you have to decide. Additional pet rent and/or deposits, if legal in your area, are a great idea. People love their pets, and will pay what you need to cover possible damage. Remember, this is your investment, protect it fiercely!

I also authorize my tenants to do minor repairs, and include the receipts with their monthly rent for reimbursement. This is a great way to get cheap labor, and avoid daily phone calls over little stuff!

CHAPTER 29

Staging, Marketing, and Selling Properties for Maximum Profit

I f your plan is to sell your property, think back to when you were buying, and remember that value is the key. You saw value in a short sale because the owner was upside-down in his or her loan, and you could get the property at a discount to true value. Or you saw an opportunity to improve the property, with your profit being the mark up after bringing it up to saleable condition. Whatever the reasoning for purchase was, you saw value in the property. Keep that in mind while I talk about being on the other side of the fence in this chapter. If you can anticipate problems, you can solve them before anyone notices. If you anticipate questions, you can have answers before they are raised.

What's It Worth?

When you did your short sale package, you put together a market analysis that used recently sold properties and currently listed properties to develop a market value for the short sale candidate. The procedure is very similar now, except that you're looking for comparable sales that will support the price at which you want to sell.

Don't cherry-pick the comps because you'll only be fooling yourself. You will not be able to choose the ones your prospective buyers are using, so get as many comps as you can in the nearby area that have sold recently.

Some considerations in what is sometimes called the *Comparative Market Analysis* (CMA):

- Select properties as similar to yours as possible.
- Where differences exist, adjust the value to make up for them.

- Be objective, and try to compare realistically.
- Drive and look at the comps, don't just use the records.

Once you have come up with a price, you can do the other analysis, the *Competitive Market Analysis*. With this process, you look at your current competition on the market. Again, drive by the competition; this is the only way that you can make a realistic comparison. We want to see where our property and pricing falls in the competitive landscape.

A mistake made by many realtors, as well as investors, is not pricing to the competition. If comparable properties that have recently sold are saying that your home should be priced at $250,000, the end result can be quite different based on the current market and competition. Here is how the number can go either direction:

- When past sales happened, there were 18 competitive properties listed, and now there are 32. With a higher inventory and more competition, your price needs to drop. More circulation equals lower prices.
- Now reverse the situation. There are only 10 active listings in competition, so supply and demand might very well dictate an increase in price.

Another thing overlooked by many investors is their cost to hold a property. Every day you still own it costs you money. Your situation and whether you have a mortgage will define these holding costs. However, consider this when you price the property. Many sellers have ended up with less by holding out too long for more. We are not in the business of being right, we're in the business of making money. Get a fair market price, and move on to the next deal.

(i) An excellent strategy is to price just under the market, perhaps by 5 percent. It's okay to state that fact in your marketing as well. Buyers are running the numbers just as you did. If you are both being realistic in your calculations, if your property appears to be a value . . . it will sell!

Get Ready, Get Set

Just like a purchase, the sale requires a plan. Walk through the property and write down all the items that might turn you off if you were a buyer. This is your property preparation checklist. We're not looking at remodel or major improvements here, but more the little things that buyers notice and that influence their expectations. Fixing the little things and creating a better first impression will go a long way.

Should you stage your property? This really isn't a question. If staging is defined as setting up the property for its best presentation, then why ask—just do it! Whether or not you know it, everything you have ever purchased was staged. Proof that staging works is the fact that you bought it!

You may be asking if you should hire professional stagers. That is not necessary if you can do some things for yourself or contract them out, for example:

- Landscaping and curb appeal should be the best it can be economically.
- Absolute cleanliness is a must.
- Furnished works better than empty space.
- No clutter and no personal belongings.

What you are trying to accomplish is to enable the buyer to envision this as his home, not yours. Any artwork should be generic and not too personal. Knickknacks and clutter need to be gone. Furniture should accent and not crowd a room. Placement should invite the buyer into a room and make it look larger and bright.

Faucets shouldn't drip. Walls shouldn't be scarred. Doors and windows should function properly. Floors should be clean. It's really not difficult to know what to do. What would you want to see if this were to be your future personal home?

 When staging a house, remember that less is more!

Marketing with a Realtor

Let's get some terminology out of the way in regards to real estate professionals:

- A realtor is a member of the National Association of Realtors and subscribes to a code of ethics and enforcement of them through the association.
- An agent is usually subordinated to and working under a sponsoring real estate broker. They cannot work outside the authority of the broker.
- A real estate broker could still be associated with a brokerage or sponsoring broker, but normally has satisfied more rigorous licensing or experience requirements.

Though they are called agents, it is much more likely today that the real estate person with whom you are working is not your agent. This is a legal status that is a lot like that of an attorney, and they are obligated to certain requirements. There is some liability on your part as well. You really don't need for them to be your agent because that usually carries with it vicarious liability on your part. If they do something illegal that you knew about, you could be held liable if they were your agent. Just have your real estate professional explain the relationship under which you will work together. There will likely be a written disclosure of some kind as well.

Only work with a realtor. You take your profession seriously, and so do they. Nothing else needs to be said!

You don't have to list with a realtor to work with them. If you choose to market your home on your own, you can still bring it to the attention of local real estate professionals. You can offer a commission to those who bring a buyer. You might even want to offer a slightly higher buyer agent commission than is common in the multiple listing service (MLS). In this dry market, you have the edge. You make the terms and can say take it or leave it. Most agents would rather make 4 percent of something than 100 percent of nothing.

The real estate professional will be hesitant to bring clients to look at your property. They view you as an unrepresented party, and they will be working in the best interests of their client. They could incur liability if you ask questions and they answer them. If you make it clear in your materials directed at agents that you will be represented by an attorney and not reliant on them for advice, it could bring you more showings.

If an agent shows your property to a prospect, they will want to know they're going to get paid. They will ask for a written agreement to do that. Figure 29.1 is a sample broker participation agreement you can use for one time showings.

Marketing It Yourself

Don't wait; start the marketing process. Short of major work or renovation, don't let minor repairs hold up your marketing. Remember that holding costs are building daily. I generally get properties on the market within a week after I own it—even if the work isn't done.

In the middle of rehabing a property several years ago, a "listed" property went up for sale across the street. I found out what the listed price was, and when they were having an open house. I priced mine 10 percent lower, had a sign in the yard that Sunday—and had a full price offer the next day. I didn't even have the new cabinets in yet!

Prepare a quality property brochure. Think like a drive-by buyer, especially if you're placing a brochure box at the sign. If you drove up and had an interest, what would you want to see in the brochure? If the lot is different, perhaps

FIGURE 29.2   Sample Classified Ads

as well. This is a service that gives you an 800 number, and even routes the caller to your custom marketing message—even allowing faxback of documents, or instant connection with your cell phone, realtor, or mortgage person. The other feature is that it will capture the phone number of the caller, so that you can call them back to see if you can get a dialogue going. The system I use is at www .CCUCallCapture.com.

The web site you build is visible to the world. Don't forget that your home may be viewed by site visitors from other countries. If your area is a draw for other countries and cultures, mention it in your site marketing.

As far as the local nature of the marketing piece, you will probably do some classified ads. If you priced below market, this is a good place to make that point, as well as on sites like eBay.com and CraigsList.com.

(i) A great way to get more bang for your buck is to place a small three-line ad that drives people to a web site. Don't try and list all the features in an expensive classified ad—create mystery and "force" people to check it out! Figure 29.2 illustrates some examples.

Finding Qualified Buyers

You are not in this to make friends, though it could and does happen. Do not fear upsetting a looker by asking him questions and for documents that will indicate he is a buyer who is qualified to purchase the property. Savvy buyers will come with a lender preapproval letter, but if they do not, ask for one before you waste a lot of time on them. Most lenders can crank one off the computer within an hour of checking their credit, so it isn't a delay you can't afford. We don't care about serving cookies and giving balloons to the kids, leave that to the circus. We are in the business of making money!

It's not difficult to get a preapproval letter, so you shouldn't entertain an offer without one. Any buyer who's unprepared may just be a casual looker, or it may be that he or she has credit and financial issues. It is best that you place the requirement for a lender preapproval letter in your marketing materials. You shouldn't have to explain or justify it if you state it upfront.

i   Send your inquiries to your mortgage broker team member to get qualified, and indicate that you don't show the home to anyone who isn't preapproved first!

Negotiating Offers

When a buyer brings an offer, there is one consideration right off the bat. Did it come with a real estate agent, or is the buyer unrepresented? First, it is a money issue for you because using a real estate agent will require a commission, thus your counteroffer might need to take that into consideration.

However, there is another consideration: if the buyer is not represented, you will want to have something in your offer or counteroffers that states clearly that you have advised the buyer to seek advice from an attorney in these dealings, and that you will not be offering him assistance in the process. Don't let the case end up in front of a judge because he didn't understand the issues involved. If it does, at least you have the "I told you so!" document.

Be courteous and business-like in your responses to offers and counteroffers. A deal that falls through in this process is wasted time for all involved. So, carefully consider offers, and do not get offended and develop an attitude. Buyers will test the water with low offers, but that doesn't mean they won't pay more. Just counteroffer where you want the price to go. The less emotional, the better. The best way to create a professional, yet courteous atmosphere during negotiations is to be professional and courteous.

Seller Financing

One of the reasons that we invest in real estate is for the higher rates of return that real estate provides. Don't overlook the opportunities presented by seller financing.

It is not a discount route for the buyer because you should charge market rates. This will be significantly more than the money would earn in a savings account or in Certificates of Deposit. If long-term, excellent interest and principal payments appeal to you, then entertain the seller financing route.

By involving an attorney with the proper safeguards, you can secure your position and have the option of repossession if the buyer defaults. The worst case might be a few months or years of nice returns, with a new opportunity to sell the property. I would strongly suggest that one of the requirements for the seller financing be that you be named as an "additional insured" on their homeowner insurance policy. That way you'll be notified if they let the insurance lapse.

i For a loan application, use a standard FNMA 1003 government application form that can be downloaded free from: https://www.efanniemae.com/sf/formsdocs/forms/1003.jsp.

Do the proper credit and background checks. Cover your interests and backside by consulting an attorney for help with the paperwork.

If you're charging market rates, the usual reason for a buyer to be interested in seller financing is a lack of a significant down payment, or a credit problem. Once you know all about him, you can make the decision whether to proceed. If he has issues with down payment and/or credit, it is likely that you can demand top price for the home by working with him. If that's the case, you may want to assign or sell the loan later.

If the problems were with credit, most buyers of loan paper will consider the loan as "seasoned" in a couple of years. So, at some point, for the right price, you may want to assign your rights or sell the loan. Figure 29.3 is a form to help you out if you're doing it right away. Why might you do that? Another investor may like this buyer's credit profile, and they may want this loan for their portfolio. If so, you can assign your rights immediately and walk away with cash.

Don't Forget Taxes

If you are the owner in a pre-foreclosure property situation, you may be able to take the steps outlined here and sell the property prior to foreclosure. If so, be sure to consider the tax consequences of selling if any debt is forgiven. If the lender reports the amount forgiven on a 1099 form, the IRS may tax you on it. However, in 2008, relief acts were placed into law that may remove this concern for you. Consult your tax professional.

ASSIGNMENT OF PURCHASE AGREEMENT

The agreement is made on this _____ Day of _____ 20__, between:

_____ hereby known as the Assignor, and

_____ hereby known as the Assignee.

In return for the consideration set for in this agreement, Assignor hereby assigns, sells, and transfers all of the Assignor's title and interest in and rights under the attached agreement entitled, "Purchase Agreement" dated: _____, hereby referred to as the "Agreement" executed by: _____ as Seller and by _____, as Buyer.   For the property commonly known as:_____
_____
_____

And legally described as: _____
_____
_____
_____

By accepting this assignment, Assignee agrees to undertake and perform the obligations imposed on Assignor, as buyer, under the aforementioned Agreement. Assignee accepts this assignment subject to all terms and conditions contained in the Agreement, or imposed by law. A copy of the Agreement is attached hereto as Exhibit "A" and incorporated herein as if fully set forth herein.

It is hereby agreed that the obligations of both Assignor and Assignee, hereunder, are not contingent upon the recordation of a deed, or other completion of the purchase of the property, under the Agreement. It is the sole responsibility of Assignee to seek legal or other relief, in the event that the agreement is not performed, as a result of the act or omission of any other party to the Agreement.

In return for the rights assigned by Assignor herein, Assignee hereby agrees to pay Assignor the sum of _____ dollars.

All of the provisions of this assignment of purchase agreement shall extend to, bind, and inure to the benefit of heirs, executors, personal representatives, successors, and assigns of Assignor and Assignee.

IN WITNESS WHEREOF, Assignor and Assignee have set their hands on this day.
The _____ Day of _____ 20__.

_____   _____
Assignor   Assignee

_____   _____
Witness   Witness

   FIGURE 29.3   Assignment of Purchase Agreement

Final Thoughts

If you've made it this far, then you have all the ammunition you need to go out into the marketplace and feel confident about your new profession. I feel privileged that you invited me in to help educate you and get you started on your road to financial freedom.

The real estate and mortgage lending worlds have been very good to me over the years, and I feel blessed by the thousands of people I have had the good fortune to meet and work with. People who've shared their insights, stories and their secrets on how to do this the right way. Now it's your turn to take this information and do something with it—nothing will happen until you do!

Now go make some money!

—Chip

When beginning as a foreclosure investor, many people will make simple mistakes that end up costing them thousands of dollars. Here is a quick checklist of amateur mistakes, and what NOT to do when dealing with foreclosure properties. You are risking your money if you are:

1. **Buying a property without researching the title;**

2. **Buying a junior lien thinking it's a senior lien;**

3. **Buying without inspecting the property;**

4. **Paying more than it's worth and/or overestimating the value;**

5. **Buying inside the redemption period instead of at the pre-foreclosure stage;**

6. **Fixing up a property before the owner is out;**

7. **Closing the transaction before the owner is out;**

8. **Underestimating the repair and holding costs;**

9. **Trusting everything the homeowner says at face value; or**

10. **Being too stubborn or getting too greedy!**

Post this list above your desk, and refer to it each and every time you're looking at a deal!

Best wishes to your success!

I t is important to understand the rules for the jurisdiction and state where the property is located prior to pursuing the foreclosure market. We have listed the current rules and regulations for all 50 states and Washington DC. Here is a guide to the listing information:

- *Type of foreclosure process:* This can be *judicial* or *nonjudicial,* or even both! A judicial process involves a lawsuit by the lender, and is handled by the court. A nonjudicial process is involved when there is a preauthorized power of sale in the mortgage document or deed of trust. This allows the lender to foreclosure directly to pay off the loan balance and any costs.

- *Process period:* The average amount of time it takes for the foreclosure to go from the initial foreclosure notice (or notice of default) through to the time possession is transferred to a new owner.

- *Type of deed:* The type of deed involved can be a *mortgage,* a *deed of trust* or both. A mortgage is a specific contract between the borrower and lender that allows the lender to foreclosure in event of default. A deed of trust is a contract that puts control of the deed with a trustee—a neutral third party. In this case, the trustee forecloses when the borrower defaults on the loan.

- *Notice of default:* Some states require that a notice of default (or simply NOD) be sent to the borrower informing them of their default status on the loan.

- *Notice of sale requirements:* A published and posted notice indicating the specific date, time, place, and terms of a foreclosure sale. Includes the property address, legal description, as well as borrower and lender information. May be overridden by mortgage documents.

- *Redemption period requirements:* A period of time after the sale, in which the foreclosed borrower has the right to redeem the property by paying off the loan and all costs—including attorney fees, penalties, and interest.

The information provided next is considered to be up-to-date and accurate as of time of publication, but as with everything, things do change. These rules and regulations can also sometimes vary from county to county, so consult the county clerk or register of deeds or a qualified real estate attorney for any clarification or additional details. Remember, never trespass on a property that you do not own unless you have obtained permission to do so.

Alabama

- *Type of foreclosure process:* Both. Nonjudicial is more common.
- *Process period:* 60–90 days average.
- *Type of deed:* Both are used.
- *Notice of default:* Not state mandated, but may be included in lender documents.
- *Notice of sale requirements:* Posted at courthouse and three other public places, 3 weeks notice in local newspaper and as directed by individual mortgage document.
- *Redemption period requirements:* 12 months.

Alaska

- *Type of foreclosure process:* Both. Nonjudicial is more common.
- *Process period:* 90 day average.
- *Type of deed:* Both are used.
- *Notice of default:* Varies by area.
- *Notice of sale requirements:* Notice in local newspaper for 4 consecutive weeks and in 3 public places—one of which has to be closest U.S. Postal office 30 days prior to the date of sale.
- *Redemption period requirements:* 12 months for judicial; none for nonjudicial.

Arizona

- *Type of foreclosure process:* Nonjudicial.
- *Process period:* 90 days.
- *Type of deed:* Both.
- *Notice of default:* None.
- *Notice of sale requirements:* Notice must be published in local newspaper for 4 consecutive weeks, with last notice appearing no less than 10 days prior to sale; mailed to all lien holders and borrower at least 3 months prior to sale; posted at courthouse and on property at least 20 days prior to sale.
- *Redemption period requirements:* None.

Arkansas

- *Type of foreclosure process:* Both.
- *Process period:* 90–120 days average.
- *Type of deed:* Both.
- *Notice of default:* Must be filed with county and mailed to borrower (nonjudicial).
- *Notice of sale requirements:* 4 consecutive weeks listed in local newspaper, and the final notice must appear at least 10 days prior to the sale; posted in the county recorders office.
- *Redemption period requirements:* 12 months for judicial, none for nonjudicial.

California

- *Type of foreclosure process:* Both. Nonjudicial is more common.
- *Process period:* 120 days.
- *Type of deed:* Both.
- *Notice of default:* Notice must be filed with county, mailed to all borrowers and lien holders.
- *Notice of sale requirements:* Published in local newspaper for 3 consecutive weeks at least 20 days prior to sale; recorded with county at least 14 days prior to sale; posted on property and in at least one public location minimum of 20 days prior to sale.
- *Redemption period requirements:* 365 days judicial; None for nonjudicial.

Colorado

- *Type of foreclosure process:* Both. Nonjudicial is more common.
- *Process period:* 45–180 days average.
- *Type of deed:* Deed of Trust.
- *Notice of default:* None.
- *Notice of sale requirements:* Mailed to borrower and published 5 weeks in local newspaper.
- *Redemption period requirements:* 75 days for residential; 180 days for agricultural.

Connecticut

- *Type of foreclosure process:* Judicial.
- *Process period:* 60–150 days average.
- *Type of deed:* Mortgage Deed.
- *Notice of default:* None.
- *Notice of sale requirements:* Notice published by attorney.
- *Redemption period requirements:* Decided by court.

Delaware

- *Type of foreclosure process:* Judicial.
- *Process period:* 210–300 days.
- *Type of deed:* Mortgage Deed.
- *Notice of default:* None.
- *Notice of sale requirements:* Notice to borrower at least 10 days prior to sale; 14 days posting on the property; published in two local newspapers no more than 3 times per week for 2 weeks prior to sale.
- *Redemption period requirements:* None. Borrower may contest sale prior to court confirmation.

Florida

- *Type of foreclosure process:* Judicial.
- *Process period:* 150–180 days average.

- *Type of deed:* Mortgage Deed.
- *Notice of default:* None required.
- *Notice of sale requirements:* Notice to be published in local newspaper for 2 consecutive weeks prior to sale—second notice to be at least 5 days prior to sale.
- *Redemption period requirements:* None.

Georgia

- *Type of foreclosure process:* Both (mostly nonjudicial).
- *Process period:* 60–90 days average.
- *Type of deed:* Both.
- *Notice of default:* None required.
- *Notice of sale requirements:* Notice to borrower at least 15 days prior to sale; publication in local newspaper for 4 weeks prior to sale.
- *Redemption period requirements:* None.

Hawaii

- *Type of foreclosure process:* Both.
- *Process period:* 180 days nonjudicial; 330 days judicial.
- *Type of deed:* Both.
- *Notice of default:* As required by mortgage clause.
- *Notice of sale requirements:* Notice to borrower at least 21 days before sale; publication in local newspaper for 3 consecutive weeks prior to sale, with final notice appearing at least 14 days prior to sale.
- *Redemption period requirements:* None.

Idaho

- *Type of foreclosure process:* Both, but mostly nonjudicial.
- *Process period:* 150–180 days for nonjudicial; 330 days for judicial.
- *Type of deed:* Both.
- *Notice of default:* Notice to be mailed to borrower and lien holders or interested parties as filed with county recorders office.
- *Notice of sale requirements:* Notice mailed to borrower 120 days prior to sale; publication in local newspaper for 4 consecutive weeks, with final notice to appear not less than 30 days prior to sale.
- *Redemption period requirements:* 365 days judicial; none for nonjudicial.

Illinois

- *Type of foreclosure process:* Judicial.
- *Process period:* 300–360 days average.

- *Type of deed:* Mortgage Deed.
- *Notice of default:* None.
- *Notice of sale requirements:* Notice sent to borrower and all lien holders; published in local newspaper for 3 consecutive weeks no more than 45 days prior to sale, with last notice appearing no less than 7 days prior to sale.
- *Redemption period requirements:* 90 days.

Indiana

- *Type of foreclosure process:* Judicial.
- *Process period:* 150–270 days average.
- *Type of deed:* Mortgage Deed.
- *Notice of default:* None.
- *Notice of sale requirements:* Personal delivery by sheriff to borrower; Notice published in local newspaper for 3 consecutive weeks no more than 30 days prior to sale; posted in at least 3 public places and in county courthouse.
- *Redemption period requirements:* None.

Iowa

- *Type of foreclosure process:* Both (nonjudicial by request).
- *Process period:* 120–180 days average.
- *Type of deed:* Mortgage Deed.
- *Notice of default:* Notice required to borrower.
- *Notice of sale requirements:* Notice delivered to borrower at least 20 days prior to sale; publication in local newspaper with first notice at least 4 weeks prior to sale and again 2 weeks prior to sale; posted in three public places including county courthouse.
- *Redemption period requirements:* Variable.

Kansas

- *Type of foreclosure process:* Judicial.
- *Process period:* 12–24 months.
- *Type of deed:* Mortgage Deed.
- *Notice of default:* Required to borrower.
- *Notice of sale requirements:* Notice to be published in local newspaper for 3 consecutive weeks prior to sale.
- *Redemption period requirements:* 90 days (if vacant); 180 days (if occupied).

Kentucky

- *Type of foreclosure process:* Judicial.
- *Process period:* 180 days.

- *Type of deed:* Mortgage Deed.
- *Notice of default:* None.
- *Notice of sale requirements:* Published in local newspaper for 3 consecutive weeks prior to sale.
- *Redemption period requirements:* 12 months.

Louisiana

- *Type of foreclosure process:* Judicial.
- *Process period:* 60–270 days (shorter is typical).
- *Type of deed:* Mortgage Deed.
- *Notice of default:* None.
- *Notice of sale requirements:* Personal service by sheriff to borrower; publication in a local newspaper twice prior to sale for minimum of 30 days.
- *Redemption period requirements:* None.

Maine

- *Type of foreclosure process:* Judicial.
- *Process period:* 180–210 days average.
- *Type of deed:* Mortgage Deed.
- *Notice of default:* Notice required to be served to borrower prior to sale.
- *Notice of sale requirements:* Published in local newspaper 3 weeks prior to sale.
- *Redemption period requirements:* 90 days.

Maryland

- *Type of foreclosure process:* Judicial.
- *Process period:* 60–90 days average.
- *Type of deed:* Both.
- *Notice of default:* None.
- *Notice of sale requirements:* Notice to borrower and all lien holders at least 10 days prior to sale; publication in local newspaper 3 weeks prior to sale.
- *Redemption period requirements:* Court mandates.

Massachusetts

- *Type of foreclosure process:* Both.
- *Process period:* 75–90 days.
- *Type of deed:* Both.
- *Notice of default:* None.

- *Notice of sale requirements:* Notice to borrower and all lien holders at least 14 days prior to sale; publication in local newspaper 3 consecutive weeks prior to sale, with first notice no less than 21 days prior.

- *Redemption period requirements:* None.

Michigan

- *Type of foreclosure process:* Both.

- *Process period:* 90–420 days.

- *Type of deed:* Both.

- *Notice of default:* None.

- *Notice of sale requirements:* Publication in local newspaper for 4 consecutive weeks prior to sale, with first notice at least 28 days prior. Posting on property for same period.

- *Redemption period requirements:* 180–365 days; none if vacant.

Minnesota

- *Type of foreclosure process:* Both but mostly nonjudicial.

- *Process period:* 120 days.

- *Type of deed:* Both.

- *Notice of default:* Required to borrower.

- *Notice of sale requirements:* Personal service to borrower at least 4 weeks prior to sale; publication in local newspaper for 6 weeks prior to sale.

  Redemption period requirements: 6–12 months.

Mississippi

- *Type of foreclosure process:* Both; mostly nonjudicial.

- *Process period:* 90–120 days.

- *Type of deed:* Both.

- *Notice of default:* 30 days prior to sale.

- *Notice of sale requirements:* Notice posted at county courthouse; published in local newspaper for 3 weeks prior to sale.

- *Redemption period requirements:* None.

Missouri

- *Type of foreclosure process:* Both; mostly nonjudicial.

- *Process period:* 21–45 days.

- *Type of deed:* Both.

- *Notice of default:* Required to borrower.

- *Notice of sale requirements:* Notice to borrower and lien holders at least 20 days prior to sale; published in local newspaper for 3 weeks prior to sale; counties with a city of greater than 50,000 residents requires published notice for 20 days (with last day on date of sale); other counties requires published notice weekly for 4 consecutive weeks, with final notice no more than 7 days prior to sale.

- *Redemption period requirements:* Borrower must declare intent with lender at least 10 days prior to sale. Borrower must post bond within 20 days after the sale of all interest, costs, damages and 6% interest—then has 12 month redemption.

Montana

- *Type of foreclosure process:* Both.
- *Process period:* 150–180 days.
- *Type of deed:* Both.
- *Notice of default:* None.
- *Notice of sale requirements:* Notice to borrower at least 120 days prior to sale; posted on property at least 20 days prior to sale; published in local newspaper for 3 consecutive weeks prior to sale.
- *Redemption period requirements:* None.

Nebraska

- *Type of foreclosure process:* Judicial.
- *Process period:* 120–180 days average.
- *Type of deed:* Mortgage Deed.
- *Notice of default:* Required to borrower.
- *Notice of sale requirements:* Judicial—publication in local newspaper 4 weeks prior to sale; nonjudicial—published in local newspaper for 5 weeks prior to sale, with final notice to appear 10–30 days prior to sale.
- *Redemption period requirements:* None.

Nevada

- *Type of foreclosure process:* Both; mostly nonjudicial.
- *Process period:* 120–180 days.
- *Type of deed:* Both; mostly Deed of Trust.
- *Notice of default:* Required to borrower.
- *Notice of sale requirements:* Notice mailed to borrower an all lien holders prior to sale; publication in local newspaper for 3 weeks prior to sale; posted in 3 public locations at least 21 days prior to sale.
- *Redemption period requirements:* Nonjudicial—none; judicial—12 months (rare).

New Hampshire

- *Type of foreclosure process:* Nonjudicial.
- *Process period:* 90 days.
- *Type of deed:* Both.
- *Notice of default:* 30-day payment notice.
- *Notice of sale requirements:* Notice to borrower at least 26 days prior to sale; publication in local newspaper for 3 weeks prior to sale—first notice at least 21 days before sale.
- *Redemption period requirements:* Nonjudicial—none; judicial—12 months (rare).

New Jersey

- *Type of foreclosure process:* Judicial.
- *Process period:* 90–270 days.
- *Type of deed:* Mortgage Deed.
- *Notice of default:* Notice to borrower at least 30 days prior to initiation of foreclosure.
- *Notice of sale requirements:* Notice to borrower at least 10 days prior to sale; posting on property and county courthouse; published in two local newspapers (one of which has to be largest in county).
- *Redemption period requirements:* 10 days.

New Mexico

- *Type of foreclosure process:* Judicial.
- *Process period:* 120 days.
- *Type of deed:* Mortgage Deed.
- *Notice of default:* None.
- *Notice of sale requirements:* Publication in local newspaper for 4 consecutive weeks, with final notice at least 3 days prior to sale.
- *Redemption period requirements:* 9 months.

New York

- *Type of foreclosure process:* Both; mostly judicial.
- *Process period:* 210–450 days.
- *Type of deed:* Both.
- *Notice of default:* None.
- *Notice of sale requirements:* Publication in local newspaper for 4 weeks.
- *Redemption period requirements:* None.

North Carolina

- *Type of foreclosure process:* Both; mostly nonjudicial.
- *Process period:* 90–120 days.
- *Type of deed:* Both.
- *Notice of default:* Required to borrower.
- *Notice of sale requirements:* Posted at county courthouse at least 20 days prior to sale; notice mailed to borrower at least 20 days prior to sale; published in local newspaper for 2 weeks.
- *Redemption period requirements:* 10 days.

North Dakota

- *Type of foreclosure process:* Judicial.
- *Process period:* 90–150 days.
- *Type of deed:* Mortgage Deed.
- *Notice of default:* 30-day notice of intent.
- *Notice of sale requirements:* Notice to borrower; published in local newspaper or legal news for 2 months, with last notice appearing at least 10 days prior to sale.
- *Redemption period requirements:* 180–365 days.

Ohio

- *Type of foreclosure process:* Judicial.
- *Process period:* 150–210 days.
- *Type of deed:* Mortgage Deed.
- *Notice of default:* Required to borrower.
- *Notice of sale requirements:* Published in local newspaper for three weeks prior to sale.
- *Redemption period requirements:* None.

Oklahoma

- *Type of foreclosure process:* Both.
- *Process period:* 90–210 days.
- *Type of deed:* Both.
- *Notice of default:* Required to borrower.
- *Notice of sale requirements:* Notice published in local newspaper for 4 consecutive weeks, with first notice at least 30 days prior to sale; recorded in county office.
- *Redemption period requirements:* None.

Oregon

- *Type of foreclosure process:* Both.
- *Process period:* 150–180 days.

- *Type of deed:* Both.
- *Notice of default:* Required—4 months prior to sale.
- *Notice of sale requirements:* Publication in local newspaper for 4 weeks, with last notice at least 20 days prior to sale.
- *Redemption period requirements:* Nonjudicial—none; judicial—180 days.

Pennsylvania

- *Type of foreclosure process:* Judicial.
- *Process period:* 90–270 days.
- *Type of deed:* Mortgage Deed.
- *Notice of default:* 4 months prior to sale.
- *Notice of sale requirements:* Notice to borrower; posted on property at least 30 days prior to sale; published in local newspaper for 3 consecutive weeks.
- *Redemption period requirements:* None.

Rhode Island

- *Type of foreclosure process:* Both; mostly nonjudicial.
- *Process period:* 90–270 days.
- *Type of deed:* Mortgage Deed.
- *Notice of default:* None.
- *Notice of sale requirements:* Notice to borrower at least 20 days prior to public notice; publication in local newspaper and legal newspaper for 3 weeks—with first notice at least 21 days prior to sale.
- *Redemption period requirements:* None.

South Carolina

- *Type of foreclosure process:* Judicial.
- *Process period:* 150–180 days.
- *Type of deed:* Mortgage Deed.
- *Notice of default:* None.
- *Notice of sale requirements:* Posted at county courthouse; published in local and legal newspapers for 3 weeks prior to sale.
- *Redemption period requirements:* 30 days with deficiency judgment; None, if waived by lender.

South Dakota

- *Type of foreclosure process:* Both; mostly judicial.
- *Process period:* 90–150 days.
- *Type of deed:* Both.
- *Notice of default:* None.

- *Notice of sale requirements:* Notice to borrower and lien holders at least 21 days prior to sale; published in local newspaper for 3 weeks prior to sale.
- *Redemption period requirements:* 60–120 days.

Tennessee

- *Type of foreclosure process:* Both; mostly nonjudicial.
- *Process period:* 60 days.
- *Type of deed:* Both.
- *Notice of default:* None.
- *Notice of sale requirements:* Published in local newspaper 3 times, with first notice at least 20 days prior to sale.
- *Redemption period requirements:* Usually none—can be up to 720 days.

Texas

- *Type of foreclosure process:* Both; mostly nonjudicial.
- *Process period:* 30–90 days.
- *Type of deed:* Both.
- *Notice of default:* Required to borrower.
- *Notice of sale requirements:* Notice mailed to borrower at least 21 days prior to sale; posted at county courthouse and filed with Clerk at least 21 days prior to sale.
- *Redemption period requirements:* None.

Utah

- *Type of foreclosure process:* Both; mostly nonjudicial.
- *Process period:* 150 days.
- *Type of deed:* Both.
- *Notice of default:* Required to borrower.
- *Notice of sale requirements:* Posted on property and in country recorders office at least 20 days prior to sale; published in local newspaper for 3 consecutive weeks, with final notice between 10–30 days prior to sale.
- *Redemption period requirements:* None—nonjudicial; judicial—court mandated.

Vermont

- *Type of foreclosure process:* Both.
- *Process period:* 90–270 days.
- *Type of deed:* Both.
- *Notice of default:* Required to borrower.

- *Notice of sale requirements:* Notice to borrower at least 60 days prior to sale; published in local newspaper for 3 weeks, with first notice at least 21 days prior to sale.
- *Redemption period requirements:* 180–365 days.

Virginia

- *Type of foreclosure process:* Both; mostly nonjudicial.
- *Process period:* 60 days.
- *Type of deed:* Both.
- *Notice of default:* Required to borrower.
- *Notice of sale requirements:* Notice to borrower at least 14 days prior to sale.
- *Redemption period requirements:* None.

Washington

- *Type of foreclosure process:* Both; mostly nonjudicial.
- *Process period:* 120 days average.
- *Type of deed:* Both.
- *Notice of default:* Required to borrower.
- *Notice of sale requirements:* Must be recorded at county minimum of 90 days prior to sale; notice to borrower and all lien holders; published in local newspaper at least once between 28th and 32nd day before sale, and again between 7th and 11th day prior to sale.
- *Redemption period requirements:* 12 months unless waived.

Washington, DC

- *Type of foreclosure process:* Nonjudicial (once in awhile judicial).
- *Process period:* 30–60 days average.
- *Type of deed:* Both.
- *Notice of default:* Notice must be sent to Borrower.
- *Notice of sale requirements:* Notice must be posted according to mortgage deed or deed of trust, or advertized in local newspaper for 5 weeks prior to sale; Certified Mail to borrowers 30 days prior to sale; recorded with county; sent to mayor or mayoral agent and all other lien holders.
- *Redemption period requirements:* None.

West Virginia

- *Type of foreclosure process:* Both.
- *Process period:* 60–90 days.

- *Type of deed:* Both.
- *Notice of default:* Required to borrower.
- *Notice of sale requirements:* Notice to borrower and lien holders at least 20 days prior to sale; published in local newspaper for 2 weeks prior to sale.
- *Redemption period requirements:* 20 days.

Wisconsin

- *Type of foreclosure process:* Both; mostly judicial.
- *Process period:* 90–290 days.
- *Type of deed:* Both.
- *Notice of default:* None.
- *Notice of sale requirements:* Varies depending on circumstances. Minimum 10 months from court ruling unless waived by all parties.
- *Redemption period requirements:* 180–365 days.

Wyoming

- *Type of foreclosure process:* Both.
- *Process period:* 60–90 days.
- *Type of deed:* Both.
- *Notice of default:* Notice to borrower at least 10 days prior to advertising sale.
- *Notice of sale requirements:* Published in local newspaper for 4 consecutive weeks.
- *Redemption period requirements:* 90–365 days.

Not surprisingly, with today's technology, the Internet will serve as your best friend in researching good foreclosure properties and structuring your deals. Here are 101 of my favorite resources which will save you a ton of time, energy, money and headaches!

Foreclosure Properties and Statistics

Foreclosure statistics   www.RealtyTrac.com
HUD homes for sale   www.hud.gov/homes/homesforsale.cfm
Gov't homes for sale   www.homesales.gov/homesales/mainAction.do
Foreclosure Search   www.ForeclosureFreeSearch.com
Foreclosure Listings   www.ForeclosureListings.com
Foreclosure Listings   www.ForeclosureS.com
Illinois Foreclosures   www.public-record.com/content/databases/foreclosures/index.asp
San Diego Foreclosures   www.ForeclosureAccess.com
Foreclosure Records   www.Records.Foreclosure.com

In addition, many lenders and banks have individual pages listing REO properties for sale.

Approximate Property Values

Zillow Property Valuation   www.Zillow.com
Multiple Listing Search   www.MLS.com
MLS – Canada   www.MLS.ca
House Values   www.HouseValues.com
Trulia   www.Trulia.com
Yahoo! Home Values   http://realestate.yahoo.com/Homevalues

Local real estate agents will still be the best source of current local market conditions and values.

Association and Regulatory Agencies

Mortgage Bankers Assn.   www.MBAA.org
Mortgage Brokers Assn.   www.NAMB.org
National Assn of Realtors®   www.Realtor.com
Fannie Mae   www.FannieMae.com
Freddie Mac   www.FreddieMac.com
FHA   www.HUD.gov
U.S. Dept of Veteran Affairs   www.VA.gov

National NREIA   www.NationalREIA.com
Rental Property Managers   www.NARPM.org
U.S. Government info site   www.USA.gov

Make sure to also check your individual state regulatory agency.

Public Property Records

Government Records   www.brbpub.com/freeresources/pubrecsites.aspx
Virtual Gumshoe   www.VirtualGumshoe.com
Public Record Finder   www.PublicRecordFinder.com
Search Systems   www.SearchSystems.com
Yellow/White Pages   www.Switchboard.com
Public Records   www.Public-Files.com
Public Records Search   www.PRSearch.com
Bankruptcy Records   http://pacer.psc.uscourts.gov/
Chapter 13 Records   www.13DataCenter.com
Tax Records Search   www.Netronline.com/public_records.htm

Most state, county and city recorder's offices also have records online.

People Searches

Intelius Search   www.Intelius.com
Web Detective   www.Web-Detective.com
ZabaSearch   www.ZabaSearch.com
People Search   www.People-Search.com
Zoom   www.ZoomInfo.com
Lycos People Search   www.WhoWhere.com
Skip Ease   www.SkipEase.com
Social Security Admin   www.SSA.gov

Demographic Information

Cost of Living Statistics   www.BestPlaces.net
U.S. Geocode Info   www.ffiec.gov/Geocode/default.aspx
Census information   www.Census.gov/
Federal Statistics   www.fedstats.gov/
Labor Statistics   www.BLS.gov
Federal Housing Oversight   www.ofheo.gov/Research.aspx

Maps and Aerial Photography

MapQuest   www.MapQuest.com
Google   www.Maps.Google.com
Aerial Maps   www.TerraServer-USA.com
Google Earth   www.Earth.Google.com
Yahoo! Maps   www.Maps.Yahoo.com

Crime Information

U.S. Dept of Justice   www.ojp.usdoj.gov/bjs/
FBI Crime Reports   www.FBI.gov/ucr/ucr.htm

State Crime Statistics   www.bestplaces.net/crime/
City Crime Statistics   www.Melissadata.com/lookups/crimecity.asp
National Sex Offender Registry   www.FBI.gov/hq/cid/cac/registry.htm

Attorney and Legal Resources

Lawyer Search   www.FindLaw.com
Legal Questions   www.LawGuru.com
Legal Forms   www.LegalZoom.com
Free Forms and Research   www.LawInfo.com
Attorney Search   www.lawyers.com

Title Insurance Research

First American   www.FirstAm.com
Property Records   www.firstam.com/list.cfm?id=70&sectionid=05
Stewart Title   www.Stewart.com
Old Republic Title   www.OldRepublicTitle.com
Chicago Title   https://www.ctic.com/
Fidelity National   https://www.fntic.com/

These are the major title insurers. There are many agents located throughout the country, including many attorney offices.

Appraisal Resources

Appraisal Institute   www.appraisalinstitute.org/
Appraiser Search   www.isa-appraisers.org/ISA_form.html
Appraisers Forum   www.AppraisersForum.com
HUD Appraisal Guidelines   www.hud.gov/offices/hsg/sfh/ref/chap1.cfm

Rehabilitation and Repair Costs

Construction Calculators   www.construction-resource.com/calculators/
Lowe's Job Estimator   www.lowesforpros.com/resourcecenter/jobestimators.cfm
Quote Estimator   www.get-a-quote.net/quickcalc/
Marshall Swift   http://marshallswift.com/
RS Means   www.RSMeans.com
Geometric Calculator   www.Blocklayer.mobi

Tax Information

Federal Tax Information   www.IRS.gov
Tax Search   www.Netronline.com/public_records.htm
Tax & Assessor Search   www.knowx.com/subreg/pr_assets.jsp
Maryland Tax Search   www.dat.state.md.us/
Miami-Dade Tax Search   www.miamidade.gov/proptax/
El Paso, Texas https://actweb.acttax.com/act_webdev/elpaso/index.jsp

Several regional examples are listed above. Most tax searches are done at the local County or City level. Check with your tax assessor or treasurer's office for their website access address.

Environmental Resources

Environmental Protection Agency   www.epa.gov/osw
Superfund Sites   www.epa.gov/superfund/
Pollution Statistics   www.Scorecard.org
Environmental Sites   www.World.org/weo/pollution
Lead-based Paint Info   www.epa.gov/lead/
Lead Disclosure Rule   www.hud.gov/offices/lead/enforcement/disclosure.cfm

Other Resource Sites

Call Capture Systems   www.CCUCallCapture.com
Credit Reports   www.AnnualCreditReport.com
Do Not Call List   www.DoNotCall.gov
Mortgage Payment Calculator   www.bankrate.com/brm/mortgage-calculator.asp
100 Mortgage Calculators   www.mortgageloan.com/calculator/
U.S. Zip Code Registry   www.zip4.usps.com/zip4/citytown_zip.jsp
Property Flipping Info   www.FlippingFrenzy.com
Mortgage Myths   www.TheMortgageMyths.com
Investors Kit   www.ChipCummings.com/CashingIn

Lenders have a language all their own. In this glossary, we present and decipher the most cryptic jargon and acronyms that lenders and their ilk are likely to toss at you.

1031   See *Tax-deferred exchange*.

Adjustable Rate Mortgage (ARM)   A mortgage in which the rate can change.

Adjusted basis   Value used in calculating the taxable gain on the sale of a property. The adjusted basis is the original cost of the property plus capital improvements minus accumulated depreciation and the cost of selling it.

Adjustment period   The length of time that determines how often the interest rate can change on an adjustable rate mortgage. See also *Index*, *Cap*, and *Margin*.

Amortization   Creative process of retiring debt through predetermined periodic payments.

Annual Percentage Rate (APR)   Calculation disclosed on the TIL which indicates the total cost of credit when costs are taken into account.

Automated Underwriting (AU)   Computerized system used by lenders to determine a borrower's eligibility for loan programs.

Automated Valuation Model (AVM)   A computerized system for determining the value of a property that sort of takes the place of an appraisal.

Back-end debt ratio   Total debt payments (including house payment with homeowner's insurance and property taxes) divided by total monthly income. According to the Federal Housing Authority (FHA), your back-end debt ratio should not exceed 43 percent. See also *Debt ratio* and *Front-end debt ratio*.

Balloon payment   A typically large final payment due on a loan that covers the remaining balance. Balloon payments are required when a loan is scheduled to be paid in full before the debt can be retired through monthly payments.

Basis   The starting point for calculating the gain or loss on an investment—usually the purchase price.

BPO   Broker Price Opinion. An informal estimate of value used for helping the lender determine the current value of a foreclosure property.

Cap   The maximum interest rate allowed for an ARM loan.

Capital gain or loss   The net profit on an investment property that's subject to tax. Capital gains can be long-term (taxed at a lower rate) or short-term.

Capital improvement   A renovation that increases the value or useful life of a property in excess of one year.

Cash flow   The net operating income (NOI) of a property minus its debt service. See also *NOI* and *DS*.

Closing   A ritual that takes place with all the parties to sign documents, disburse funds, and transfer the ownership of real estate.

Closing Costs   Costs incurred by a borrower, or paid on their behalf, to close on a real estate transaction. Listed on the GFE and the HUD-1.

Combined Loan To Value (CLTV)   The total LTV with all mortgages included.

Commercial property   Property used for business as opposed to living quarters. Technically, however, the term also covers residential real estate having five units or more.

Comps or comparables   Properties that are similar to the property in question and can be used to estimate its value.

Conforming loan   A loan that adheres to all Fannie Mae and Freddie Mac requirements. See also *Sub-prime loan*.

Contract for deed   See *Land contract*.

Conventional loan   A loan that doesn't require underwriting or insuring by the government (such as FHA or VA underwriting).

Cost approach   An appraisal method that starts with what it would cost to build the same structure today, depreciates it, and then adds in the value of the land.

Cross-collateralization   Using two or more properties to secure the repayment of a loan.

Debt ratio   A formula that lenders often use to determine a borrower's ability to afford monthly payments on a loan:

Debt ratio   = Total Monthly Payments / Total Monthly Income
See also   *Back-end debt ratio* and *Front-end debt ratio*.

Deed of trust   A legal document that functions much like a mortgage in that it secures the repayment of a loan. In deed of trust states, a trustee holds the deed until the loan is paid back in full. If the borrower defaults on the loan, the trustee can then sell the property to help the lender recoup any loss.

Department of Housing and Urban Development (HUD)   Part of the federal government that oversees FHA.

Department of Veteran Affairs (VA)   Insures loans made by lenders to eligible Veterans.

Depreciation   The decline in value of a property over time usually due to wear and tear.

Discount rate   Rate that is used by banks and financial institutions when lending money between themselves. Sometimes used as an index for ARM loan adjustments.

Due on sale clause   Wording in most mortgages that requires the borrower to pay the balance in full in the event that the property changes hands.

Earnest Money Deposit (EMD)   Funds put up by a prospective purchaser as a commitment to follow through on the purchase of a property.

Equity   The amount of money remaining if you sold the property today and paid off any loans taken out against the property.

Estoppel certificate   Legal document that tenants use to acknowledge agreements or changes in the lease or the status of rent payments.

Federal Housing Administration (FHA)   Part of the Department of Housing and Urban Development that insures home mortgage loans.

Fair Isaac & Company (FICO) score   A credit scoring system commonly used by lenders to determine the risk a borrower represents related to repayment.

Fixed-rate loan   A loan for which the interest rate remains unchanged over the life of the loan. See also *ARM*.

Forfeiture clause   Legal wording commonly used in a land contract or lease option agreement that entitles the seller to repossess the property in the event that the buyer fails to comply with the terms of the agreement.

Front-end debt ratio   House payment alone (including property taxes and insurance) divided by total monthly income. According to the FHA, your front-end debt ratio should not exceed 31 percent. See also *Debt ratio* and *Back-end debt ratio*.

Good Faith Estimate (GFE)   A list of estimated costs involved in the loan transaction that the lender provides to the borrower prior to, or within three days of application.

Hard money   A typically short-term, high-interest loan that investors often use to score some quick cash to move forward on an investment opportunity.

Home-Equity-Line-Of-Credit (HELOC)   Credit line secured by a piece of real property. With a HELOC, you pay interest on only the amount of money you actually draw against the credit line.

HUD-1   Settlement statement used at closing to disclose all costs and credits for borrowers and sellers involved in a real estate transaction.

Hybrid loan   A combination of an ARM and a fixed-rate loan; for example, with a 3/1 hybrid, the interest rate would remain fixed for three years and then become an adjustable-rate loan in which the rate could be adjusted every year. See also *ARM* and *Fixed-rate loan*.

Income approach   A real estate appraisal method that focuses more on the revenue-generating potential of rental property than the property's value.

Index   An indicator used to calculate rates on some mortgage loan products, notably ARM loans. See also *Adjustment period*, *Cap*, and *Margin*.

Land contract   A legal instrument that enables the seller to finance the purchase of his property. The seller functions as the lender, and the contract takes the place of a mortgage or deed of trust.

Lease option agreement   A legal instrument that enables a buyer to rent a property for a certain amount of time at the end of which she has the option to purchase it for the pre-agreed-upon price.

Leverage   The use of borrowed money to increase purchase power.

Lien   A claim against a property. A mortgage is a type of lien.

Limited Liability Corporation (LLC)   A legal structure that protects the owner's personal assets from any loss that the business incurs.

Loan officer   Someone who works for a lending institution or mortgage broker to assist borrowers in selecting and applying for loans. See also *Mortgage broker*.

Loan-To-Value (LTV)   A ratio expressing the loan amount divided by the property's current market value. For example, the LTV on an $80,000 loan to purchase a $100,000 property would be 80 percent. Lenders use LTV as one way to measure risk – the lower the LTV, the less the risk.

Long-term capital gain The realized profit on an investment property held more than 12 months.

Management expenses (ME) Whatever you pay yourself or others to care for a property.

Margin An amount added to an index to calculate an adjustment for an ARM loan. The margin remains constant over the life of the loan. See also *Adjustment period*, *Index*, and *Cap*.

Mortgage A loan secured by real estate. States which are not trust states use a mortgage as the legal instrument to secure a lien against the property.

Mortgage broker A licensed professional who assists borrowers in shopping for loans made available through multiple lenders.

Mortgage Insurance Premium (MIP) Term used for insurance required for FHA-insured loans.

Net Operating Income (NOI) The amount of money left over after all expenses are deducted from a property's gross income.

Net worth The value of everything you own minus everything you owe.

Non-conforming loan See *Sub-prime loan*.

Note Legal instrument that describes the terms of the mortgage loan.

Operating expenses Costs for maintaining a property such as taxes, insurance, maintenance and upkeep.

Pass-through expenses Costs that a landlord incurs and then charges the tenant to pay in full or a portion of in addition to paying rent.

Points Interest paid on a loan up front rather than monthly. One point is one percent of the total loan amount.

Pre-approval A lender's agreement to finance the purchase of an investment property up to a certain amount, assuming the property meets certain conditions. See also *Prequalification*.

Prequalification A lender's assurance that a borrower probably would qualify for a particular loan. See also, *Pre-approval*.

Prepaids Costs of a transaction listed on the GFE or HUD-1 which are paid in advance for the benefit of the borrower.

Prepayment penalty A clause in some mortgage agreements that requires the borrower to pay additional money if she pays back the loan early.

Principal + Interest + Taxes + Insurance (PITI) Term used to describe a payment that covers the principal and interest due on a loan along with taxes and insurance to be placed in escrow.

Private Mortgage Insurance (PMI) Insurance required on high LTV conventional loans.

Pro forma A statement projecting the future performance of an income-producing property.

Promissory note A legal document borrower's sign as their personal agreement to pay back a loan according to the terms specified in the note.

Real Estate Owned (REO) Property owned by the bank. Sometimes, you can get the bank to finance the purchase of these properties.

Real Estate Settlement and Procedures Act (RESPA)   Federal law which requires lenders to disclose settlement costs (GFE and HUD-1) as well as the procedures for consumer disclosure.

Reserves   Amount of liquid assets that a borrower has left after paying all costs for the transaction.

Resource clause   Legal language in a loan contract that stipulates what a lender can do to collect on a borrower who's in default on a loan.

Seller financing   A process by which the seller of a property agrees to loan the buyer the money to purchase it. See also *Land contract* and *Lease-option agreement*.

Short-term capital gain   The realized profit on an investment property held fewer than 12 months.

Sub-prime loan   A loan that does not adhere to Fannie Mae or Freddie Mac requirements and, as a result, typically charges more in interest and upfront costs.

Tax-deferred exchange   A provision of the tax code that allows investors to exchange like-kind properties instead of selling those properties and exposing the profits to capital gains taxes. Often referred to as a 1031 in reference to this section of the tax code.

Title insurance   Insurance that covers the lender and/or new owner of real estate against any title defects, such as an overlooked claim to the property.

Title   The owner of record for a parcel of real estate.

Truth-In-Lending-Act (TIL or TILA)   Federal law that requires lenders to follow certain guidelines for disclosing loan terms, including the APR. Not used on commercial properties.

Yield Spread Premium (YSP)   An amount paid by a lender to a broker as compensation for origination and delivery services.

Ana → Freedom Plus
480 880 9466

SPECIAL BONUS!

Downloadable Investor Tool Kit!

Get online access to over 40 customizable:

- ✓ Documents
- ✓ Checklists
- ✓ Letters
- ✓ Forms
- ✓ Inspections
- ✓ Agreements

Word and PDF format

Access Online Support Services:

- Conference Calls
- Foreclosure Updates
- Investor Education Events
- Marketing Strategies

You Can Get Instant Access NOW at:

www.ChipCummings.com/CashingIn
Password: INTEGRITY

Chip@ChipCummings.com   (616) 977-7900